Law and Order

CYNTHIA NITZ RIS
University of Cincinnati

Pearson

Boston   Columbus   Indianapolis   New York   San Francisco   Upper Saddle River
Amsterdam   Cape Town   Dubai   London   Madrid   Milan   Munich   Paris   Montreal   Toronto
Delhi   Mexico City   Sao Paulo   Sydney   Hong Kong   Seoul   Singapore   Taipei   Tokyo

Senior Sponsoring Editor: Katharine Glynn
Senior Marketing Manager: Sandra McGuire
Assistant Editor: Rebecca Gilpin
Production Manager: Fran Russello
Project Coordination, Text Design, and Electronic Page Makeup:
  Sandeep Rawat / Aptara®, Inc.
Cover Design Manager: Jayne Conte
Cover Designer: Karen Salzbach
Cover Illustration/Photo: Fotolia: © Junial Enterprises
Printer and Binder: RR Donnelley and Sons Company

Credits and acknowledgments for materials borrowed from other sources and reproduced, with permission, in this textbook appear on the appropriate page within text.

Every effort has been made to provide accurate and current Internet information in this book. However, the Internet and information posted on it are constantly changing, so it is inevitable that some of the Internet addresses listed in this textbook will change.

Library of Congress Cataloging-in-Publication Data

Ris, Cynthia Nitz.
  Law and order/Cynthia Nitz Ris.
    p. cm.
  Includes bibliographical references.
  ISBN-13: 978-0-205-64458-2
  ISBN-10: 0-205-64458-9
  1. Legal composition. 2. Law—United States. I. Title.
  KF250.R57 2012
  349.73—dc23

                                        2011024885

1 2 3 4 5 6 7 8 9 10—DOH—14 13 12 11

PEARSON   ISBN-13: 978-0-205-64458-2
                         ISBN-10:   0-205-64458-9

When you hear the word *law*, what do you think of? Chances are, each of us has a variety of responses, including contradictory ones, based on our experiences with the law. As a driver, I appreciate laws against jaywalking; on foot, I might view those laws as a nuisance. If I'm hurt by someone else's negligence, I'm glad I can bring a lawsuit to recover damages; if I accidentally hurt someone else, I might think not only that there are too many lawyers, but that the legal system is broken. We also receive a fair amount of partial or misinformation through second-hand experiences of others and from what seems the most common source of our legal knowledge: television and movies. We might assume that most law takes place in the course of a trial since courtroom scenes are ubiquitous, yet 80–90% of all cases don't go to trial. We might also think that something is either legal or illegal. Most legal disputes, however, are the result of a lack of such bright lines, or clearly defined standards that leave little room for interpretation. Instead, such disputes often result from gray areas where it is unclear what is legal, or what a controlling word such as *obscenity* might mean in a particular case.

Whatever our understanding of the law, we will be actively affected by it throughout our lives. From the legal certificate recording our birth, to that which declares our death, we are bookended by the law. Even the simple birth certificate reflects the momentous impact the law can have in our lives: consider the controversy over whether President Barack Obama could prove his citizenship with a birth certificate and hence confirm his legal ability to be president of the United States. This is only one instance of many in which the law has the potential to affect our destinies.

This reader focuses on a few select areas of the law's impact to illustrate its complexity, import, and relevance. Chapter 1 ("The Rule of Law") provides an idea of the challenges of building a society from the legal ground up and suggests that, no matter how well built, a system of laws is fraught with questions of interpretation. In Chapter 2 ("The Stories We Tell: Law as Narrative") we hear the voices of those affected by the law, including those with varying agency in the law—a lawyer, judges, a defendant, a police officer, and an average citizen. To bring the law closer to home for students, Chapter 3 ("When Law Comes to Campus") reminds us that the ivory tower is not immune from legal constraints. Within and outside academia, technology is rapidly changing our concepts about many things, including the law; Chapter 4 ("Can My Avatar Serve My Sentence? Real Laws in a Virtual World") considers this impact in areas familiar to many students, including music downloads, Second Life, and social networks. Finally, given this connected society in which we live, Chapter 5 ("Reconsidering Laws: In Search of Global Values") asks us to consider how law can and should operate on a global level, or at least with global concerns in mind.

Each chapter contains at least five main readings, many with supplementary material such as state laws or court documents to help support, explain, or enlarge the primary texts under discussion. Even though the readings are neither unduly complicated nor chock-full of legalese, notes are included where they may be useful to connect readers to related online material that may help provide context as well as additional support and perspectives. To provide yet another medium by which to experience the law, a final endnote refers readers to a compendium of television shows and movies that represent both the potency of law and its more entertaining aspects.

This text is meant to encourage readers to engage in close reading and careful analysis. Attention to the writing down to the word level is, therefore, a good place to start. Many of the documents refer to language that is specialized—what is the difference between a plaintiff and a defendant? What is a misdemeanor or a hung jury? Looking up words can move you beyond definitions to allow you to enter the world of a particular discourse community—the legal one. Attention to rhetorical considerations—such as who the audience is for a particular reading, what the author's goals are, and how each text is constructed for those purposes—is also crucial. Such analysis can help us break down the complexity of issues by considering them from different perspectives. This is a useful practice for any discipline or profession, including the law, where lawyers must consider their clients' perspectives as well as the responses of a variety of audiences to the arguments on behalf of the lawyers' clients. Such attention to perspective and the details of a case, including an understanding of the relevancy of those details, is a critical skill to master. In what ways can you see utilizing this skill in your chosen discipline and profession as well as in your daily life?

Throughout the text, you'll hear from a variety of individuals, including legal scholars, language experts, Supreme Court justices, and social critics. These writers work in multiple genres, from *The New York Times* and *Scientific American* to books, law journal articles, blogs, court documents, and transcripts of interviews and speeches. These readings—which inform, proclaim, prescribe and proscribe, argue, and predict—offer a variety of ways to consider the law. Coupled with the introductions to and questions about the readings, you are encouraged to add yet another reasoned perspective—your own—as you engage with, learn more about, and analyze the texts and their authors and this complicated entity we call the law.

ACKNOWLEDGMENTS

Just as the law shapes us in countless ways, I realize I am shaped by the institutions of which I have been a part and by those colleagues, students, friends, and family for whom I am so grateful. I appreciate the support of the institutions in which I have learned and worked, including the guidance of many exemplary professors at the University of Michigan Law School; their questions helped me better understand the law as a wonderfully complicated enterprise and appreciate that what we ask is often as important as any answer we can provide. I'm indebted to the National Endowment for the Humanities and its seminar on the rule of law, to Matthew Anderson and Cathrine Frank for their guidance in that setting, and to the many participants for ideas that directly shaped this text. I'd like to thank those friends and colleagues I met at the University of Cincinnati who have encouraged my work, especially in the intersection of law and English studies; these include Michael Delaney, Jonathan Kamholtz, Tom LeClair, Maggy Lindgren, and Laura Micciche. I especially want to thank my students whose curiosity and enthusiasm keep fueling mine. For editorial assistance on this text, and for helping to remind me of the importance of detail, I'd like to thank Pearson Longman and especially Ginny Blanford, Rebecca Gilpin, and the remarkably thorough Mary Benis, and Sandeep Rawat at Aptara for his care and patience. A very special thanks to Cathy Piha Huffman not only for her insightful suggestions for this book, but for her invaluable friendship since law school. Special thanks also to Michele Griegel-McCord and Lisa Beckelhimer and to many other friends and colleagues whose ideas and dedication have been truly inspirational. And my greatest thanks to my family: to my parents for their generosity of spirit and love of learning, and to my sons—Geoff, Greg, and Andrew—with more admiration, appreciation, and love than any words can express.

The Rule of Law

"The first thing we do, let's kill all the lawyers."
William Shakespeare, *Henry VI* (Act IV, Scene 2)

When one of Shakespeare's characters utters this line, it is not merely another jab at lawyers. Here, revolt is in the offing, and if the characters are to succeed in taking power, they must do away with those who have installed and protected the current rule of law. This quotation, therefore, reflects both the power of law and the sometimes-vehement opposition to it. Although law is seen by most as a necessary component of an ordered society, beyond that common perspective lies controversy. Which laws are needed, to whom they should apply, how they should be expressed, by whom they should be determined, and how they should be understood and enforced—these are only some of the questions that anyone who seeks to write or critique laws needs to consider.

Having been born into a world where laws already exist, we may not have considered the difficulty of creating laws, especially those required to establish a new society. The late professor and legal scholar Lon Fuller helps provide that perspective in his allegory of the challenges a new king faces in his kingdom. That king, Rex, encounters many pitfalls, especially in ignoring the citizens who would be governed. Fuller's analysis helps us realize that the rule of law must be many things, including clear, consistent, and applicable to everyone in society, even those who would be king.

In addition, an array of documents created to establish a new society—the Declaration of Independence, the Constitution, and the Bill of Rights—help remind us how the fledgling "united States" attempted to identify and establish the rule of law in its new government. Even though the Declaration of Independence does not establish specific laws, it clearly sets out "the consent of the governed" as a crucial prerequisite to a stable society and as insurance that important rights will be protected. These rights are secured through the institutions set out in the Constitution—

within the legislative, executive, and judicial branches—and in the idea that all people, perhaps especially those who write the laws, are held accountable to those same laws. If you think this provides tension, or some temptation for those writing the rules to avoid the yoke of the rules, you're right. That's one reason the broad strokes of the Constitution were offset by the Bill of Rights, an antidote to what some feared was too much power held in the federal offices.

Once established, existing laws must be enforced and interpreted to continue to be fair, just, and faithful representations of the values of that culture. New laws may need to be written to respond to unforeseen situations. Former Supreme Court Justice Sandra Day O'Connor examines these requirements in light of a new war in which governing laws don't appear to anticipate the new circumstances our military may encounter. How do we know when existing laws become insufficient for new situations? Who decides in the meantime how to respond to changing events?

Finally, Lera Boroditsky raises compelling concerns about our ability to reach consensus on these and other questions. She focuses on how language differences among cultures can affect perceptions of reality. If various cultures perceive the world differently, how can they agree on what rules are necessary, let alone how to apply and interpret them? Does our present-day culture define *freedom* and what is "unreasonable" differently than our framers did? Whether or not we can or should interpret documents strictly, without being affected by our perceptual differences, continues to be the subject of debate among legal scholars.

As you read through this chapter and the questions for the individual texts, pay close attention to the words they employ. Are you sure that the word *happiness* in the excerpt from the Constitution has the same meaning for another student in your class or a student across the globe as it has for you? What are the implications if we cannot agree on the meaning, or significance, of what our laws are trying to protect?

The Morality That Makes Law Possible

LON L. FULLER

Lon L. Fuller was a legal philosopher who began teaching as a professor of law at Harvard Law School in 1940. Of Fuller's time at that law school, former Dean Albert M. Sacks noted that Fuller's success lay not necessarily in having the right answers but "in convincing me that the questions were right—that they had to be faced and that they deserved careful thought." His questions about the law, and his famous debate with fellow legal scholar and British legal philosopher H. L. A. Hart, helped shape the current controversy over the role of morality in the law. Followers of Hart, or legal positivists, consider law as less morality-bound and more language- and logic-bound, whereas those adhering to the concept of natural law, like Fuller, consider moral questions to be at the heart of our creation and interpretation of laws. In this reading, Fuller describes an allegorical ruler and suggests questions to consider: What happens if laws are not known, understood, or fairly administered? Under what conditions are citizens obliged to follow the law?

---◆---

This chapter will begin with a fairly lengthy allegory. It concerns the unhappy reign of a monarch who bore the convenient, but not very imaginative and not even very regal sounding name of Rex.

EIGHT WAYS TO FAIL TO MAKE LAW

Rex came to the throne filled with the zeal of a reformer. He considered that the greatest failure of his predecessors had been in the field of law. For generations the legal system had known nothing like a basic reform. Procedures of trial were cumbersome, the rules of law spoke in the archaic tongue of another age, justice was expensive, the judges were slovenly and sometimes corrupt. Rex was resolved to remedy all this and to make his name in history as a great lawgiver. It was his unhappy fate to fail in this ambition. Indeed, he failed spectacularly, since not only did he not succeed in introducing the needed reforms, but he never even succeeded in creating any law at all, good or bad.

His first official act was, however, dramatic and propitious. Since he needed a clean slate on which to write, he announced to his subjects the immediate repeal of all existing law, of what-ever kind. He then set about drafting a new code. Unfortunately, trained as a lonely prince, his education had been very defective. In particular he found himself incapable of making even the simplest generalizations. Though not lacking in confidence when it came to deciding specific controversies, the effort to give articulate reasons for any conclusion strained his capacities to the breaking point.

Becoming aware of his limitations, Rex gave up the project of a code and announced to his subjects that henceforth he would act as a judge in any disputes that might arise among them. In this way under the stimulus of a variety of cases he hoped that his latent powers of generalization might develop and, proceeding case by case, he would gradually work out a system of rules that could be incorporated in a code. Unfortunately the defects in his education were more deep-seated than he had supposed. The venture failed completely. After he had handed down literally hundreds of decisions neither he nor his subjects could detect in those decisions any pattern whatsoever. Such tentatives toward generalization as were to be found in his opinions only compounded the confusion, for they gave false leads to his subjects and threw his own meager powers of judgment off balance in the decision of later cases.

After this fiasco Rex realized it was necessary to take a fresh start. His first move was to subscribe to a course of lessons in generalization. With his intellectual powers thus fortified, he resumed the project of a code and, after many hours of solitary labor, succeeded in preparing a fairly lengthy document. He was still not confident, however, that he had fully overcome his previous defects. Accordingly, he announced to his subjects that he had written out a code and would henceforth be governed by it in deciding cases, but that for an indefinite future the contents of the code would remain an official state secret, known only to him and his scrivener. To Rex's surprise this sensible plan was deeply resented by his subjects. They declared it was very unpleasant to have one's case decided by rules when there was no way of knowing what those rules were.

Stunned by this rejection Rex undertook an earnest inventory of his personal strengths and weaknesses. He decided that life had taught him one clear lesson, namely, that it is easier to decide things with the aid of hindsight than it is to attempt to foresee and control the future. Not only did hindsight make it easier to decide cases, but—and this was of supreme importance to Rex—it made it easier to give reasons. Deciding to capitalize on this insight, Rex hit on the following plan. At the beginning of each calendar year he would decide all the controversies that had arisen among his subjects during the preceding year. He would accompany his decisions with a full statement of reasons. Naturally, the reasons thus given would be understood as not controlling decisions in future years, for that would be to defeat the whole purpose of the new arrangement, which was to gain the advantages of hindsight. Rex confidently announced the new plan to his subjects, observing that he was going to publish the full text of his judgments with the rules applied by him, thus meeting the chief objection to the old plan. Rex's subjects received this announcement in silence, then quietly explained through their leaders that when they said they needed to know the rules, they meant they needed to know them *in advance* so they could act on them. Rex muttered something to the effect that they might have made that point a little clearer, but said he would see what could be done.

Rex now realized that there was no escape from a published code declaring the rules to be applied in future disputes. Continuing his lessons in generalization, Rex worked diligently on a revised code, and finally announced that it would shortly be published. This announcement was received with universal gratification. The dismay of Rex's subjects was all the more intense, therefore, when his code became available and it was discovered that it was truly a masterpiece of obscurity. Legal experts who studied it declared that there was not a single sentence in it that could be understood either by an ordinary citizen or by a trained lawyer. Indignation became general and soon a picket appeared before the royal palace carrying a sign that read, "How can anybody follow a rule that nobody can understand?"

The code was quickly withdrawn. Recognizing for the first time he needed assistance, Rex put a staff of experts to work on a revision. He instructed them to leave the substance untouched, but to clarify the expression throughout. The resulting code was a model of clarity, but as it was studied it became apparent that its new clarity had merely brought to light that it was honeycombed with contradictions. It was reliably reported that there was not a single provision in the code that was not nullified by another provision inconsistent with it. A picket again appeared before the royal residence carrying a sign that read, "This time the king made himself clear—in both directions."

Once again the code was withdrawn for revision. By now, however, Rex had lost his patience with his subjects and the negative attitude they seemed to adopt toward everything he tried to do for them. He decided to teach them a lesson and put an end to their carping. He instructed his experts to purge the code of contradictions, but at the same time to stiffen drastically every requirement contained in it and to add a long list of new crimes. Thus, where before the citizen summoned to the throne was given ten days in which to report, in the revision the time was cut to ten seconds. It was made a crime, punishable by ten years' imprisonment, to cough, sneeze, hiccough, faint or fall down in the presence of the king. It was made treason not to understand, believe in, and correctly profess the doctrine of evolutionary, democratic redemption.

When the new code was published a near revolution resulted. Leading citizens declared their intention to flout its provisions. Someone discovered in an ancient author a passage that seemed apt: "To command what cannot be done is not to make law; it is to unmake law, for a command that cannot be obeyed serves no end but confusion, fear and chaos." Soon this passage was being quoted in a hundred petitions to the king.

The code was again withdrawn and a staff of experts charged with the task of revision. Rex's instructions to the experts were that whenever they encountered a rule requiring an impossibility, it should be revised to make compliance possible. It turned out that to accomplish this result every provision in the code had to be substantially rewritten. The final result was, however, a triumph of draftsmanship. It was clear, consistent with itself, and demanded nothing of the subject that did not lie easily within his powers. It was printed and distributed free of charge on every street corner.

However, before the effective date for the new code had arrived, it was discovered that so much time had been spent in successive revisions of Rex's original draft, that the substance of the code had been seriously overtaken by events. Ever since Rex assumed the throne there had been a suspension of ordinary legal processes and this had brought about important economic and institutional changes within the country. Accommodation of these altered conditions required many changes of substance in the law. Accordingly as soon as the new code became legally effective, it was subjected to a daily stream of amendments. Again popular discontent mounted; an anonymous pamphlet appeared on the streets carrying scurrilous cartoons of the king and a leading article with the title: "A law that changes every day is worse than no law at all."

Within a short time this source of discontent began to cure itself as the pace of amendment gradually slackened. Before this had occurred to any noticeable degree, however, Rex announced an important decision. Reflecting on the misadventures of his reign, he concluded that much of the trouble lay in bad advice he had received from experts. He accordingly declared he was reassuming the judicial power in his own person. In this way he could directly control the application of the new code and insure his country against another crisis. He began to spend practically all of his time hearing and deciding cases arising under the new code.

As the king proceeded with this task, it seemed to bring to a belated blossoming his long dormant powers of generalization. His opinions began, indeed, to reveal a confident and almost exuberant virtuosity as he deftly distinguished his own previous decisions, exposed the principles on which he acted, and laid down guide lines for the disposition of future controversies. For Rex's subjects a new day seemed about to dawn when they could finally conform their conduct to a coherent body of rules.

This hope was, however, soon shattered. As the bound volumes of Rex's judgments became available and were subjected to closer study, his subjects were appalled to discover that there existed no discernible relation between those judgments and the code they purported to apply. Insofar as it found expression in the actual disposition of controversies, the new code might just as well not have existed at all. Yet in virtually every one of his decisions Rex declared and redeclared the code to be the basic law of his kingdom.

Leading citizens began to hold private meetings to discuss what measures, short of open revolt, could be taken to get the king away from the bench and back on the throne. While these discussions were going on Rex suddenly died, old before his time and deeply disillusioned with his subjects.

The first act of his successor, Rex II, was to announce that he was taking the powers of government away from the lawyers and placing them in the hands of psychiatrists and experts in public relations. This way, he explained, people could be made happy without rules.

THE CONSEQUENCES OF FAILURE

Rex's bungling career as legislator and judge illustrates that the attempt to create and maintain a system of legal rules may miscarry in at least eight ways; there are in this enterprise, if you will, eight distinct routes to disaster. The first and most obvious lies in a failure to achieve rules at all, so that every issue must be decided on an ad hoc basis. The other routes are: (2) a failure to publicize, or at least to make available to the affected party, the rules he is expected to observe; (3) the abuse of retroactive legislation, which not only cannot itself guide action, but undercuts the integrity of rules prospective in effect, since it puts them under the threat of retrospective change; (4) a failure to make rules understandable; (5) the enactment of contradictory rules or (6) rules that require conduct beyond the powers of the affected party; (7) introducing such frequent changes in the rules that the subject cannot orient his action by them; and, finally, (8) a failure of congruence between the rules as announced and their actual administration.

A total failure in any one of these eight directions does not simply result in a bad system of law; it results in something that is not properly called a legal system at all, except perhaps in the Pickwickian sense in which a void contract can still be said to be one kind of contract. Certainly there can be no rational ground for asserting that a man can have a moral obligation to obey a legal rule that does not exist, or is kept secret from him, or that came into existence only after he had acted, or was unintelligible, or was contradicted by another rule of the same system, or commanded the impossible, or changed every minute. It may not be impossible for a man to obey a rule that is disregarded by those charged with its administration, but at some point obedience becomes futile—as futile, in fact, as casting a vote that will never be counted. As the sociologist Simmel has observed, there is a kind of reciprocity between government and the citizen with respect to the observance of rules.[1] Government says to the citizen in effect, "These are the rules we expect you to follow. If you follow them, you have our assurance that they are the rules that will be applied to your conduct." When this bond of reciprocity is finally and completely ruptured by government, nothing is left on which to ground the citizen's duty to observe the rules.

The citizen's predicament becomes more difficult when, though there is no total failure in any direction, there is a general and drastic deterioration in legality, such as occurred in Germany under Hitler. A situation begins to develop, for example, in which though some laws are published, others, including the most important, are not. Though most laws are prospective in effect, so free a use is made of retrospective legislation that no law is immune to change ex post facto if it suits the convenience of those in power. For the trial of criminal cases concerned with loyalty to the regime, special military tribunals are established and these tribunals disregard, whenever it suits their convenience, the rules that are supposed to control their decision. Increasingly the principle object of government seems to be, not that of giving the citizen rules by which to shape his conduct, but to frighten him into impotence. As such a situation develops, the problem faced by the citizen is not so simple as that of a voter who knows with certainty that his ballot will not be counted. It is more like that of the voter who knows that the odds are against his ballot being counted at all, and that if it is counted, there is a good chance that it will be counted for the side against which he actually voted. A citizen in this predicament has to decide for himself whether to stay with the system and cast his ballot as a kind of symbolic act expressing the hope of a better day. So it was

---

[1]*The Sociology of Georg Simmel* (1950), trans. Wolff, §4, "Interaction in the Idea of 'Law,'" pp. 186–89; see also Chapter 4, "Subordination under a Principle," pp. 250–67. Simmel's discussion is worthy of study by those concerned with defining the conditions under which the ideal of "the rule of law" can be realized.

with the German citizen under Hitler faced with deciding whether he had an obligation to obey such portions of the laws as the Nazi terror had left intact.

In situations like these there can be no simple principle by which to test the citizen's obligation of fidelity to law, any more than there can be such a principle for testing his right to engage in a general revolution. One thing is, however, clear. A mere respect for constituted authority must not be confused with fidelity to law. Rex's subjects, for example, remained faithful to him as king throughout his long and inept reign. They were not faithful to his law, for he never made any.

From Fuller, Lon L. "The Morality That Makes Law Possible." The Morality of Law. *New Haven, CT: Yale University Press, 1964. Copyright 1964. Reprinted by permission of Yale University Press.*

Questions to Consider

1. Fuller calls this a "lengthy allegory." What is an allegory, and how is it different from other representations, such as a short story or an extended hypothetical? How are we to interpret this?

2. The title of the first section sounds like a how-to guide: "Eight Ways to Fail to Make Law." Would anyone actually set out to fail? In what way is this title satirical? Why do you think Rex goes to his deathbed "deeply disillusioned with his subjects"?

3. Fuller notes that Rex's successor did away with rules. Is this the better solution? Does Fuller think it is?

4. How does the tone Fuller uses change between the allegory and the analysis sections? Point to language choices or examples Fuller uses that represent the difference.

5. What examples can you think of, historically or in contemporary society, that represent individuals being faithful to a ruler (or government) but not faithful to that society's laws? How can you resolve this apparent paradox?

The Declaration of Independence

A declaration does not have the same force and effect a law would have, but those who sign such a document commit to the provisions within it. Among the signers of the Declaration of Independence is John Hancock, whose large, flourishing signature has become synonymous with adding one's name to a document. Similarly, this entire document has, for many, become synonymous with bold action founded on deliberate and clear argumentation; in fact, much of this text is familiar to most Americans and many others around the world. "When in the Course of human events, it becomes necessary for one people to dissolve the political bands which have connected them with another" begins the commitment that led to a break with what was then generally considered the most powerful country in the world, in turn leading to the creation of another country that many would argue has since supplanted the former in power and prestige. As you read this still-dynamic document, consider how it sets out an argument for the action the signers are about to undertake. What rhetorical strategies do they employ to make their decision to "throw off" their king seem almost inevitable? Are these mere "Facts" or something else?

---- ◆ ----

IN CONGRESS, JULY 4, 1776

The unanimous Declaration of thethirteen united States of America

When in the Course of human events, it becomes necessary for one people to dissolve the political bands which have connected them with another, and to assume among the powers of the earth, the separate and equal station to which the Laws of Nature and Nature's God entitle them, a decent respect to the opinions of mankind requires that they should declare the causes which impel them to the separation.

We hold these truths to be self-evident, that all men are created equal, that they are endowed by their Creator with certain unalienable Rights, that among these are Life, Liberty, and the pursuit of Happiness.—That to secure these rights, Governments are instituted among Men, deriving their just powers from the consent of the governed,—That whenever any Form of Government becomes destructive of these ends, it is the Right of the People to alter or to abolish it, and to institute new Government, laying its foundation on such principles and organizing its powers in such form, as to them shall seem most likely to effect their Safety and Happiness. Prudence, indeed, will dictate that Governments long established should not be changed for light and transient causes; and accordingly all experience hath shewn, that mankind are more disposed to suffer, while evils are sufferable, than to right themselves by abolishing the forms to which they are accustomed. But when a long train of abuses and usurpations, pursuing invariably the same Object evinces a design to reduce them under absolute Despotism, it is their right, it is their duty, to throw off such Government, and to provide new guards for their future security.—Such has been the patient sufferance of these colonies; and such is now the necessity which constrains them to alter their former Systems of Government. The history of the present King of Great Britain is a history of repeated injuries and usurpations, all having in direct object the establishment of an absolute Tyranny over these States. To prove this, let Facts be submitted to a candid world.

He has refused his Assent to Laws, the most wholesome and necessary for the public good.

He has forbidden his Governors to pass Laws of immediate and pressing importance, unless suspended in their operation till his Assent should be obtained; and when so suspended, he has utterly neglected to attend to them.

He has refused to pass other Laws for the accommodation of large districts of people, unless those people would relinquish the right of Representation in the Legislature, a right inestimable to them and formidable to tyrants only.

He has called together legislative bodies at places unusual, uncomfortable, and distant from the depository of their public Records, for the sole purpose of fatiguing them into compliance with his measures.

He has dissolved Representative Houses repeatedly, for opposing with manly firmness his invasions on the rights of the people.

He has refused for a long time, after such dissolutions, to cause others to be elected; whereby the Legislative powers, incapable of Annihilation, have returned to the People at large for their exercise; the State remaining in the mean time exposed to all the dangers of invasion from without, and convulsions within.

He has endeavoured to prevent the population of these States; for that purpose obstructing the Laws for Naturalization of Foreigners; refusing to pass others to encourage their migrations hither, and raising the conditions of new Appropriations of Lands.

He has obstructed the Administration of Justice, by refusing his Assent to Laws for establishing Judiciary powers.

He has made Judges dependent on his Will alone, for the tenure of their offices, and the amount and payment of their salaries.

He has erected a multitude of New Offices, and sent hither swarms of Officers to harrass our people, and eat out their substance.

He has kept among us, in times of peace, Standing Armies without the Consent of our legislatures.

He has affected to render the Military independent of and superior to the Civil power.

He has combined with others to subject us to a jurisdiction foreign to our constitution, and unacknowledged by our laws; giving his Assent to their Acts of pretended Legislation:

For Quartering large bodies of armed troops among us:

For protecting them, by a mock Trial, from punishment for any Murders which they should commit on the Inhabitants of these States:

For cutting off our Trade with all parts of the world:

For imposing Taxes on us without our Consent:

For depriving us in many cases, of the benefits of Trial by Jury:

For transporting us beyond Seas to be tried for pretended offences

For abolishing the free System of English Laws in a neighbouring Province, establishing therein an Arbitrary government, and enlarging its Boundaries so as to render it at once an example and fit instrument for introducing the same absolute rule into these Colonies:

For taking away our Charters, abolishing our most valuable Laws, and altering fundamentally the Forms of our Governments:

For suspending our own Legislatures, and declaring themselves invested with power to legislate for us in all cases whatsoever.

He has abdicated Government here, by declaring us out of his Protection and waging War against us.

He has plundered our seas, ravaged our Coasts, burnt our towns, and destroyed the lives of our people.

He is at this time transporting large Armies of foreign Mercenaries to compleat the works of death, desolation and tyranny, already begun with circumstances of Cruelty & perfidy scarcely paralleled in the most barbarous ages, and totally unworthy the Head of a civilized nation.

He has constrained our fellow Citizens taken Captive on the high Seas to bear Arms against their Country, to become the executioners of their friends and Brethren, or to fall themselves by their Hands.

He has excited domestic insurrections amongst us, and has endeavoured to bring on the inhabitants of our frontiers, the merciless Indian Savages, whose known rule of warfare, is an undistinguished destruction of all ages, sexes and conditions.

In every stage of these Oppressions We have Petitioned for Redress in the most humble terms: Our repeated Petitions have been answered only by repeated injury. A Prince whose character is thus marked by every act which may define a Tyrant, is unfit to be the ruler of a free people.

Nor have We been wanting in attentions to our Brittish brethren. We have warned them from time to time of attempts by their legislature to extend an unwarrantable jurisdiction over us. We have reminded them of the circumstances of our emigration and settlement here. We have appealed to their native justice and magnanimity, and we have conjured them by the ties of our common kindred to disavow these usurpations, which, would inevitably interrupt our connections and correspondence. They too have been deaf to the voice of justice and of consanguinity. We must, therefore, acquiesce in the necessity, which denounces our Separation, and hold them, as we hold the rest of mankind, Enemies in War, in Peace Friends.

We, therefore, the Representatives of the united States of America, in General Congress, Assembled, appealing to the Supreme Judge of the world for the rectitude of our intentions, do, in the Name, and by Authority of the good People of these Colonies, solemnly publish and declare, That these United Colonies are, and of Right ought to be Free and Independent States; that they are Absolved from all Allegiance to the British Crown, and that all political connection between them and the State of Great Britain, is and ought to be totally dissolved; and that as Free and Independent States, they have full Power to levy War, conclude Peace, contract Alliances, establish Commerce, and to do all other Acts and Things which Independent States may of right do. And for the support of this Declaration, with a firm reliance on the protection of divine Providence, we mutually pledge to each other our Lives, our Fortunes and our sacred Honor.

[Following this declaration are the signatures of fifty-six representatives.]

NOTE: Reproductions of the original documents of this and the Constitution, as well as transcripts, can be found at the National Archives *online (www.archives.gov). A transcript comparing the different versions of this text—Jefferson's main text; a copy with Benjamin Franklin's, John Adams's, and Jefferson's revisions; and the version that resulted from the Continental Congress—can be viewed at* USHistory.org, *a site created by the Independence Hall Association (www.ushistory.org/declaration/document/ compare.htm).*

Questions to Consider

1. Why do you think this document is described as "The unanimous Declaration" rather than just "A Declaration of Independence"? Notice the use of adjectives throughout the document. How do they help impel a reader to agree with the authors' points?
2. In 1776, spelling, capitalization, and punctuation were not yet as uniform as they are today; hence, you find "our Brittish brethren" and words such as "Object" and "Facts" capitalized. Some of these words may have been capitalized as a point of emphasis; how else is emphasis employed in this document and to what ends?
3. In what ways do the framers both argue for the ability to rebel and limit their argument so that not every disagreement would lead to an overthrow of the government? Why do they do this?
4. How would you describe the organization employed in this document? Note, especially, the contrasting use of "We" and "He"; how does this serve to frame the document?
5. Who do you think the framers anticipated the various audiences of this document would be? How do their rhetorical strategies reveal this awareness?

The Constitution of the United States and the Bill of Rights

On September 17, 1787, a document was signed that would establish the general system of government that has remained relatively intact ever since. In the handwritten original, the words "We the People" are written large, and what follows, in a relatively short document of seven articles, is the formation of the three major branches of the federal government and general rules governing their establishment and powers; the balance of power between Congress and the states and among the states themselves; the manner in which debts are to be engaged; and the methods for ratification of, and amendments to, the Constitution. Less than two years later, on March 4, 1789, the first ten amendments to the Constitution, known as the Bill of Rights, were signed; they were ratified by the end of 1791. Though only slightly newer than the Declaration of Independence, these documents may seem more contemporary than the Declaration. Why is this, and with what wording and phrases are you familiar?

———— ✦ ————

THE CONSTITUTION OF THE UNITED STATES (Excerpts)

We the People of the United States, in Order to form a more perfect Union, establish Justice, insure domestic Tranquility, provide for the common defence, promote the general Welfare, and secure the Blessings of Liberty to ourselves and our Posterity, do ordain and establish this Constitution for the United States of America.

Article I

SECTION 1

All legislative Powers herein granted shall be vested in a Congress of the United States, which shall consist of a Senate and House of Representatives. [There follows the manner in which legislators can and should serve, and their powers, as well as how impeachment, including that of the President, shall be accomplished.] . . .

Article II

SECTION 1

The executive Power shall be vested in a President of the United States of America. He shall hold his Office during the Term of four Years, and, together with the Vice President, chosen for the same Term, be elected, as follows: [there follows the manner of election through an Electoral College]. . . .

No Person except a natural born Citizen, or a Citizen of the United States, at the time of the Adoption of this Constitution, shall be eligible to the Office of President; neither shall any Person be eligible to that Office who shall not have attained to the Age of thirty five Years, and been fourteen Years a Resident within the United States. . . .

Before he enter on the Execution of his Office, he shall take the following Oath or Affirmation: —"I do solemnly swear (or affirm) that I will faithfully execute the Office of President of the United States, and will to the best of my Ability, preserve, protect and defend the Constitution of the United States.". . .

SECTION 4

The President, Vice President and all civil Officers of the United States, shall be removed from Office on Impeachment for, and Conviction of, Treason, Bribery, or other high Crimes and Misdemeanors.

Article III

SECTION 1

The judicial Power of the United States shall be vested in one supreme Court, and in such inferior Courts as the Congress may from time to time ordain and establish. The Judges, both of the supreme and inferior Courts, shall hold their Offices during good Behavior, and shall, at stated Times, receive for their Services, a Compensation, which shall not be diminished during their Continuance in Office.

SECTION 2

The judicial Power shall extend to all Cases, in Law and Equity, arising under this Constitution, the Laws of the United States, and Treaties made, or which shall be made, under their Authority; [there follow other cases to which judicial power shall extend and the kind of jurisdiction courts will have]. . . .

The Trial of all Crimes, except in Cases of Impeachment, shall be by Jury; and such Trial shall be held in the State where the said Crimes shall have been committed; but when not committed within any State, the trial shall be at such Place or Places as the Congress may by Law have directed.

SECTION 3

Treason against the United States, shall consist only in levying War against them, or in adhering to their Enemies, giving them Aid and Comfort. No Person shall be convicted of Treason unless on the Testimony of two Witnesses to the same overt Act, or on Confession in open Court. . . .

Article IV

[This article includes the Full Faith and Credit Clause, allowing reciprocity between states, and the Privileges and Immunities Clause, requiring citizens of various states to be held by the laws of the various states.]

Article V

The Congress, whenever two thirds of both Houses shall deem it necessary, shall propose Amendments to this Constitution, or, on the Application of the Legislatures of two thirds of the several States, shall call a Convention for proposing Amendments, which, in either Case, shall be valid to all Intents and Purposes, as Part of this Constitution, when ratified by the Legislatures of three fourths of the several States, or by Conventions in three fourths thereof, as the one or the other Mode of Ratification may be proposed by the Congress; Provided that no Amendment which may be made prior to the Year One thousand eight hundred and eight shall in any Manner affect the first and fourth Clauses in the Ninth Section of the first Article; and that no State, without its Consent, shall be deprived of its equal Suffrage in the Senate.

Article VI

. . . This Constitution, and the Laws of the United States which shall be made in Pursuance thereof; and all Treaties made, or which shall be made, under the Authority of the United States, shall be the supreme Law of the Land; and the Judges in every State shall be bound thereby, any Thing in the Constitution or Laws of any State to the Contrary notwithstanding.

The Senators and Representatives before mentioned, and the Members of the several State Legislatures, and all executive and judicial Officers, both of the United States and of the several States, shall be bound by Oath or Affirmation, to support this Constitution; but no religious Test shall ever be required as a Qualification to any Office or public Trust under the United States.

Article VII

[This article clarifies ratification establishing the Constitution.]

[The document is attested to and signed by the president of the Constitutional Convention, George Washington, and thirty-eight witnesses from twelve states.]

THE BILL OF RIGHTS

The Preamble to The Bill of Rights

Congress of the United States begun and held at the City of New-York, on Wednesday the fourth of March, one thousand seven hundred and eighty nine.

THE Conventions of a number of the States, having at the time of their adopting the Constitution, expressed a desire, in order to prevent misconstruction or abuse of its powers, that further declaratory and restrictive clauses should be added: And as extending the ground of public confidence in the Government, will best ensure the beneficent ends of its institution.

RESOLVED by the Senate and House of Representatives of the United States of America, in Congress assembled, two thirds of both Houses concurring, that the following Articles be proposed to the Legislatures of the several States, as amendments to the Constitution of the United States, all, or any of which Articles, when ratified by three fourths of the said Legislatures, to be valid to all intents and purposes, as part of the said Constitution; viz.

ARTICLES in addition to, and Amendment of the Constitution of the United States of America, proposed by Congress, and ratified by the Legislatures of the several States, pursuant to the fifth Article of the original Constitution.

Amendment I

Congress shall make no law respecting an establishment of religion, or prohibiting the free exercise thereof; or abridging the freedom of speech, or of the press; or the right of the people peaceably to assemble, and to petition the Government for a redress of grievances.

Amendment II

A well regulated Militia, being necessary to the security of a free State, the right of the people to keep and bear Arms, shall not be infringed.

Amendment III

No Soldier shall, in time of peace be quartered in any house, without the consent of the Owner, nor in time of war, but in a manner to be prescribed by law.

Amendment IV

The right of the people to be secure in their persons, houses, papers, and effects, against unreasonable searches and seizures, shall not be violated, and no Warrants shall issue, but upon probable cause, supported by Oath or affirmation, and particularly describing the place to be searched, and the persons or things to be seized.

Amendment V

No person shall be held to answer for a capital, or otherwise infamous crime, unless on a presentment or indictment of a Grand Jury, except in cases arising in the land or naval forces, or in the Militia, when in actual service in time of War or public danger; nor shall any person be subject for the same offence to be twice put in jeopardy of life or limb; nor shall be compelled in any criminal case to be a witness against himself, nor be deprived of life, liberty, or property, without due process of law; nor shall private property be taken for public use, without just compensation.

Amendment VI

In all criminal prosecutions, the accused shall enjoy the right to a speedy and public trial, by an impartial jury of the State and district wherein the crime shall have been committed, which district shall have been previously ascertained by law, and to be informed of the nature and cause of the accusation; to be confronted with the witnesses against him; to have compulsory process for obtaining witnesses in his favor, and to have the Assistance of Counsel for his defence.

Amendment VII

In Suits at common law, where the value in controversy shall exceed twenty dollars, the right of trial by jury shall be preserved, and no fact tried by a jury, shall be otherwise re-examined in any Court of the United States, than according to the rules of the common law.

Amendment VIII

Excessive bail shall not be required, nor excessive fines imposed, nor cruel and unusual punishments inflicted.

Amendment IX

The enumeration in the Constitution, of certain rights, shall not be construed to deny or disparage others retained by the people.

Amendment X

The powers not delegated to the United States by the Constitution, nor prohibited by it to the States, are reserved to the States respectively, or to the people.

Questions to Consider

1. The framers noted their goals to be "establish[ing] Justice" and "insur[ing] domestic Tranquility." Did the acceptance of the Constitution achieve this? Do you think the framers thought it would? Why else might they begin a document like this with words that aspired to so much?
2. Every four years when a President takes the oath of office, he (as of this printing, it has always been a male to do so) repeats the words prescribed in Article II, Section 1. When President Obama took the oath, much media attention surrounded the mistakes Supreme Court Chief Justice Roberts made when administering the oath of office to him. What would you argue is the power of historical continuity and of attention to accuracy in that continuity?
3. What rhetorical characteristics would you say identify these Articles and Amendments as rules to be obeyed? How do these characteristics lend a more contemporary style to these documents than is evident in the Declaration of Independence?
4. What purpose do the introductory paragraphs to the Bill of Rights serve?
5. Consider the structure of the sentences within the Bill of Rights. How does each suggest a focus and potential aid to interpretation, and in what ways might the structures impede interpretation? Overall, how do these statements serve to "amend" the Constitution?

We Need a Clear Set of Rules to Reaffirm Our Values as a Nation

SANDRA DAY O'CONNOR

Sandra Day O'Connor rose to prominence as the first female Supreme Court justice, appointed in 1981 by President Ronald Reagan. Although O'Connor had graduated from Stanford Law School, where she had served on the Law Review, many law firms were not hiring female attorneys in 1952, so O'Connor took a position in public practice as a deputy county attorney for San Mateo County. Afterward, she held a number of positions, including state senator and judge, before she was appointed to the Supreme Court. This 2006 text was excerpted by Army Magazine *from an address made by O'Connor to cadets at the U.S. Military Academy at West Point. O'Connor warns that, despite the Constitution and judicial interpretation of that document, as well as other guiding military rules such as the Geneva Conventions, military personnel often move ahead without clear guidance. What rules are to be used when none seem to exist or when the circumstances of the situation are vastly different from those under which the rules were written?*

❖

Each of the West Point Cadets here today joined the long gray line after 9/11. Each of you chose in the aftermath of that terrible September day to come here, to train and to serve your country, braving the risks and the challenges of future conflicts with a shadowy, unidentified enemy and a war like no other we have seen. Your years here are marked by where you will go afterwards: Iraq, Afghanistan, or other unknown places to which the service calls you. As you head out into that future, you will face profoundly difficult choices. You will perhaps also come across the old Roman maxim "in time of war the laws are silent." That maxim seems almost quaint today. The Romans had no Geneva Conventions, nor did they have a JAG Corps (or for that matter, a press corps). Today, law and war seem inseparable. But there is still some truth to that old saying, because to the extent that there is a law of war, it is always the law of the *last* war. So there is some tension there. Today, this tension is made most clear when we talk about how the United States treats its prisoners in the war on terror. What law governs the detention and interrogation of terrorist suspects? And how are you to know what standards apply? What does your *duty* demand? What does your *honor* demand? And what does your *country* demand? It is hard enough to answer the first two questions, but harder still when the nation's elected leaders are silent about the last.

The Geneva Conventions and their Protocols were not made for conflicts between a state and an international terrorist network. For the most part, they were drafted with traditional armies of nation states in mind. Some have said that we need to rethink these Conventions and amend them. But that is a daunting process and takes many years. And what are soldiers meant to do in the meantime? For many years, the Conventions have set the basic ground rules for the U.S. armed forces in matters related to the treatment of prisoners. The Army has devoted a great deal of effort to implementing and specifying the standards set out in the Conventions in its field manuals and manuals about intelligence interrogation. But no one has yet written the book for the rules that apply when the Geneva Conventions do not. That is a very difficult situation. And there has been a lot of confusion about what roles apply to whom, and where.

As a result, military personnel from the front lines in Iraq have reported that they do not know what rules apply, and that they have not received clear guidelines from their superior officers. Some of their superior officers are saying that they were not able to get clear guidelines from people higher up in the chain of command. This is clearly not a good situation. When soldiers are being told to go out and get intelligence, but not told the limits on how they may do so, they may overstep the bounds. That in turn may lead to both legal and diplomatic difficulties. And if our military is not treating prisoners of war "properly," that may also increase the dangers to U.S. soldiers if they are captured by the enemy. Often it is the low-ranking soldiers that are blamed for the abuses. They, of course, have to take responsibility for their own actions, but those that would lead them also need to take responsibility. Finally, it seems to me we need a clear set of rules to reaffirm our values as a nation. This is crucial in the ongoing war of ideas. We have to demonstrate two things in particular: First, this country believes in protecting the basic humanity of all people, and that includes even our adversaries. Second, we will not stoop to the atrocities and inhumane tactics of some of our adversaries.

But where will we get specific guidance? Our Supreme Court has said very little about what the government may and may not do to people captured by U.S. forces on the battlefield. The Supreme Court takes cases that have arisen in the lower courts, which are often decided some years after the events being litigated. In a case in 2003 called *Hamdi* we said that U.S. citizens who are being held on U.S. soil as enemy combatants have to be given some minimal due process of law. But we were cautious about putting too much of a burden on the military, and deciding too much. So the command of that case is modest. The military must give citizens who are being detained—not at the moment they are captured on the battlefield, but later, when the military makes the decision to hold onto them—a "meaningful opportunity" to challenge the factual basis for their detention. It must tell them why they are being held, and give them a fair opportunity to contest the facts before an impartial adjudicator. We did not decide if this process could be achieved through a military tribunal. We simply said that there has to be some way for a U.S. citizen who is being indefinitely detained to have some outside review—a second look if you will.

In another case that we decided at the same time, called *Rasul,* we said even less. *Rasul* held that detainees held as enemy combatants at the Guantanamo Bay Naval Base could bring an action in federal courts challenging the legality of their detention. This also was a narrow decision. It said *only that in a place like Guantanamo, which is under the "complete jurisdiction and control"* of the United States, could prisoners who are being held indefinitely bring a challenge to their detention. But we said nothing about what kinds of claims will succeed once the detainees get to federal court.

These were limited steps and decisions. Some criticized the Court for doing too much. But the Court was bound by the Constitution and by the historical events of the Court to do no less. Some criticized the Court for doing too little. But the Court is naturally reluctant to rule more broadly than necessary. The Court is only one branch of government, and it cannot, and should not, give broad answers to the difficult policy questions that face our nation today.

So the Supreme Court treads cautiously. One of the architectural features of the Supreme Court are the small bronze turtles that hold up the lampposts in our courtyards. They symbolize the pace of justice: slow but steady. And that is the nature of *our* duty, *our* honor, and *our* service to country, as members of the Supreme Court. We move slowly, but steadily, under the light shed by our Constitution. Sometimes that light does not illuminate very much. It is an old document—and it is very short. But with good reason: It is designed primarily not to govern the people, but to allow the people to govern themselves.

We guard the ground rules, so that the people, through their elected representatives, can run the country. This is where we expect Congress to step in. But it has done surprisingly little to date to clarify United States policy towards prisoners in the war on terror. That may be changing, of course. The Senate recently voted to insert an amendment into a military spending bill to make the U.S. policy on interrogations clear. The bill would establish that it is the same as in the U.S. Army Field Manual on Intelligence Interrogation. The bill also states that this country will not engage in cruel and degrading treatment of prisoners under any circumstances. It is not my place to express views about the merits of this or any other legislation, but I think it is not too much to say that I believe some clarity from Congress and the President would be welcomed by our armed forces.

Justice Brandeis once said, "In most matters it is more important that the applicable rule of law be settled than that it be settled right." That statement is true in many circumstances. But this is not one of them. Here, it is important that the law be settled, *and* that it be settled right. So perhaps Congress will continue to try to get the law right, and, from time to time, these kinds of questions will end up back before the federal courts.

Insofar as the courts have not delimited with clarity the standards and the limits, it is more likely that the other branches will step in and make the political choices that at the end of the day in their application may return to the courts in a different form—but it takes years for most of these matters to be resolved.

In the meantime, the nation has placed an enormous burden upon our armed forces. We have asked you to be our soldiers and our statesmen, to be our combatants and our conscience. This burden has been placed upon you with only limited guidance. But the history and honor of this institution suggests that if anyone can bear this responsibility, it is the Corps of Cadets, and your previous graduates. This institution has been producing our nation's military leaders for more than 200 years. It has done so during times of peace and times of war. It has always done so with skill and distinction. We are facing military challenges today unlike any in the past. Our nation will rely on you new young military leaders to do as you have done in the past—to defend our nation here and abroad, to conduct yourselves honorably with or without specific guidelines, and to enable our nation to survive in some of the most challenging times we have faced. Our military personnel have had to become more than soldiers. Now they are our diplomats, our peacekeepers, our nation builders as well. There is much to do and no blueprints for doing it.

May I say as someone without a military background that we citizens are deeply grateful and appreciative for your courage and dedication. Without you, we would not long survive.

May God bless you—each and every one.

O'Connor, Sandra Day. "We Need a Clear Set of Rules to Reaffirm Our Values as a Nation." Army Magazine. 56:1 (January 2006): 9–10, 12. Excerpt from "Remarks by Sandra Day O'Connor: Upon Receiving the Sylvanus Thayer Award, West Point, October 20, 2005." West Point Association of

Questions to Consider

1. O'Connor notes the role of the Supreme Court as providing guidance bound by the Constitution that "cannot, and should not, give broad answers to the difficult policy questions that face our nation today." From whom does she suggest those answers should come?

2. Despite the existence and interpretation of military rules, O'Connor agrees with the Roman maxim that during war "the laws are silent." What does she mean by this?

3. Supreme Court rulings, such as those in *Hamdi* and *Rasul*, are noted by O'Connor. This use of precedent, or stare decisis, is the practice of following previous decisions in cases with similar fact situations. Why does O'Connor say that these rulings cannot govern new cases? What does this suggest about the importance of the distinct facts of each new situation that arises?

4. Note the structure of O'Connor's argument. How are the demands of duty, honor, and country reflected in the responsibilities of both the soldier and the Supreme Court? Why does she make this comparison?

5. What is O'Connor's purpose in this address? Although this speech seems to be to one particular audience, is this really her only audience?

How Does Our Language Shape the Way We Think?

LERA BORODITSKY

If we are what we eat, are we what we say as well? In this essay, Dr. Lera Boroditsky, a professor of psychology, neuroscience, and symbolic systems at Stanford, provides examples of the ways in which various cultures describe the world around them in astonishingly different ways. Not only are their words different, but how they are used in other circumstances strongly suggests that such differences in words shape perspectives in a broader sense. As support for her analysis, Boroditsky, winner of the McDonnell Scholar Award and the CAREER award from the National Science Foundation, has collected data from around the world. This article is taken from a collection entitled What's Next? Dispatches on the Future of Science *and subtitled* Original Essays from a New Generation of Scientists. *What is new about this way of thinking, and why might it be especially important in our increasingly global future?*

---- ✦ ----

Humans communicate with one another using a dazzling array of languages, each differing from the next in innumerable ways. Do the languages we speak shape the way we see the world, the way we think, and the way we live our lives? Do people who speak different languages think differently simply because they speak different languages? Does learning new languages change the way you think? Do polyglots think differently when speaking different languages?

These questions touch on nearly all of the major controversies in the study of mind. They have engaged scores of philosophers, anthropologists, linguists, and psychologists, and they have important implications for politics, law, and religion. Yet despite nearly constant attention and debate, very little empirical work was done on these questions until recently. For a long time, the idea that language might shape thought was considered at best untestable and more often simply wrong. Research in my labs at Stanford University and at MIT has helped reopen this question. We have collected data around the world: from China, Greece, Chile, Indonesia, Russia, and Aboriginal Australia. What we have learned is that people who speak different languages do indeed think differently and that even flukes of grammar can profoundly affect how we see the world. Language is a uniquely human gift, central to our experience of being human. Appreciating its role in constructing our mental lives brings us one step closer to understanding the very nature of humanity.

I often start my undergraduate lectures by asking students the following question: which cognitive faculty would you most hate to lose? Most of them pick the sense of sight; a few pick hearing. Once in a while, a wisecracking student might pick her sense of humor or her fashion sense. Almost never do any of them spontaneously say that the faculty they'd most hate to lose is language. Yet if you lose (or are born without) your sight or hearing, you can still have a wonderfully rich social existence. You can have friends, you can get an education, you can hold a job, you can start a family. But what would your life be like if you had never learned a language? Could you still have friends, get an education, hold a job, start a family? Language is so fundamental to our experience, so deeply a part of being human, that it's hard to imagine life without it. But are languages merely tools for expressing our thoughts, or do they actually shape our thoughts?

Most questions of whether and how language shapes thought start with the simple observation that languages differ from one another. And a lot! Let's take a (very) hypothetical example. Suppose you want to say, "Bush read Chomsky's latest book." Let's focus on just the verb, "read." To say this sentence in English, we have to mark the verb for tense; in this case, we have to pronounce it like "red" and not like "reed". In Indonesian you need not (in fact, you can't) alter the verb to mark tense. In Russian you would have to alter the verb to indicate tense and gender. So if it was Laura Bush who did the reading, you'd use a different form of the verb than if it was George. In Russian you'd also have to include in the verb information about completion. If George read only part of the book, you'd use a different form of the verb than if he'd diligently plowed through the whole thing. In Turkish you'd have to include in the verb how you acquired this information: if you had witnessed this unlikely event with your own two eyes, you'd use one verb form, but if you had simply read or heard about it, or inferred it from something Bush said, you'd use a different verb form.

Clearly, languages require different things of their speakers. Does this mean that the speakers think differently about the world? Do English, Indonesian, Russian, and Turkish speakers end up attending to, partitioning, and remembering their experiences differently just because they speak different languages?

For some scholars, the answer to these questions has been an obvious yes. Just look at the way people talk, they might say. Certainly, speakers of different languages must attend to and encode strikingly different aspects of the world just so they can use their language properly.

Scholars on the other side of the debate don't find the differences in how people talk convincing. All our linguistic utterances are sparse, encoding only a small part of the information we have available. Just because English speakers don't include the same information in their verbs that Russian and Turkish speakers do doesn't mean that English speakers aren't paying attention to the same things; all it means is that they're not talking about them. It's possible that everyone thinks the same way, notices the same things, but just talks differently.

Believers in cross-linguistic differences counter that everyone does *not* pay attention to the same things: if everyone did, one might think it would be easy to learn to speak other languages. Unfortunately, learning a new language (especially one not closely related to those you know) is never easy; it seems to require paying attention to a new set of distinctions. Whether it's distinguishing modes of being in Spanish, evidentiality in Turkish, or aspect in Russian, learning to speak these languages requires something more than just learning vocabulary: it requires paying attention to the right things in the world so that you have the correct information to include in what you *say*.

Such a priori arguments about whether or not language shapes thought have gone in circles for centuries, with some arguing that it's impossible for language to shape thought and others arguing that it's impossible for language *not* to shape thought. Recently my group and others have figured out ways to empirically test some of the key questions in this ancient debate, with fascinating results. So instead of arguing about what must be true or what can't be true, let's find out what *is* true.

Follow me to Pormpuraaw, a small Aboriginal community on the western edge of Cape York, in northern Australia. I came here because of the way the locals, the Kuuk Thaayorre, talk about space. Instead of words like "right," "left," "forward," and "back," which, as commonly used in English, define space relative to an observer, the Kuuk Thaayorre, like many other Aboriginal groups, use cardinal-direction terms—north, south, east, and west—to define space.[1] This is done at all scales, which means you have to say things like "There's an ant on your southeast leg" or "Move the cup to the north-northwest a little bit." One obvious consequence of speaking such a language is that you have to stay oriented at all times, or else you cannot speak properly. The normal greeting in Kuuk Thaayorre is "Where are you going?" and the answer should be something like "South-southeast, in the middle distance." If you don't know which way you're facing, you can't even get past "Hello."

---

[1] S.C. Levinson and D.P. Wilking, eds., *Grammars of Space: Explorations in Cognitive Diversity* (New York: Cambridge University Press, 2006).

The result is a profound difference in navigational ability and spatial knowledge between speakers of languages that rely primarily on absolute reference frames (like Kuuk Thaayorre) and languages that rely on relative reference frames (like English).[2] Simply put, speakers of languages like Kuuk Thaayorre are much better than English speakers at staying oriented and keeping track of where they are, even in unfamiliar landscapes or inside unfamiliar buildings. What enables them—in fact, forces them—to do this is their language. Having their attention trained in this way equips them to perform navigational feats once thought beyond human capabilities.

Because space is such a fundamental domain of thought, differences in how people think about space don't end there. People rely on their spatial knowledge to build other, more complex, more abstract representations. Representations of such things as time, number, musical pitch, kinship relations, morality, and emotions have been shown to depend on how we think about space. So if the Kuuk Thaayorre think differently about space, do they also think differently about other things, like time? This is what my collaborator Alice Gaby and I came to Pormpuraaw to find out.

To test this idea, we gave people sets of pictures that showed some kind of temporal progression (e.g., pictures of a man aging, or a crocodile growing, or a banana being eaten). Their job was to arrange the shuffled photos on the ground to show the correct temporal order. We tested each person in two separate sittings, each time facing in a different cardinal direction. If you ask English speakers to do this, they'll arrange the cards so that time proceeds from left to right. Hebrew speakers will tend to lay out the cards from right to left, showing that writing direction in a language plays a role.[3] So what about folks like the Kuuk Thaayorre, who don't use words like "left" and "right"? What will they do?

The Kuuk Thaayorre did not arrange the cards more often from left to right than from right to left, nor more toward or away from the body. But their arrangements were not random: there was a pattern, just a different one from that of English speakers. Instead of arranging time from left to right, they arranged it from east to west. That is, when they were seated facing south, the cards went left to right. When they faced north, the cards went from right to left. When they faced east, the cards came toward the body, and so on. This was

[2]Levinson, *Space in Language and Cognition: Explorations in Cognitive Diversity* (New York: Cambridge University Press, 2003).

[3]B. Tversky et al., "Cross-Cultural and Developmental Trends in Graphic Productions," *Cognitive Psychology* 23(1991): 515–57; O. Fuhrman and L. Boroditsky, "Mental Time-Lines Follow Writing Direction: Comparing English and Hebrew Speakers," *Proceedings of the 29th Annual Conference of the Cognitive Science Society* (2007): 1007–10.

true even though we never told any of our subjects which direction they faced. The Kuuk Thaayorre not only knew that already (usually much better than I did), but they also spontaneously used this spatial orientation to construct their representations of time.

People's ideas of time differ across languages in other ways. For example, English speakers tend to talk about time using horizontal spatial metaphors (e.g., "The best is *ahead* of us," "The worst is *behind* us"), whereas Mandarin speakers have a vertical metaphor for time (e.g., the next month is the "down month" and the last month is the "up month"). Mandarin speakers talk about time vertically more often than English speakers do, so do Mandarin speakers think about time vertically more often than English speakers do? Imagine this simple experiment. I stand next to you, point to a spot in space directly in front of you, and tell you, "This spot, here, is today. Where would you put yesterday? And where would you put tomorrow?" When English speakers are asked to do this, they nearly always point horizontally. But Mandarin speakers often point vertically, about seven or eight times more often than do English speakers.[4]

Even basic aspects of time perception can be affected by language. For example, English speakers prefer to talk about duration in terms of length (e.g., "That was a *short* talk," "The meeting didn't take *long*"), while Spanish and Greek speakers prefer to talk about time in terms of amount, relying more on words like "much," "big," and "little" rather than "short" and "long." Our research into such basic cognitive abilities as estimating duration shows that speakers of different languages differ in ways predicted by the patterns of metaphors in their language. (For example, when asked to estimate duration, English speakers are more likely to be confused by distance information, estimating that a line of greater length remains on the test screen for a longer period of time, whereas Greek speakers are more likely to be confused by amount, estimating that a container that is fuller remains longer on the screen.)[5]

An important question at this point is: are these differences caused by language per se or by some other aspect of culture? Of course, the lives of English, Mandarin, Greek, Spanish, and Kuuk Thaayorre speakers differ in a myriad of ways. How do we know that it is language itself that creates these differences in thought and not some other aspect of their respective cultures?

[4]L. Boroditsky, "Do English and Mandarin Speakers Think Differently About Time?" *Proceedings of the 48th Annual Meeting of the Psychonomic Society* (2007): 34.
[5]D. Casasanto et al., "How Deep Are Effects of Language on Thought? Time Estimation in Speakers of English, Indonesian, Greek, and Spanish," *Proceedings of the 26th Annual Conference of the Cognitive Science Society* (2004): 575–80.

One way to answer this question is to teach people new ways of talking and see if that changes the way they think. In our lab, we've taught English speakers different ways of talking about time. In one such study, English speakers were taught to use size metaphors (as in Greek) to describe duration (e.g., a movie *is larger than* a sneeze), or vertical metaphors (as in Mandarin) to describe event order. Once the English speakers had learned to talk about time in these new ways, their cognitive performance began to resemble that of Greek or Mandarin speakers. This suggests that patterns in a language can indeed play a causal role in construct-ing how we think.[6] In practical terms, it means that when you're learning a new language, you're not simply learning a new way of talking, you are also inadvertently learning a new way of thinking.

Beyond abstract or complex domains of thought like space and time, languages also meddle in basic aspects of visual perception—our ability to distinguish colors, for example. Different languages divide up the color continuum differently: some make many more distinctions between colors than others, and the boundaries often don't line up across languages.

To test whether differences in color language lead to differ-ences in color perception, we compared Russian and English speakers' ability to discriminate shades of blue. In Russian there is no single word that covers all the colors that English speakers call "blue." Russian makes an obligatory distinction between light blue (*goluboy*) and dark blue (*siniy*). Does this distinction mean that *siniy* blues look more different from *goluboy* blues to Russian speakers? Indeed, the data say yes. Russian speakers are quicker to distinguish two shades of blue that are called by the different names in Russian (i.e., one being *siniy* and the other being *goluboy*) than if the two fall into the same category. For English speakers, all these shades are still designated by the same word, "blue," and there are no comparable differences in reaction time.

Further, the Russian advantage disappears when subjects are asked to perform a verbal interference task (reciting a string of digits) while making color judgments but not when they're asked to perform an equally difficult spatial interference task (keeping a novel visual pattern in memory). The disappearance of the advan-tage when performing a verbal task shows that language is nor-mally involved in even surprisingly basic perceptual judgments—and that it is language per se that creates this differ-ence in perception between Russian and English speakers. When

[6]Ibid., "How Deep Are Effects of Language on Thought? Time Estimation in Speakers of English and Greek" (in review); L. Boroditsky, "Does Language Shape Thought? English and Mandarin Speakers' Conceptions of Time," *Cognitive Psychology* 43, no. 1(2001): 1–22.

Russian speakers are blocked from their normal access to language by a verbal interference task, the differences between Russian and English speakers disappear.

Even what might be deemed frivolous aspects of language can have far-reaching subconscious effects on how we see the world. Take grammatical gender. In Spanish and other Romance languages, nouns are either masculine or feminine. In many other languages, nouns are divided into many more genders ("gender" in this context meaning class or kind). For example, some Australian Aboriginal languages have up to sixteen genders, including classes of hunting weapons, canines, things that are shiny, or, in the phrase made famous by cognitive linguist George Lakoff, "women, fire, and dangerous things."

What it means for a language to have grammatical gender is that words belonging to different genders get treated differently grammatically and words belonging to the same grammatical gender get treated the same grammatically. Languages can require speakers to change pronouns, adjective and verb endings, possessives, numerals, and so on, depending on the noun's gender. For example, to say something like "my chair was old" in Russian (*moy stul bil' stariy*), you'd need to make every word in the sentence agree in gender with "chair" (*stul*), which is masculine in Russian. So you'd use the masculine form of "my," "was," and "old." These are the same forms you'd use in speaking of a biological male, as in "my grandfather was old." If, instead of speaking of a chair, you were speaking of a bed (*krovat'*), which is feminine in Russian, or about your grandmother, you would use the feminine form of "my," "was," and "old."

Does treating chairs as masculine and beds as feminine in the grammar make Russian speakers think of chairs as being more like men and beds as more like women in some way? It turns out that it does. In one study, we asked German and Spanish speakers to describe objects having opposite gender assignment in those two languages. The descriptions they gave differed in a way predicted by grammatical gender. For example, when asked to describe a "key"— a word that is masculine in German and feminine in Spanish—the German speakers were more likely to use words like "hard," "heavy," "jagged," "metal," "serrated," and "useful," whereas Spanish speakers were more likely to say "golden," "intricate," "little," "lovely," "shiny," and "tiny." To describe a "bridge," which is feminine in German and masculine in Spanish, the German speakers said "beautiful," "elegant," "fragile," "peaceful," "pretty," and "slender," and the Spanish speakers said "big," "dangerous," "long," "strong," "sturdy," and "towering." This was true even though all testing was done in English, a language without grammatical gender. The same pattern of results also emerged in entirely nonlinguistic tasks (e.g., rating similarity between pictures). And we can also show that it is aspects of language per se that shape how people think: teaching English speakers new grammatical gender systems influences mental representations of objects in the same way it does with German and Spanish speakers. Apparently even small flukes of grammar, like the seemingly arbitrary assignment of gender to a noun, can have an effect on people's ideas of concrete objects in the world.[7]

In fact, you don't even need to go into the lab to see these effects of language; you can see them with your own eyes in an art gallery. Look at some famous examples of personification in art—the ways in which abstract entities such as death, sin, victory, or time are given human form. How does an artist decide whether death, say, or time should be painted as a man or a woman? It turns out that in 85 percent of such personifications, whether a male or female figure is chosen is predicted by the grammatical gender of the word in the artist's native language. So, for example, German painters are more likely to paint death as a man, whereas Russian painters are more likely to paint death as a woman.

The fact that even quirks of grammar, such as grammatical gender, can affect our thinking is profound. Such quirks are pervasive in language; gender, for example, applies to all nouns, which means that it is affecting how people think about anything that can be designated by a noun. That's a lot of stuff!

I have described how languages shape the way we think about space, time, colors, and objects. Other studies have found effects of language on how people construe events, reason about causality, keep track of number, understand material substance, perceive and experience emotion, reason about other people's minds, choose to take risks, and even in the way they choose professions and spouses.[8] Taken together, these results show

---

[7]L. Boroditsky et al., "Sex, Syntax, and Semantics," in D. Gentner and S. Goldin-Meadow, eds., *Language in Mind: Advances in the Study of Language and Cognition* (Cambridge, MA: MIT Press, 2003), 61–79.

[8]L. Boroditsky, "Linguistic Relativity," in L. Nadel, ed., *Encyclopedia of Cognitive Science* (London: MacMillan, 2003), 917–21; B. W. Pelham et al., "Why Susie Sells Seashells by the Seashore: Implicit Egotism and Major Life Decisions," *Journal of Personality and Social Psychology* 82, no. 4(2002): 469–86; A. Tversky and D. Kahneman, "The Framing of Decisions and the Psychology of Choice," *Science* 211(1981): 453–58; P. Pica et al., "Exact and Approximate Arithmetic in an Amazonian Indigene Group," *Science* 306(2004): 499–503; J.G. de Villiers and P.A. de Villiers, "Linguistic Determinism and False Belief," in P. Mitchell and K. Riggs, eds., *Children's Reasoning and the Mind* (Hove, UK: Psychology Press, in press); J.A. Lucy and S. Gaskins, "Interaction of Language Type and Referent Type in the Development of Nonverbal Classification Preferences," in Gentner and Goldin-Meadow, 465–92; L. F. Barrett et al., "Language as a Context for Emotion Perception," *Trends in Cognitive Sciences* 11(2007): 327–32.

that linguistic processes are pervasive in most fundamental domains of thought, unconsciously shaping us from the nuts and bolts of cognition and perception to our loftiest abstract notions and major life decisions. Language is central to our experience of being human, and the languages we speak profoundly shape the way we think, the way we see the world, the way we live our lives.

Questions to Consider

1. How do the questions with which Boroditsky opens her essay help frame her argument? At what point in this essay is her position on these questions clear?

2. Boroditsky claims that the intersection of language and thinking has "important implications for politics, law, and religion." In what ways do you see these institutions affected by the questions raised?

3. This text is replete with examples to help support Boroditsky's argument. How would you characterize the different kinds of examples? With what other kinds of strategies does she build her article?

4. At various times in our culture, there have been movements to change the way we refer to certain professions, people, or concepts in an overt effort to also change perspectives; consider efforts to change *fireman* to *firefighter*. How might certain words relating to these concepts represent, and/or come to create, different perspectives?

5. Although Boroditsky is an expert in technical and scientific areas, this essay is relatively accessible. Where do you see evidence of this, and why do you think Boroditsky wrote for a general audience?

Making Connections

1. Lon Fuller's essay is from his book *The Morality of Law*. How does his exploration of Rex represent a certain morality, or at least unstated assumptions, about the decision to establish rules and what rules to create? What morals and values are represented in the Constitution and the Bill of Rights?
2. Boroditsky asserts that languages "profoundly shape the way we think, the way we see the world, the way we live our lives." How does the language you speak, compared with what your parents or grandparents speak, affect your perceptions about the world you share?
3. If you look up the original Declaration of Independence, you'll see evidence of revisions and collaboration. Why are both important, especially in creating a text with which you want others to agree?
4. Although it's clear that most of the texts in this chapter are arguments, note that the Bill of Rights was the framers' response to those who argued that the Constitution granted too much power to the government. Where can you see this power struggle reflected in these two documents?
5. O'Connor notes that gaps exist in the law the West Point cadets are required to follow. Can laws ever cover all situations to which they theoretically apply? Why or why not?
6. What current controversies represent soldiers or governments being unsure about what their scope should be during armed conflict? What do these controversies have in common with other historical examples? Consider, for example, the My Lai incident during the Vietnam War and the internment of Japanese- and German-Americans during WWII.
7. The Constitution sets out many mandates that are not fully developed, such as the requirements of inferior courts and of trials by jury. How can understanding the purpose behind broad mandates help in creating specific rules to implement such requirements?
8. Many legal scholars and groups debate what constitutes "the rule of law." One such group that uses Fuller's requirements as an example is the student-driven University of Iowa Center for International Finance and Development, which has created a web page to help the layperson understand laws as they relate to the goals of international finance (see blogs.law.uiowa.edu/ebook/faqs/what-is-the-rule-of-law). How would you explain to a general audience how your university's rules help promote educational goals?

The Stories We Tell:
Law as Narrative

But this too is true: stories can save us.
               Tim O'Brien, The Things They Carried

Law relies on stories in many ways: how an accident occurred, why a defendant claims innocence, how an injurious product was made. That narrative must include relevant information in order for a trier of fact to decide on issues of guilt or liability. In other words, the story must prove something—it must have probative value—in order for it to have legal effect. Yet even then, a story's usefulness may be limited. How that narrative is interpreted and what it proves are subject to debate. Thus, we might use multiple judges or jury members in making a determination; even so, we have hung juries and dissenting judicial opinions. Moreover, these measures don't ensure "correct" results—Innocence Projects around the country unearth old DNA samples and help to prove innocent an uncomfortable number of prisoners whom the courts had labeled guilty.

Stories not only reveal a culture, but can also help to shape one. These narratives can serve as a window into how the legal system works, as well as how it fails to work, and into the cultural values we have and aspire to, as well as where those values fail to be realized. In turn, these stories can motivate change that can reshape an institution such as the law. What do the stories in this chapter tell us? How can our understanding of them promote change? Each narrative should be read critically, keeping in mind the singular perspective represented. It will help to ask questions—Why is this individual telling this story at this particular time? Who would have different stories to tell on this subject, and why? What kinds of practices and culture would give rise to different end results?

We begin with narratives written in the context of legal cases. The first is delivered by a lawyer during the long-delayed retrial of a suspect in the murder of a prominent civil rights activist killed in Mississippi in 1963. The prosecutor, Bobby DeLaughter, only a boy at the time of the murder, provides his closing argument—summing up the case and attempting to persuade the jury that they need to find this defendant guilty, thirty-one years and two mistrials after the murder. DeLaughter explained that his argument was a response to questions he had jotted down over the years from people wondering why anyone would care about this case; if they wondered, DeLaughter thought, so too would this jury. The set of narratives that comprise the second selection are written for a broader legal community. In the various opinions by the Supreme Court in the *DeShaney* case, the justices seem to speak to each other as much as to a wider audience in describing their perspectives regarding the abuse of a young boy by his father. In each of these first two cases, the final decision may surprise you.

More personal reflections are encountered in the remaining readings. Dennis Barrie looks back on his experience as a defendant in the case against him and the Contemporary Arts Center in Cincinnati, Ohio, in 1990. The defendants had exhibited works by the controversial artist and photographer Robert Mapplethorpe; for this, obscenity charges were brought against them. In another essay, Dwayne Franklin recalls various encounters with the law that highlight the potentially paradoxical relationships an average citizen might have with the legal system. Finally, then-Police Captain Mike Gauldin is asked to recall an investigation he led of a rape case. The defendant was convicted and imprisoned for eleven years before being exonerated. Gauldin argues that the investigation could not have turned out any other way.

Speaking on a variety of legal issues in very different contexts, these narrators may help you appreciate both the pervasiveness and the complicated nature of law. Keep in mind, however, that these stories reflect individual perspectives. What is your personal narrative of the law?

Closing Argument in *The State of Mississippi v. Byron De La Beckwith*
DELIVERED BY BOBBY DELAUGHTER

This closing argument appears in Ladies and Gentlemen of the Jury: Greatest Closing Arguments in Modern Law *by attorneys Michael S. Lief, H. Mitchell Caldwell, and Benjamin Bycel. Despite two trials of Byron De La Beckwith, the juries had not been able to unanimously decide on this white man's guilt or innocence in the murder of black civil rights activist Medgar Evers. Many commentators would agree that the 1960s were a difficult time, and the deep South a difficult place, to find justice for blacks—a time when lynchings of blacks and civil rights workers still occurred. The authors of the text contend that for the all-white, all-male juries, it was not a question of whether the defendant had murdered Evers, but whether such an incident was truly a crime. Although new evidence had allowed the case to be reopened in a more progressive era, the passage of time always impedes criminal trials. Witnesses' memories fade and defendants grow old—De La Beckwith was seventy-four at this final retrial. Pay attention to the strategies Bobby DeLaughter employs in his attempt to persuade the jury to find the defendant, Byron De La Beckwith, guilty as charged.*

---------------- ◆ ----------------

When we started the testimony a little over a week ago now, I stood before you and I told you what the evidence would show in this case. I told you then that when all the evidence was in, you would see what this case was about; you would see what this case was not about; it is about an unarmed man, arriving home [in] the late hours of the night, having been working, coming home to his family, his wife, three small children that were staying up, waiting on him to get home inside the home there, getting out of his automobile with his back turned, and being shot down by a bushwacker from ambush. And that he dropped T-shirts in his arms, and he crawled from that automobile where he was gunned down, down the side of that carport, into the carport, trying to make it to his door, in this puddle of blood, with his keys in his hand, and his wife and children coming out when they hear the shot, and his three children pleading over and over, "Daddy, Daddy, please get up." And that's what the case is about. This man being gunned down and shot down in the back in the dark from ambush, not able to face his self-appointed accuser, his judge, and his executioner.

And the court has given you several instructions. And this instruction here tells you what the case is about legally. Legally, it's about whether or not this defendant killed and murdered Medgar Evers on June the twelfth, 1963. And you've taken an oath to make that determination, not on speculation, not on conjecture, and not on guesswork, and not "what if" and not "what maybe," but on the evidence. And this doesn't say unless the defendant is of a certain age, because no man, ladies and gentlemen, is above the law. And if we start making decisions like that, that doesn't have anything to do with the law, eventually, where do we draw the line? Do we say in this case, "We're gonna draw the line when the person is seventy-something," and in another case if they're sixty-five. No man, regardless of his age, is above the law. And it doesn't say, "Unless you find that this offense was committed thirty year[s] ago." It says, "If you believe from the evidence that he did it on June 12 of 1963, he's guilty, and it's your duty to find him guilty."

Because you see, ladies and gentlemen, what we're talking about here, this type of offense, this type of murder, this assassination by a sniper from ambush is something that's timeless. This is something that spans the races. It is something that every decent human being should absolutely be sickened by, whether you be black, white, Hispanic; it doesn't matter. Murder by ambush is the most vile, savage, reprehensible type of murder that one can imagine. And that's what you've got here.

This isn't about black versus white or white versus black. This is about something that is reprehensible to decent minds. This is about society, civilized society, versus the vile, society versus the reprehensible, society versus the shocking. This, ladies and gentlemen, is about the state of Mississippi versus this defendant, Byron De La Beckwith.

Now, who could do such a thing? I'll tell you. [*Reading*] "The foul, contemptible, selfish person who continually tells the Negro that America is equally his; that he's as good as anybody; that he has the right to govern this land should be ashamed to lie like that. Believing such a lie has put many a darkie in the river late at night, some at the end of a rope, stirring others of their race to unrest. The Negro in our country is as helpful as a boll weevil to cotton. Some of these weevils are puny little runts and can't create the volume of damage that others can. Some are powerful, becoming mad monsters, snapping and snarling and biting the cotton. They must be destroyed with their wretched remains burned, lest the pure white cotton bolls be destroyed."

Well, in Medgar Evers, the field secretary for the NAACP, the focal point of integration in 1963, the boll weevil that fit the scope of this defendant's rifle was done exactly, what this defendant said in Exhibit 7, should be done. Eliminated, lest the pure white cotton bolls be destroyed.

Exhibit 69, submitted by this defendant, [*reading*] "Believe it or not, the NAACP, under the direction of its leaders, is doing a first-class job of getting itself in a position to be exterminated." So who could do such a shocking thing? And his opinion has not changed one iota from those words up until 1963.

How do we know that? Exhibit 71, written in November of 1976, [*reading*] "as much involved in Klan activity as a person can be." He hadn't mellowed one bit. That is what the words are that this defendant submitted, and whosoever—whatsoever a man thinks in his heart, so shall he become. And that's exactly what he became. He was on a one-man mission to exterminate what he considered to be the most important, in his words, "boll weevil" of that time. Lest the pure white bolls be destroyed.

And so we know from the evidence that on Saturday before Medgar Evers was gunned down, this defendant was in Jackson, Mississippi; couldn't find his prey's residence. Why? Because Medgar Evers, by that time, had to get an unlisted phone number. He couldn't just go to a phone book and look up his number and his address. And so he was down there at the Continental Trailways bus station trying to find out where he lived. And we know from the evidence that he went up to some cab drivers trying to find out. And then, we know after that his car was seen parked on the north side of Pittman's grocery, right there in the area. And so we know he was here on Saturday trying to find where Medgar Evers lived; drove to the location; walked into that vacant lot, getting things ready and set up. And then we know he went back to Greenwood; got this rifle; went out; target practiced; getting those crosshairs, those sights, set in for his target; got that scar over his right eye when the recoil of that rifle, when that scope jammed his eyeball there; went to work on Monday; worked all day; but what was on his mind? What did John Book tell you? All he wanted to do was talk about integration and guns. Couldn't even keep his mind on his business that day.

And so the next day was the day. The next day was the day, and his car is seen by those then-teenage boys in that area again. His car is seen by Barbara Holder who worked at times at Joe's Drive-In. This car, his car, is seen parked in that corner with the rear end backed into it, where all he's got to do is get out of that car right here in the corner where [it] was parked, walk down that path as shown in the pictures, get to this clump of trees, and wait. And he waited, and while he's waiting, he takes his hand and he breaks off this branch here, and what does he have? He has a hole.

And what do you see in that hole? His perfect view of the driveway of Medgar Evers, and he waits.

And after midnight that night, Medgar Evers, unsuspecting, gets out; gets his T-shirts out of the car; and this rifle was propped up against this sweet gum tree that we know from the testimony of Officer Luke and the other detectives that were in the area that described the scratch mark in the bark there. And so he takes this rifle, and he braces it up against a tree, and he finds Medgar Evers, his prey, in this scope, and he pulls the trigger, and ends his life in one fatal shot.

He gets in his car. On the way out, he cannot be found holding that weapon in his car. No matter what his planning, no matter his effort—remember what Barbara Holder told you of when he pulled into this area, instead of driving up in here, instead of coming around the front, the car came from around the back. And so after he does his dirty work and he's on the way back to his car, perchance if he's seen or stopped, he can't afford to have this rifle with him in that automobile. And so he takes it, and he sticks it in the honeysuckle vines right here behind this hedge row. Gets in his car, and leaves directly, and he's heading north on Delta Drive, Highway 49, back to his home in Greenwood.

And so the gun is found in the search the next day. His gun. The same gun that he had traded, had obtained from Ennis Thorn McIntyre. We know that how? Several ways. The serial number on this gun matches the serial number on the invoice where Mr. McIntyre first purchased it from International Firearms. We also know from the testimony of that FBI agent at the crime lab, Richard Poppleton. Remember when he told you that he compared the cartridges that had been removed from this weapon with cartridges that McIntyre had provided to the FBI, and from comparing the individual microscopic characteristics that would be caused by that firing pin, and that breech face, and that firing pin and that breech face alone matched. Those cartridges came from one and the same gun, and you're looking at it. Exhibit 36. This defendant's gun. This defendant's scope. His gun. His fingerprint. His car.

We're not just talking about some 1960s model. We're talking about a 1962 white Valiant that witnesses say, what? It also had a long aerial on it. And we're not even talking about a car that witnesses say was a 1960s white Valiant with a long aerial. What did they say? What did they say, not only in this courtroom, but in the courtroom thirty years ago and to the police, it was a white Valiant—Ronald Pittman said it was a white Valiant, a 1962 white Valiant, long antenna on it, long aerial, and what else? "The thing I remember most about it, when we got up close was that emblem on the rearview mirror."

And so what did the police do? What did we have the police do? What did we have the FBI do in recent years? To go back and get this photograph, the negative from this photograph, enlarge this area here, and let's see if it has any type of emblem hanging from it. And so, lo and behold, there she is. Now a person's words may be one thing, but a picture speaks a thousand words.

His gun. His scope. His fingerprint. His car. And lastly, but certainly not least, his mouth. When he thought he had beat the system thirty years ago, he couldn't keep his mouth shut with people that he thought were gonna be impressed by him, and that he thought were his buddies and comrades, two of them from the Klan, one in Florida, one from Mississippi, testified. At least six people have given you sworn testimony that at various times in different locations, none of whom knew each other or came across each other at any time, told you what he has said about this. He wants to take credit for what he has claimed should be done, but he just don't want to pay the price for it. And so he hasn't been able to keep his mouth shut.

And so not only do we have his car, his gun, his scope, his fingerprint, his mouth, we've got his own venom. His venom has come back to poison him just as effectively as anything else.

And why did this happen? Why did any of this happen? For what reason was Medgar Evers assassinated? For what he believed. Not in necessary self-defense was this done. Medgar Evers didn't do anything of a violent nature to this defendant. What he did was to have the gall, the "uppityness" to want for his people things like what? To be called by name, instead of "boy."

To go in a restaurant, to go in a department store, to vote, and for your children to get a decent education in a decent school. For wanting some degree of equality for himself, his family, and his fellowman, and for them to be accepted as human beings with some dignity. This kind of murder, ladies and gentlemen, no matter who the victim, no matter what his race; this kind of murder, when you're talking about somebody that's assassinated, shot down in the back for what they believe, for such meager things as wanting some dignity, when that kind of murder happens, there is just a gaping wound laid open on society as a whole. And even where justice is fulfilled, that kind of murder, that kind of wound will always leave a scar that won't ever go away. We have to learn from the past, folks, that where justice is never fulfilled—justice has sometimes been referred to as that soothing balm to be applied on the wounds inflicted on society—where justice is never fulfilled and that wound can never be cleansed, all it does is just fester and fester and fester over the years.

And so it is up to the system; it's up to the law-abiding citizens, and the law of the state of Mississippi that the perpetrator of such an assassination be brought to justice. This defendant. So that the decent law-abiding people of this state will maintain a new respect for the value of human life, and that our state will truly be one that is of the people, for the people, and by the people, no matter what you[r] race, color, or creed is.

One of the defense attorneys early on in the jury selection process asked whether or not any of you had heard something to the effect of the eyes being on Mississippi; Mississippi on trial. Mississippi is not on trial. And I'm not sure what eyes are on Mississippi, but this I do know. Justice in this case, in whatever case, is what the jury says it is. Justice in this case is what you twelve ladies and gentlemen say it is. So in this case, in effect, you are Mississippi. So what is Mississippi justice in this case, ladies and gentlemen? What is Mississippi justice for this defendant's hate-inspired assassination; assassination of a man that just desired to be free and equal?

If you analyze the evidence, use your common sense that God gave you, examine your heart, your consciences, and base your verdict on the evidence and the law, then you will have done the right thing. If you base it on the law and the evidence, and in the spirit of human dignity, there's no question in my mind that whatever you come out with, it'll be the right thing, because I have faith that it will be to hold him accountable. And the only way to do that is to find him guilty.

Remember the words of the Psalms, as I have over the past four years: "Commit your way to the Lord, trust in Him, and He will act. He will make your vindication shine like the light, and the justice of your cause as the noon day." From the evidence in this case, the law that you've sworn to apply, it can't be but one way if justice is truly going to be done.

And so on behalf of the state of Mississippi, I'm gonna do what I told you I was gonna do in the very beginning. I'm gonna ask you to hold this defendant accountable. You have no part in sentencing. That's something that the law will take care of. It's up to the court.

But to hold him accountable, find him guilty, simply because it's right, it's just, and Lord knows, it's just time. He has danced to the music for thirty years. Isn't it time that he pay the piper? Is it ever too late to do the right thing? For the sake of justice and the hope of us as a civilized society, I sincerely hope and pray that it's not.

Reprinted with the permission of Scribner, a Division of Simon & Schuster, Inc., from LADIES AND GENTLEMEN OF THE JURY:

Questions to Consider

(*Spoiler alert:* The jury's decision is noted in the last question.)

1. What story does DeLaughter open with, and why?
2. What is the impact of the questions DeLaughter uses in his argument? Remember that the jury has already heard all the information in this case— none of the facts DeLaughter is bringing up are new at this point.
3. DeLaughter uses specific and vivid details throughout his argument. What details does he choose to focus on, and why? Keep in mind that this is the last chance DeLaughter has to convince the jury to find the defendant guilty.
4. Were you surprised by the lawyer's diction? DeLaughter asks if "'we're gonna draw the line'"; says "Lord knows, it's just time"; and peppers his text with fragments. Why did he choose this tone? What other rhetorical strategies are used to persuade his audience?
5. How does DeLaughter engage the jurors in feeling responsible to come to the "right" decision? Their decision, after five and a half hours, was to find the defendant guilty.

Opinion of the Supreme Court of the United States in *DeShaney, a Minor, by His Guardian ad Litem, et al. v. Winnebago County Department of Social Services, et al.*

This case, brought on behalf of Joshua DeShaney, was appealed to the Supreme Court after both the original and the appellate courts denied the petitioners' claim—in other words, DeShaney had lost. Here, you'll read why the Court decides to hear the case even though fewer than two percent of cases appealed to the Supreme Court are granted certiorari, or a review, before the Court. Not all the justices were in agreement with the final decision; you'll see excerpts from the majority as well as the dissenting opinions. You will need to read these carefully; court opinions are not always easy to understand. What accounts for that difficulty, and what accounts for the different ways the facts are represented in the various opinions?

◆

CHIEF JUSTICE REHNQUIST delivered the opinion of the Court.

Petitioner is a boy who was beaten and permanently injured by his father, with whom he lived. Respondents are social workers and other local officials who received complaints that petitioner was being abused by his father and had reason to believe that this was the case, but nonetheless did not act to remove petitioner from his father's custody. Petitioner sued respondents claiming that their failure to act deprived him of his liberty in violation of the Due Process Clause of the Fourteenth Amendment to the United States Constitution. We hold that it did not.

I

The facts of this case are undeniably tragic. Petitioner Joshua DeShaney was born in 1979. In 1980, a Wyoming court granted his parents a divorce and awarded custody of Joshua to his father, Randy DeShaney. The father shortly thereafter moved to Neenah, a city located in Winnebago County, Wisconsin, taking the infant Joshua with him. There he entered into a second marriage, which also ended in divorce.

The Winnebago County authorities first learned that Joshua DeShaney might be a victim of child abuse in January 1982, when his father's second wife complained to the police, at the time of their divorce, that he had previously "hit the boy causing marks and [was] a prime case for child abuse." App. 152–153. The Winnebago County Department of Social Services (DSS) interviewed the father, but he denied the accusations, and DSS did not pursue them further. In January 1983, Joshua was admitted to a local hospital with multiple bruises and abrasions. The examining physician suspected child abuse and notified DSS, which immediately obtained an order from a Wisconsin juvenile court placing Joshua in the temporary custody of the hospital. Three days later, the county convened an ad hoc "Child Protection Team"—consisting of a pediatrician, a psychologist, a police detective, the county's lawyer, several DSS caseworkers, and various hospital personnel—to consider Joshua's situation. At this meeting, the Team decided that there was insufficient evidence of child abuse to retain Joshua in the custody of the court. The Team did, however, decide to recommend several measures to protect Joshua, including enrolling him in a preschool program, providing his father with certain counselling services, and encouraging his father's girlfriend to move out of the home. Randy DeShaney entered into a voluntary agreement with DSS in which he promised to cooperate with them in accomplishing these goals.

Based on the recommendation of the Child Protection Team, the juvenile court dismissed the child protection case and returned Joshua to the custody of his father. A month later, emergency room personnel called the DSS caseworker handling Joshua's case to report that he had once again been treated for suspicious injuries. The caseworker concluded that there was no basis for action. For the next six months, the caseworker made monthly visits to the DeShaney home, during which she observed a number of suspicious injuries on Joshua's head; she also noticed that he had not been enrolled in school, and that the girlfriend had not moved out. The caseworker dutifully recorded these incidents in her files, along with her continuing suspicions that someone in the DeShaney household was physically abusing Joshua, but she did nothing more. In November 1983, the emergency room notified DSS that Joshua had been treated once again for injuries that they believed to be caused by child abuse. On the caseworker's next two visits to the DeShaney home, she was told that Joshua was too ill to see her. Still DSS took no action.

In March 1984, Randy DeShaney beat 4-year-old Joshua so severely that he fell into a life-threatening coma. Emergency brain surgery revealed a series of hemorrhages caused by traumatic injuries to the head inflicted over a long period of time. Joshua did not die, but he suffered brain damage so severe that he is expected to spend the rest of his life confined to an institution for the profoundly retarded. Randy DeShaney was subsequently tried and convicted of child abuse.

Joshua and his mother brought this action under 42 U.S.C. § 1983 in the United States District Court for the Eastern District of Wisconsin against respondents Winnebago County, DSS, and various individual employees of DSS. The complaint alleged that respondents had deprived Joshua of his liberty without due process of law, in violation of his rights under the Fourteenth Amendment, by failing to intervene to protect him against a risk of violence at his father's hands of which they knew or should have known. The District Court granted summary judgment for respondents.

The Court of Appeals for the Seventh Circuit affirmed, 812 F. 2d 298 (1987), holding that petitioners had not made out an actionable § 1983 claim for two alternative reasons. First, the court held that the Due Process Clause of the Fourteenth Amendment does not require a state or local governmental entity to protect its citizens from "private violence, or other mishaps not attributable to the conduct of its employees." *Id.*, at 301. In so holding, the court specifically rejected the position endorsed by a divided panel of the Third Circuit in *Estate of Bailey by Oare* v. *County of York,* 768 F. 2d 503, 510–511 (1985), and by dicta in *Jensen* v. *Conrad,* 747 F. 2d 185, 190–194 (CA4 1984), cert. denied, 470 U.S. 1052 (1985), that once the State learns that a particular child is in danger of abuse from third parties and actually undertakes to protect him from that danger, a "special relationship" arises between it and the child which imposes an affirmative constitutional duty to provide adequate protection. 812 F. 2d, at 303–304. Second, the court held, in reliance on our decision in *Martinez* v. *California,* 444 U.S. 277, 285 (1980), that the causal connection between respondents' conduct and Joshua's injuries was too attenuated to establish a deprivation of constitutional rights actionable under § 1983. 812 F. 2d, at 301–303. The court therefore found it unnecessary to reach the question whether respondents' conduct evinced the "state of mind" necessary to make out a due process claim after *Daniels* v. *Williams,* 474 U.S. 327 (1986), and *Davidson* v. *Cannon,* 474 U.S. 344 (1986). 812 F. 2d, at 302.

Because of the inconsistent approaches taken by the lower courts in determining when, if ever, the failure of a state or local governmental entity or its agents to provide an individual with adequate protective services constitutes a violation of the individual's due process rights, see *Archie* v. *Racine,* 847 F. 2d 1211, 1220–1223, and n. 10 (CA7 1988) (en banc) (collecting cases), cert. pending, No. 88–576, and the importance of the issue to the administration of state and local governments, we granted certiorari. 485 U.S. 958 (1988). We now affirm.

II

The Due Process Clause of the Fourteenth Amendment provides that "[n]o State shall . . . deprive any person of life, liberty, or property, without due process of law." Petitioners contend that the State[1] deprived Joshua of his liberty interest in "free[dom] from . . . unjustified intrusions on personal security," see *Ingraham* v. *Wright*, 430 U.S. 651, 673 (1977), by failing to provide him with adequate protection against his father's violence. The claim is one invoking the substantive rather than the procedural component of the Due Process Clause; petitioners do not claim that the State denied Joshua protection without according him appropriate procedural safeguards, see *Morrissey* v. *Brewer*, 408 U.S. 471, 481 (1972), but that it was categorically obligated to protect him in these circumstances, see *Youngberg* v. *Romeo*, 457 U.S. 307, 309 (1982).[2]

But nothing in the language of the Due Process Clause itself requires the State to protect the life, liberty, and property of its citizens against invasion by private actors. The Clause is phrased as a limitation on the State's power to act, not as a guarantee of certain minimal levels of safety and security. It forbids the State itself to deprive individuals of life, liberty, or property without "due process of law," but its language cannot fairly be extended to impose an affirmative obligation on the State to ensure that those interests do not come to harm through other means. Nor does history support such an expansive reading of the constitutional text. . . .

It is well to remember that the harm was inflicted not by the State of Wisconsin, but by Joshua's father. The most that can be said of the state functionaries in this case is that they stood by and did nothing when suspicious circumstances dictated a more active role for them. In defense of them it must also be said that

---

[1] As used here, the term "State" refers generically to state and local governmental entities and their agents.

[2] Petitioners also argue that the Wisconsin child protection statutes gave Joshua an "entitlement" to receive protective services in accordance with the terms of the statute, an entitlement which would enjoy due process protection against state deprivation under our decision in *Board of Regents of State Colleges* v. *Roth*, 408 U.S. 564 (1972). Brief for Petitioners 24–29. But this argument is made for the first time in petitioners' brief to this Court: it was not pleaded in the complaint, argued to the Court of Appeals as a ground for reversing the District Court, or raised in the petition for certiorari. We therefore decline to consider it here. See *Youngberg* v. *Romeo*, 457 U.S., at 316, n. 19; *Dothard* v. *Rawlinson*, 433 U.S. 321, 323, n. 1 (1977); *Duignan* v. *United States*, 274 U.S. 195, 200 (1927); *Old Jordan Mining & Milling Co.* v. *Société Anonyme des Mines*, 164 U.S. 261, 264–265 (1896).

had they moved too soon to take custody of the son away from the father, they would likely have been met with charges of improperly intruding into the parent-child relationship, charges based on the same Due Process Clause that forms the basis for the present charge of failure to provide adequate protection.

The people of Wisconsin may well prefer a system of liability which would place upon the State and its officials the responsibility for failure to act in situations such as the present one. They may create such a system, if they do not have it already, by changing the tort law of the State in accordance with the regular lawmaking process. But they should not have it thrust upon them by this Court's expansion of the Due Process Clause of the Fourteenth Amendment.

Affirmed

JUSTICE BRENNAN, with whom JUSTICE MARSHALL and JUSTICE BLACKMUN join, dissenting.

The specific facts before us bear out this view of Wisconsin's system of protecting children. Each time someone voiced a suspicion that Joshua was being abused, that information was relayed to the Department for investigation and possible action. When Randy DeShaney's second wife told the police that he had "'hit the boy causing marks and [was] a prime case for child abuse,'" the police referred her complaint to DSS. *Ante,* at 192. When, on three separate occasions, emergency room personnel noticed suspicious injuries on Joshua's body, they went to DSS with this information. *Ante,* at 192–193. When neighbors informed the police that they had seen or heard Joshua's father or his father's lover beating or otherwise abusing Joshua, the police brought these reports to the attention of DSS. App. 144–145. And when respondent Kemmeter, through these reports and through her own observations in the course of nearly 20 visits to the DeShaney home, *id.,* at 104, compiled growing evidence that Joshua was being abused, that information stayed within the Department— chronicled by the social worker in detail that seems almost eerie in light of her failure to act upon it. (As to the extent of the social worker's involvement in, and knowledge of, Joshua's predicament, her reaction to the news of Joshua's last and most devastating injuries is illuminating: "'I just knew the phone would ring some day and Joshua would be dead.'" 812 F. 2d 298, 300 (CA7 1987).)

Even more telling than these examples is the Department's control over the decision whether to take steps to protect a particular child from suspected abuse. While many different people contributed information and advice to this decision, it was up to the people at DSS to make the ultimate decision (subject to the approval of the local government's corporation counsel) whether to disturb the family's current arrangements. App. 41, 58. When Joshua first appeared at a local hospital with injuries signaling physical abuse, for example, it was DSS that made the decision to take him into temporary custody for the purpose of studying his situation—and it was DSS, acting in conjunction with the corporation counsel, that returned him to his father. *Ante,* at 192. Unfortunately for Joshua DeShaney, the buck effectively stopped with the Department.

In these circumstances, a private citizen, or even a person working in a government agency other than DSS, would doubtless feel that her job was done as soon as she had reported her suspicions of child abuse to DSS. Through its child-welfare program, in other words, the State of Wisconsin has relieved ordinary citizens and governmental bodies other than the Department of any sense of obligation to do anything more than report their suspicions of child abuse to DSS. If DSS ignores or dismisses these suspicions, no one will step in to fill the gap. Wisconsin's child-protection program thus effectively confined Joshua DeShaney within the walls of Randy DeShaney's violent home until such time as DSS took action to remove him. Conceivably, then, children like Joshua are made worse off by the existence of this program when the persons and entities charged with carrying it out fail to do their jobs.

It simply belies reality, therefore, to contend that the State "stood by and did nothing" with respect to Joshua. *Ante,* at 203. Through its child-protection program, the State actively intervened in Joshua's life and, by virtue of this intervention, acquired ever more certain knowledge that Joshua was in grave danger. These circumstances, in my view, plant this case solidly within the tradition of cases like *Youngberg* and *Estelle.*

It will be meager comfort to Joshua and his mother to know that, if the State had "selectively den[ied] its protective services" to them because they were "disfavored minorities," *ante,* at 197, n. 3, their § 1983 suit might have stood on sturdier ground. Because of the posture of this case, we do not know why respondents did not take steps to protect Joshua; the Court, however, tells us that their reason is irrelevant so long as their inaction was not the product of invidious discrimination. Presumably, then, if respondents decided not to help Joshua because his name began with a "J," or because he was born in the spring, or because they did not care enough about him even to formulate an intent to discriminate against him based on an arbitrary reason, respondents would not be liable to the DeShaneys because they were not the ones who dealt the blows that destroyed Joshua's life.

I do not suggest that such irrationality was at work in this case; I emphasize only that we do not know whether or not it was. I would allow Joshua and his mother the opportunity to show that respondents' failure to help him arose, not out of the sound exercise of professional judgment that we recognized in *Youngberg* as sufficient to preclude liability, see 457 U.S., at 322–323, but from the kind of arbitrariness that we have in the past condemned. . . .

As the Court today reminds us, "the Due Process Clause of the Fourteenth Amendment was intended to prevent government 'from abusing [its] power, or employing it as an instrument of oppression.'" *Ante*, at 196, quoting *Davidson, supra,* U.S., at 348. My disagreement with the Court arises from its failure to see that inaction can be every bit as abusive of power as action, that oppression can result when a State undertakes a vital duty and then ignores it. Today's opinion construes the Due Process Clause to permit a State to displace private sources of protection and then, at the critical moment, to shrug its shoulders and turn away from the harm that it has promised to try to prevent. Because I cannot agree that our Constitution is indifferent to such indifference, I respectfully dissent.

JUSTICE BLACKMUN, dissenting

Today, the Court purports to be the dispassionate oracle of the law, unmoved by "natural sympathy." *Ante*, at 202. But, in this pretense, the Court itself retreats into a sterile formalism which prevents it from recognizing either the facts of the case before it or the legal norms that should apply to those facts. As JUSTICE BRENNAN demonstrates, the facts here involve not mere passivity, but active state intervention in the life of Joshua DeShaney— intervention that triggered a fundamental duty to aid the boy once the State learned of the severe danger to which he was exposed.

The Court fails to recognize this duty because it attempts to draw a sharp and rigid line between action and inaction. But such formalistic reasoning has no place in the interpretation of the broad and stirring Clauses of the Fourteenth Amendment. Indeed, I submit that these Clauses were designed, at least in part, to undo the formalistic legal reasoning that infected antebellum jurisprudence, which the late Professor Robert Cover analyzed so effectively in his significant work entitled *Justice Accused* (1975).

Like the antebellum judges who denied relief to fugitive slaves, see *id.*, at 119–121, the Court today claims that its decision, however harsh, is compelled by existing legal doctrine. On the contrary, the question presented by this case is an open one, and our Fourteenth Amendment precedents may be read more broadly or narrowly depending upon how one chooses to read them. Faced with the choice, I would adopt a "sympathetic" reading, one which comports with dictates of fundamental justice and recognizes that compassion need not be exiled from the province of judging. Cf. A. Stone, *Law, Psychiatry, and Morality* 262 (1984) ("We will make mistakes if we go forward, but doing nothing can be the worst mistake. What is required of us is moral ambition. Until our composite sketch becomes a true portrait of humanity we must live with our uncertainty; we will grope, we will struggle, and our compassion may be our only guide and comfort").

Poor Joshua! Victim of repeated attacks by an irresponsible, bullying, cowardly, and intemperate father, and abandoned by respondents who placed him in a dangerous predicament and who knew or learned what was going on, and yet did essentially nothing except, as the Court revealingly observes, *ante*, at 193, "dutifully recorded these incidents in [their] files." It is a sad commentary upon American life, and constitutional principles—so full of late of patriotic fervor and proud proclamations about "liberty and justice for all"—that this child, Joshua DeShaney, now is assigned to live out the remainder of his life profoundly retarded. Joshua and his mother, as petitioners here, deserve—but now are denied by this Court—the opportunity to have the facts of their case considered in the light of the constitutional protection that 42 U.S.C. § 1983 is meant to provide.

From DeShaney v. Winnebago County Department of Social Services. *No. 87–154. Supreme Ct. of the US. 22 February 1989.*

NOTE: In order to find more information on Supreme Court decisions—including original documents and transcripts, information on individual justices, status updates, and analyses of cases—you might start with the following: the Supreme Court's website at www.supremecourt.gov; the Oyez Project at www.oyez.org; the Legal Information Institute, published by Cornell Law School, at www.law.cornell.edu/; and SCOTUSblog, an extensive blog by lawyers about the Supreme Court, at www.scotusblog.com.

Questions to Consider

1. Why does the tone of the language differ among opinions, as well as the choice and characterization of the facts that have been incorporated?
2. Who would you say the probable audience is for these opinions? What purposes are served by publishing these opinions?
3. All the justices in this civil trial seem to agree that this is a tragic case. The majority, however, say that the Due Process Clause doesn't protect private citizens (e.g., Joshua) against private citizens (e.g., his father who was convicted in a criminal court), and this is where the real conflict lies. The dissenters see

others as equally culpable, including the state agency whose failure to act, according to Justice Brennan, "can be every bit as abusive of power as action." Notice how interpretation of which laws and cases apply may depend on which facts are deemed relevant. Which facts seem important to you, and why?

4. In the separate dissent, Justice Blackmun notes that he would adopt a "sympathetic" reading. How could you argue that both Joshua and the county's Department of Social Services deserve our sympathy?

5. Justice Blackmun claims that Joshua and his mother were "denied by this Court . . . the opportunity to have the facts of their case considered." Whether or not you agree with the Court's controlling decision, do you think Joshua and his mother had their case adequately considered? Is the outcome of the case a measure of adequacy, or is something else?

The Scene of the Crime
DENNIS BARRIE

*In 1990 some Cincinnatians stood in line to see the Robert Map-
plethorpe photography exhibit at the Contemporary Arts Center
(CAC), while others picketed the exhibit as being obscene. The
exhibit, entitled* The Perfect Moment, *resulted in a perfect storm
between the factions who did not think this was art, or at least not
protected art, and others, such as Barrie, who argued that the
exhibit should be protected. The CAC and Dennis Barrie, then director of the CAC, were both indicted for pandering obscenity and use
of a minor in pictures depicting nudity. Barrie, a distinguished
museum director and art historian who had previously been with
the Smithsonian Institute and who went on to become director of
Cleveland's Rock 'n' Roll Hall of Fame and Museum and then the
Las Vegas Museum of Organized Crime and Law Enforcement (the
"Mob Museum"), was acquitted in a trial that made national head-
lines. This article in* Art Journal *was taken from a keynote address
Barrie gave just a year after his acquittal at a meeting of the College
Art Association in Washington, DC.*

--------------- ◆ ---------------

You know, every day I think I'm going to leave this behind, that
I'm going to leave the events of last year behind and get on with
my life. I like museum work, I like putting exhibitions together,
and I like our professions—plural—in this room. Every day I
think I'll leave it behind, but it won't let me leave it behind.

When I went to the airport this morning, the clerk at the air-
line counter said, "I want to thank you for what you did last
year." I opened the paper, and there was Pat Buchanan talking
about striptease dancers in Indiana and free speech. I see the
Washington Post and there's the Chrysler Corporation withdraw-
ing from advertising in *Playboy,* and Donald Wildman (as we like
to call him) claiming another victory against free speech. I was a
little late for this awards ceremony because I was on the phone
with a program called "Trial Watch," which replaced a couple of
soaps on NBC in the daytime. They want me to appear on it, and
the leverage they were using was that I could be on the same program with Zsa Zsa. Well, it's an "honor," and I'm still thinking
about it. Then I open up other publications and see that the story
of what happened at the Contemporary Arts Center is a story that
won't die. For me, having been a part of it, it is a little strange that
it won't die. Just in the last few weeks *Life* magazine, *Playboy, Art*

in America, Artnews, and other, more scholarly publications have published articles on what happened in Cincinnati. My favorite, actually, is not in the art publications, but in *Sports Illustrated,* which I have here for those of you in the fiftieth row back there. It's an article called "Sex, Lies, and Baseball," and it's a profile of the city of Cincinnati, last year's City of the Year. My city. I can't go into all the details, or read it all to you, but suffice it to say that it's loaded with illustrations and caricatures of many of the characters who made news in our city. Among them are Pete Rose, with a very long nose; Sam Wyche, naked because he tossed the women reporters out of the locker room; and Charles Keating— most of you forget that Charles Keating, who people think is from California, is really a Cincinnati boy—with two hands over his mouth. Then there's a picture of our sheriff, Simon Leis, with two hands over his eyes, and there's a picture of yours truly with a halo over my head. Now, I guarantee you that this will be the one and only time in history you'll ever see a museum director with a halo over his or her head.

I think this event draws so much attention because it really did have profound significance, and lasting significance. It certainly has lasting significance for my city, for Cincinnati. I think it has lasting significance for the nation. I know it has lasting significance for my institution, for the people who work there, the people who support it, and the people who believe in it. And it certainly has lasting significance for me, my friends, and my family. I know that, personally, I will never be the same, much though I would sometimes like just to go on and do exhibitions, talk to artists, and do the wonderful things that we all enjoy. I can't do that anymore. The world won't let us do that anymore. It won't let me do that anymore.

One of the writers in our city said that last year's obscenity trial was the event that, in his forty years in Cincinnati, had most divided the population. The event. Not racial warfare in the sixties; not Democrats versus Republicans. It still divides the city.

When we took the Mapplethorpe show, it was not a controversial show, and it certainly wasn't anything extraordinary for the Contemporary Arts Center. My institution is fifty-two years old. It's one of the oldest institutions in the United States devoted to the showing or presenting of contemporary art. We've had many controversial shows, many that have contained work as disturbing and challenging as Mapplethorpe's. We've never had a reaction like that we experienced this last year. But Mapplethorpe's "The Perfect Moment" did not appear in Cincinnati— nor was it presented in Cincinnati—in a vacuum. It appeared in a time of hysteria over the arts, created just a couple of miles away from here. We're in the land, folks, of Jesse Helms. The hysteria that was generated created the right moment for what happened in Cincinnati, for forces to be released that were quite terrible—and believe me, they were quite terrible. And these forces still exist. It also was the right moment for forces who believe in freedom to be unleashed, and for the reaction to take effect and to combat what has been happening in the nation in this past year.

I've told the story of what happened to us so many times that it's hard to repeat it again. So I'm not going to. But what I'm going to give you are a few images that stay with me. Some haunt me and some move me to this day. There are the bad images, the horrible images: there is the image of members of a board of trustees who were attacked—their jobs, their livelihoods, their credibility in the community; the image of a board chairman who had to resign because his very livelihood was threatened; the image of bomb threats, of threats against my life and the lives of my family and the lives of the people who work with me; the image of a near riot that almost occurred when thirty or forty police officers in their dress uniforms walked into the Contemporary Arts Center. More than anything, that image—that image of policemen in uniforms pushing patrons out of a museum, closing a museum because of what is on the walls—is the image that's going to haunt me for the rest of my life. Because that isn't our country, or it shouldn't be our country. You know, when you see it on film (I happened to watch it again the other day; you kind of get into these things every now and then) it looks like something from some other time; it really does. It looks a preview for *Hitler: The Last Ten Years.* It doesn't look like the United States, and yet it was the United States. It's very scary to contemplate, and it's something I never want to see again. Hopefully, what we did in Cincinnati will keep it from ever happening again in this country.

Some of the images are wonderful: the image of four thousand people, the night the exhibition opened to our membership, standing in line, in some cases for two and one-half hours, to see the exhibition. You know, we're a very small museum; we could fit into this room many times over. So we had to be careful of the fire code. We didn't want to break any more laws—God knows, I didn't want to go to jail for that one. So people had to wait; as people exited, others went in. And there were all sorts of people in that line—there were old and young, black and white and yellow and all kinds; there were artists and there were business people. And I think they were there not because there was such a sensational show up in the galleries, but to show their colors, to show that they believed in freedom and they believed in the stand that the Contemporary Arts Center was taking that night.

There are other images: the witnesses, the jury. Some of those people are in this room tonight. And I remember sitting in the trial. I don't recommend it to anyone; it's not fun, it's not glamorous, and it isn't like "L. A. Law." It's hard to be in that courtroom. But it's interesting, in my experience, to remember what did happen in that room.

You know, we were slated to lose. If you looked at the odds the bookmakers were giving in Las Vegas, they were bad. And if you watched and listened to the national press, you were sure there was no way the Contemporary Arts Center could win. The judge was against us. We've been in the city for fifty-two years, yet he declared that we were not a museum because we are not a collecting institution. He declared that the seven Mapplethorpe photographs in question could be presented at trial out of the context of the exhibition, even out of the context of their portfolios. And he agreed with the prosecution that exhibitions have no intellectual rhyme or thought behind them. But he didn't see that an exhibition has content, like a movie or a play or a book.

It was fascinating to watch Jacquelynn Baas, John Walsh, Martin Friedman, Evan Turner, Janet Kardon, and other museum people testifying in the courtroom before the jury made up of people who were not museum goers, who had never been to the Contemporary Arts Center (anyone who had been to the Contemporary Arts Center couldn't get on the jury), who didn't read the paper, who had very little college education, who were from the suburbs, who were thought to be conservative, who were thought to be the "right" kind of people to be horrified by the art of Robert Mapplethorpe. It was fascinating to watch those jurors listen to our colleagues speaking to them in plain and direct terms, telling them that sometimes art is not beautiful, and sometimes it's challenging, and sometimes it's even offensive, and yet it can be art, even if it's all those things. I was watching there—I sat in the front row, folks—and you could see in their eyes that they got it, and obviously they did get it because they acquitted us.

It was also interesting to sit in on the *voir dire*—the selection of the jurors. I sat there while our counsel asked prospective jurors the following question: "Mr. Jones—or Mrs. Jones—do you believe that adults have the right to decide for themselves what they can read, or what they can see, or what they can listen to?" Invariably, the vast majority of people who got up on that stand said yes. Some of them hesitated for a few moments. They said, "Well, I don't want children to see certain things. I'm not sure I'm comfortable with certain things being on television, but I can understand how a certain thing could be in a museum, or why it might be in some other kind of institution." And then the prosecutor got up (he was a study, let me tell you, but that's another talk) and said, "Well, Mr. Jones—or Mrs. Jones—you know that if something is obscene it doesn't matter whether you are over twenty-one or not; the people showing it to you are breaking the law, and you, by being there, are breaking the law!" And they looked at him quizzically as if to ask, "What are you telling me? Am I expected to believe this, or to buy into this?" It was evident to me (though it wasn't evident, I think, to a lot of reporters in that room) that a great demonstration of tolerance was being shown in that room at that point. I remember when my lawyer, Lou Serkin, sat down with me, after we had selected the jurors, and said, "We will win this case." I said, "Lou, you and I are the only two people in this room who believe that."

We did win the case. The day we won, the Reds were playing the Pirates at Riverfront Stadium. You have to understand that the Mapplethorpe case was *the* case in our city at that time, even though the Reds were on their way to the World Series. They broadcast the decision over the radios at Riverfront Stadium, and people stood up and cheered. Horns honked all over the city. It was a moment of such exhilaration in our city. I walked into a newsroom at channel 9, a CBS affiliate, and all the staff members stood up and cheered and said, "The city has been redeemed." That's an image that will stay with me for a long time.

Standing here, I think about Hans Haacke, who came to Cincinnati because he wanted to help. He brought five thousand dollars from Austrian artists, who had collected it for our defense, and presented us with two of his *Helmsboro* masterpieces. It was fascinating to hear Hans recall that, as a boy in Austria in 1945, when the Allies and the GIs arrived, they all looked to the United States as a beacon of freedom, and he didn't want that beacon to go out in 1990. That was a very moving experience, and stays with me now.

Finally, I'd like to mention an upbeat experience (actually, the whole event was upbeat, but this one is a little more fun): the jurors. We've gotten to know some of them. The only motion that we won during the trial was the right to have the jurors visit the scene of the crime—the scene-of-the-crime museum, folks. The judge readily agreed to that. He's an old prosecutor and is used to going out and looking at murder sites with the chalk drawings and all. So the jurors piled on a bus, and the prosecutors, the judge, my defense attorneys, one of my staff members, and I piled on another bus, and we made a field trip to the Contemporary Arts Center. However, the jurors were not allowed to ask questions; they were to remain silent at all times. And they were not allowed to go beyond the front desk. By request of the prosecution, they were not allowed to look at anything on the walls, I guess for fear that this would in some way sway them in the wrong direction. So these eight jurors stood at our reception desk in silence for, I believe, forty-five seconds, with people snapping pictures and the *New York Times* and the *Washington Post* writing everything down. Then we all got back on the buses and went back to the courtroom.

After the trial was over, and those jurors had made what many thought was a difficult decision, two of them called us up and said, "We never got to see the Contemporary Arts Center. Could we come down and see it now?" So on November 17, Amy Bannister, who's my PR/development person, and I took those two ex-jurors through the Contemporary Arts Center, and the two of them became members of the Contemporary Arts Center. They said that they had been frustrated that the judge had not let them see the other photographs in the exhibition, and they said everybody had gotten to see the photographs but the jury. They thought this was an absurdity. They knew that things couldn't be judged out of context.

Some things will stay with me for a long time. Some lessons will stay with me long after this is, I hope, over with in my life. Some things become evident as I look back at the controversy and the trial. I wish all of you could have been in the courtroom when we selected the jury and heard the following: that they didn't go to museums; that they didn't go to art galleries; that they didn't go to ballets; that they didn't go to symphonies; that most of them hadn't been to the kind of institution that many of us represent since their seventh-grade bus trip. I learned a lesson in that room. I learned that we're doing something terribly wrong. Our education system, our institutions—your institutions, my institution—we're all doing something terribly wrong, because there is indeed a growing gap, and it's real. Thank God we had the moment of the trial to bridge that gap for some of those people. But people have no involvement in the cultural institutions of our country anymore, and I think that's scary. Now, Cincinnati prides itself on being a cultural city, and indeed it is. But here we have this incredible gap. It's scary to think of the media exploiting the them-versus-us mentality. It is good fodder for the media, and we were vulnerable to it. We're all vulnerable to it. The media could see that it was them versus us, so they could say that the jury was not a jury of my peers, and they could say that Dennis Barrie and the Contemporary Arts Center didn't have a chance. Just look at the profiles of the jurors; it's a different world than our world. And I think it's incredible that the art world has distanced itself so much that a man like Jesse Helms can make us vulnerable.

What we do is so wonderful that we should share it, we should expose the world to it. Sometimes that's not easy to do. Sometimes we have to think of a different language than the language we use in our scholarly journals and exhibition catalogues. But we *must* make that communication. It's critical for your future and for our future.

I also have absorbed the lasting lesson that—how do I put this in a nice way?—that we need to work together, we need to be united. In the year that this controversy consumed my life, I saw that there was a reluctance on the part of many of my colleagues to make the Contemporary Arts Center's fight their fight: "Oh, I'm a ballerina; it doesn't affect me." "Oh, I only play Shostakovich; it doesn't affect me." "Oh, I only show van Dyck; it doesn't affect me." It does affect you. It's your freedom we're talking about, it's your right to show van Dyck, your ability to dance that dance. These are basic freedoms, and if we had lost our case those freedoms would have been taken away from all of you. Whether you like Robert Mapplethorpe or don't like Robert Mapplethorpe, whether you're disgusted by some of his work or embrace his work is not the issue. The issue is much more fundamental than that. The issue is about being able to see Robert Mapplethorpe's work if you want to see Robert Mapplethorpe's work.

Today an old friend of mine came up to me and said, "You're my hero!" I'm always embarrassed when that happens, and also a little bit moved. I don't think of myself as a hero, and I don't think of my staff, the people I work with, or my board as heroes. I do think of us as people dedicated to our profession, dedicated to our city and our community, and dedicated to the principles of this country. That's why we made our stand. We weren't out there to be heroes. We didn't choose this battle; I guess the battle chose us. But we were willing to go all the way. We thought it was that critical, that important. So I honor and applaud the dedication of those around me and of my institution. We're not heroes, but we did the right thing. Now I'm going to ask you to do something: I'm going to ask you to be my heroes, to go out of this room and think about what your commitments are to the fundamentals of this country, the freedoms that we have. Be politically involved; don't go back to your colleges and universities and museums and say that this world doesn't affect you. It does affect you. It's important that what we do reach the wider world and that it be expressed openly and without restriction. It's important that the Jesse Helmses of the world not have the stronger voice, especially in these times, when so many freedoms are in peril. You can be heroes because you can make that stand. You can stand whenever an exhibition is threatened, whenever a play is threatened, whenever a work is not hung in your institution. Stand there. Make your voices heard. Write those letters. You know, it actually does work. I saw eight people who were going to vote against us, vote for us. They got the message. They wanted freedom. They were willing to make a stand for it, and they took some heat for it. I see eighteen hundred people in this room. Please do the same.

Barrie, Dennis. "The Scene of the Crime." Art Journal 50.3 (Autumn 1991): 29–32. Copyright 1991 by Dennis Barrie. Reprinted by permission of the author.

NOTE: State obscenity laws such as those under which Barrie was tried can be found online; one source that includes links to state and federal laws and other important documents, as well as overviews of different types of law, is the Legal Information Institute of Cornell Law School at www.law.cornell. edu. The following is the current law in Ohio on pandering obscenity:

OHIO REVISED CODE, TITLE [29] XXIX—CRIMES, PROCEDURE, CHAPTER 2907: SEX OFFENSES

2907.32 Pandering obscenity

(A) No person, with knowledge of the character of the material or performance involved, shall do any of the following:
   (1) Create, reproduce, or publish any obscene material, when the offender knows that the material is to be used for commercial exploitation or will be publicly disseminated or displayed, or when the offender is reckless in that regard;
   (2) Promote or advertise for sale, delivery, or dissemination; sell, deliver, publicly disseminate, publicly display, exhibit, present, rent, or provide; or offer or agree to sell, deliver, publicly disseminate, publicly display, exhibit, present, rent, or provide, any obscene material;
   (3) Create, direct, or produce an obscene performance, when the offender knows that it is to be used for commercial exploitation or will be publicly presented, or when the offender is reckless in that regard;
   (4) Advertise or promote an obscene performance for presentation, or present or participate in presenting an obscene performance, when the performance is presented publicly, or when admission is charged;
   (5) Buy, procure, possess, or control any obscene material with purpose to violate division (A)(2) or (4) of this section.
(B) It is an affirmative defense to a charge under this section, that the material or performance involved was disseminated or

presented for a bona fide medical, scientific, educational, religious, governmental, judicial, or other proper purpose, by or to a physician, psychologist, sociologist, scientist, teacher, person pursuing bona fide studies or research, librarian, clergyman, prosecutor, judge, or other person having a proper interest in the material or performance.

(C) Whoever violates this section is guilty of pandering obscenity, a felony of the fifth degree. If the offender previously has been convicted of a violation of this section or of section 2907.31 of the Revised Code, then pandering obscenity is a felony of the fourth degree. Effective Date: 07-01-1996.

Questions to Consider

1. From Barrie's description of the events, who would you categorize as stakeholders in this issue? What do you think were their various concerns?

2. Given your reading of the language of the current Ohio Revised Code on Pandering Obscenity, under what subsections, or parts of a subsection, under section (A) do you think a museum director might be charged? Which of the relevant words and/or phrases would be the most subject to interpretation? Under what circumstances do you think a person might argue a defense under section (B)?

3. In discussing the jury who were going to decide on Barrie's guilt or innocence, why do you think Barrie's attorney, Louis Sirkin, said to him, "We will win this case," after they had completed jury selection? What was Sirkin looking for in the jurors, and why?

4. Barrie's account is also an argument; at one point he tells his listeners, "It's your freedom we're talking about." What does he mean, and what does he want his audience to do?

5. Barrie's address was to a group that consisted predominantly of artists, teachers of art, and other supporters of the arts. In what ways do Barrie's rhetorical strategies reflect an awareness of the common views of this group? Of their differences?

Dwayne Franklin
Patricia Ewick and Susan S. Silbey

This excerpt is taken from The Common Place of Law: Stories from Everyday Life *by Patricia Ewick and Susan S. Silbey. Patricia Ewick is a professor of sociology at Clark University and Susan Silbey is a professor of sociology and anthropology at MIT. Both have written extensively on legal issues; in this co-authored text, the authors represent their findings about how citizens use the law in both formal and informal situations and how those experiences color their perceptions of the law. The authors' primary method of obtaining information is through qualitative investigation—asking interviewees to talk at length about their experiences. Hearing directly from individuals can be invaluable in uncovering events and perspectives that researchers might not think to include in more quantitative research measures such as large-scale surveys. We hear in this selection from Dwayne Franklin. Which of Franklin's experiences and perspectives do you think might be surprising or useful to the researchers?*

◆

Dwayne Franklin lives on the edge. "This is the borderline," he says, between one city and the next, between safety and danger, respect and uncaring. Keeping an eye on his neighbors' properties, as they in turn watch over his, Dwayne Franklin and his neighbors "police the neighborhood . . . observe any criminal activity," building a barrier to keep Newark's problems from spilling across the divide that marks Irvington as a separate, cleaner, and safer place to live. "Its like you're living in a fort . . . you are behind this wall . . . It's safe around here, but yet it is not." The boundary between Dwayne Franklin's fortress and the world beyond is both spatial and metaphorical.

Dwayne moved to this detached two-family row house shortly after it was built a dozen years ago, having lived in Newark for the first twenty-seven years of his life. He lives in one apartment with his parents; his sister and her children live in the other.

An exact replica of all the other houses on the block, the Franklins' house sits on a small yard separated from its neighbors by narrow alleyways that punctuate the rhythm of the high white brick stairs and ground floor garages running the full length of Exeter Street. There are many tidy gardens, but Dwayne's is outstanding: a precisely ordered plot of begonias and Daisy Millers in a succession of alternating rows. The carefully maintained gardens and newly paved driveways stand in contrast to the street itself, littered with broken glass and crowded with cars.

Exeter Street appears to be an island of respectability in a rough and menacing surround. Bounded by a highway on one end and Newark's city limits on the other, the transition from homeowner pride to urban decay is marked by tall apartment buildings on the corners. Once inside Newark, the street is a procession of shabby retail shops, empty lots, and abandoned cars. It is an effort, Dwayne Franklin suggests, holding on to middle-class propriety and security with the city lapping at your door.

When asked, "What do you like most about this neighborhood?" Dwayne said, "The cleanliness, okay, because right across the street is Newark . . . And, I guess not just the cleanliness, but the cooperation since we are on a borderline street . . . People pretty much know each other." He disliked the cars that go racing up and down the street. "We do have a tendency to get people who come by at four o'clock in the morning doing spinouts at the intersection" where Irvington meets Newark. "Those noisy cars are stolen cars . . . Nobody would burn that much rubber off their own tires and expect to drive to work the next day." The problem, of course, is that "by the time the Irvington police arrive, and they do things very rapidly, the guy has spun out and gone across the border. And the police have to get permission to go across the border."

Crime and fear figure prominently in Dwayne Franklin's stories. He told us about an incident of vandalism and theft from his sister's apartment that was thwarted by a formidable series of locks and dead bolts.

> The police were called. The perpetrator left a wine bottle . . . I don't know how this person could have done it, but, well, my sister had a roommate at the time so it was probably someone [the roommate] knew or someone that had something against him. And it was the roommate's stuff that was taken. [Interviewer: Nothing else was taken?] He couldn't go any further than that room because he had a lock on the side door, a shackle lock, so the vandal had no access to any other parts of the house.

He seems matter of fact about crime and calls the police frequently. Dwayne

> asked the police if they were going to take the wine bottle left by the intruder and check it for prints. Of course, they said no. I mean it is a possibility that this person has a prior record. They ended up taking the bottle with them, but I think they threw it in the garbage because when I looked out front I saw them do that.

Many years earlier, Dwayne was

> downtown with a friend. We ran into these guys at the market, and went down about a block with them. The guy pulled a gun. I

looked down the barrel of a gun. I fought one of them and he ran . . . I went to the police department and reported it but they didn't believe me . . . They just didn't take a report. . . Back then I was a little younger. Because of the guy I had with me, I think they didn't believe me . . . Had they checked our job IDs, they might have acted a little differently. He worked for AT&T, but he didn't look like it.

More recently, Dwayne Franklin faced a gun again. He was accompanying his niece back from a Halloween costume party around the corner.

We passed this group of guys. They spoke, so my niece spoke back. We got to the corner downhill, she looked back, she said run, here they come, and I said, well, go ahead. And so she ran to a neighbor's house and starting knocking on the door and ringing the bell. I didn't know where she went because down that way at night, it used to be dark before they cut the trees so the lights could show through. There was three of them, two of us. Two were chasing me, one was chasing her. I managed to get over to where she was, just to the neighbor's house, which was close to the corner down there. Before I did, though, I had to pass someone holding a gun. I had a knife. He fired the gun, and he missed me at close range, so I think it was a starter pistol. I went up on the porch and finally the neighbor stuck her head out the window and said what is going on here? And they left.

This time he didn't report the incident to the police. He could offer them nothing to go on and thought they wouldn't believe him.

We didn't call the police on that one because we couldn't identify those people. And it was dark. It happened so quickly. It would have been no way that I could have even given them a description of what the people had on . . . Plus, I had had a few drinks, so, you know, while I wasn't intoxicated, when you talk to a policeman and you've had a drink, they think you're drunk.

Despite his experiences, Dwayne believes "the police generally do a good job in the community." During the last five years, he estimated that he has called the police four or five times, complaining to the taxicab commission, reporting a tree fallen across the street during a storm, reporting an accident on the corner. He is unwilling, he said, to ignore crime or corruption.

Calling the police is simply good sense, and like not burning good rubber off new tires, "it is the proper thing to do." You pay a price, he said, for not following through with legal matters. When we asked Dwayne a question about a hypothetical accident in which one of the children in the family was hit by an automobile, but not injured, he replied,

> I would tell the driver that things relating to the accident are being handled by my attorney and if he wanted to know information pertaining to the child's condition, he should contact the lawyer. You know, if you tell the driver that the child is all right, you don't know who is sitting in there with him. You know, if anything goes wrong you have a problem . . . I've seen people in that predicament where they were the friends of drivers and experienced very serious injuries, and they didn't do anything about it. And they are paying a price today.

According to Dwayne Franklin, the law and courts are there to protect. Although they, like the police, don't always succeed, they are worth the cost, Dwayne Franklin said. He was emphatic that courts can "handle the problems of ordinary people" fairly well and that minorities didn't necessarily have a harder time. Courts are fairly predictable, he added, and "judges are generally honest in dealing with each case." Courts are expensive, Dwayne commented, but not so much that you would not use them if you really needed to. "You see," he explained to us, "I was afraid at one point when I first started going into court. I was very nervous about it . . . It was a new experience, you know, so I was a little nervous. Court is always looked upon as this force." But with experience you discover, he said, that "It's a place you go to get justice. It is for you to get justice." Emphasizing the role of initiative and the sense of a layered organization, Dwayne added, at least "it is a good place to start."

Dwayne Franklin has always worked at several jobs simultaneously. As a consequence, at thirty-nine years old, he has had many and varied positions. When we interviewed him, Dwayne was leaving a five-year stint as a welfare investigator for the city. Prior to that he had worked as a ward clerk keeping medical records in the county hospital and as a paralegal for the Rutgers University legal services bureau. When he was younger, Dwayne worked for a trucking company and for a chemical company, but for the past ten years or so he has settled into his public service work. "You know, it's always helping people who can't help themselves."

During this period, Dwayne also worked part-time as a private detective for local attorneys, and when we spoke he was completing the paperwork to obtain his private investigator's license. Unwilling to rely on the income from just one job, however, he is also about to begin another position, "moving across the desk," he told us, to represent the client rather than the government. Dwayne is joining a new program housed in the hospitals to help patients manage their medical payments and the associated paperwork. In addition, Dwayne Franklin is in the Air Force Reserve. The current four-year tour of duty follows eight years in the naval reserve and two years of active duty in the Navy. He also volunteers as a tutor and counselor at the local junior high school.

It is clear that the rules and regulations of formal organizations, such as welfare offices, hospitals, schools, courts, and the military, are Dwayne Franklin's métier. His familiarity with law and courts matured with his various jobs, and from those employment-related experiences Dwayne developed personal relationships with many of the people working in the courthouse. Nonetheless, Dwayne does not present or seem to regard himself as an insider. He is a user of the system, he suggests, but his use, as was evident in his decisions about when to call the police, is careful, measured, and varied.

Rules and regulations define situations, and according to Dwayne Franklin, the prudent actor works within those constraints. Dwayne described several situations in which he defined his options and rights in terms of a formal rule or law. In the past, he explained, his easy deference was a matter of inexperience. For example, when he was much younger, working for the chemical company, he "had gotten some chemicals on my skin, and also my fingers smashed." He went to the doctor but,

> It wasn't a situation where workman's compensation would apply . . . A lot of the chemical smell had actually gotten into my body so that when I left work, I took the smell with me. It also got into my system internally, you could tell from when you go to the bathroom, the color. So, I quit . . . Had I been thinking I would have called OSHA because it was an occupational hazard to work there. And the company did blow up. Yeah, right after I left . . . I quit because I felt like it was endangering my life. I knew enough to quit and find a better job. I wish I had been a little smarter back then.

At other times, Dwayne treats the existing rules as intractable facts—not because he still lacks experience, but because there seem to be no sensible alternatives. Thus, as he was leaving his position as a welfare investigator with the city, he was owed sixteen days' vacation pay that he did not collect either as days off or as compensation. "They have in our contract that they prorate our vacation days. When I left, I had sixteen, they prorated it to ten days, so they took six days away. But it is in the contract. There is nothing I can do about it."

Although experience and rules may limit possible and practical action, Dwayne Franklin acknowledges that the rules can be changed. Dwayne told us about a time that TRW provided a mistaken credit report about him. When he inquired, he discovered that the company had a rather long delay between receiving and posting new information. He wrote to the company.

> But there was not much you could do, you know . . . They said that that was their recording procedures. They also said that the companies submit their information to them. They try and say it is the companies' problems and not theirs.

Now, Dwayne said, the situation is different.

> Since then, people have taken them to court . . . I read in the newspaper yesterday, in the business section, that New Jersey is not one of the states involved in the action against TRW although I believe the attorney general is looking into it now. But at this point, it has something to do with the Fair Credit [Reporting] Act. They are saying that TRW is not complying with the Fair Credit [Reporting] Act.

Accepting the boundaries drawn by law, Dwayne recognizes that there are alternatives within the law when things do not work out satisfactorily the first time. Thus, he was ordered to pay child support for his ex-wife's child by a previous husband. He appealed the decision and although he did not get all the money back, and it seemed that "too much time had lapsed between the time they told me I didn't have to pay and when the light went off in my head telling me to go back and get my money," the court order was eventually withdrawn. Another time, when his veteran's disability benefits were stopped because he and the doctor had failed to connect on two different appointments, he appealed the decision to the Veterans Administration. "I was seen by the local hearing board. They denied it, so I appealed to Washington . . . The local decision was reversed. I was reinstated."

Dwayne Franklin acknowledges that he may be more willing than others to work through legal channels. When we asked if he had ever been discriminated against or treated unfairly because of his age, sex, race, religion, or nationality, Dwayne Franklin said that he thought that he had been unable to rent an apartment once because he was African American. Despite his desire to take legal action, however, he deferred to his girlfriend's reluctance to formally complain.

> I went to the apartment complex in Irvington and I noticed that no other black people live there. The super on the premises was very nosy. I was going to move in with my girlfriend and he asked if my girlfriend was going to work or to be home all day. The kind of questions the guy was asking was like, you know, why do you need to know that? The people that lived on the premises were

coming out of their apartments to see if he was going to rent an apartment to us . . . We wanted to rent it, but then a lady came and said that it had been promised to someone else.

I wanted to look into it a little further . . . I did contact the tax [bureau] and tried to find out who the actual property owner was, but because it was my girlfriend, we just didn't pursue it. A lot of people do not have faith in the judicial system for some reason. She may have faith in it now but she didn't back then.

Dwayne explained that his girlfriend had been raised, as he had, as a Muslim but more strictly.

She was raised in that religion by her father. They told her, they taught me at one point, and they teach their followers, to distrust Caucasian people, and the court system seemed to them to be run by Caucasian people. So, they thought they would not be treated justly . . . I think she is still being pulled that way, but she is . . . now a Sunni Muslim, so they think differently. It is not as strict as it was.

Dwayne Franklin's ex-girlfriend is currently appealing a ruling of the welfare department. He has been helping her with an administrative hearing because now "she realizes that you can't get what you want unless you go for help . . . especially the problem with welfare. You've got to request a hearing."

Despite Dwayne's advice to seek legal counsel, his father like his ex-girlfriend also refused to appeal what he thought was a costly error from the water department. Even though the elder Mr. Franklin owns several shops around the corner as well as the house the family lives in, the water bill of several thousand dollars was ridiculously excessive. When the Franklins complained, the city installed a new meter and reduced the bill because there clearly had been something wrong. In the end, however, the elder Mr. Franklin paid the adjusted bill, although Dwayne thought that they should appeal and get a further reduction. He went so far as to consult a lawyer, a friend at Seton Hall Law School, but his father declined the help and advice.

My parents, they are like this: they would rather not pursue the legal route. I think they don't feel like being tied up in court. If it were me I would have done it. I really believe they were in the wrong. Unless you take them to court, you are almost telling them that they are right. If you're going to challenge them, you have to challenge them on a legal level. You can't just walk into the office and say, "We don't owe you money." Because even if you talk to that person, the best way to resolve it is in front of a judge. Let the jury decide whether we owe them money or not. There is a possibility that the company is negligent.

Dwayne Franklin's confidence in "pursuing the legal route," as he calls it, is not, as we have already seen, a rigid insistence that it is the only way to do things. He is not unaware of the downside. "We were going to go the legal route with it, but . . . time and cost."

> You know, the Irvington court system, you spend a day over there before the case is called. Chances are for one case you might have to go back two or three times. It's a big waste of time. Time is money.

Moreover, he recognizes the need to work around as well as through the rules, explicitly confessing ambivalence about people who always "go by the book." Describing the way he handled some welfare fraud cases, he explained how you can sometimes do better and achieve your goals by working more informally.

> I chose not to take the people to court because they get put on probation, they pay the money to probation, the money that probation collects takes ten years for the welfare department to get it, and chances are if the person doesn't pay the complete restitution, the money goes to the county. So already you have lost control of the money. The department did pretty good with collecting the money outright.

As a welfare officer, Dwayne is rather proud of the various efficiencies he was able to achieve. Yet his efforts have been hampered by his superior's tendency to "always goes by 'it's the guideline'. . . [even though] his interpretation of the guidelines have oftentimes been incorrect." His boss

> likes to run [the department] like you are helping them, but you're not . . . wants the kind of investigator that is going to take somebody to court. If you ask him to write a letter, he'll give you a letter of rhetoric. I'll give you a letter spelling out exactly what you need to know . . . There were situations where we'd get calls from hospitals' collection agencies wanting to know when they were going to get paid. I'd be told, "Tell them to call back" or "Tell them to send a bill." Why get them to send a bill if you are not going to do anything with it? When we got the computer system, I set up certain programs on the word processor so that if a bill came in you could find out if we were responsible for it.

In contrast to what Dwayne sees as mindless rule-following, he explained his approach.

> I grew up and I was told that you had to have initiative in doing things. You had to improvise if other things didn't work. When you go to work, you go to work to get a job done. You don't go to work to shuffle paper around on a desk from one side to the

other. You go to work to complete a project and move on to something else. And for the five years that I was there I would say that three of the years was spent shuffling paper around on the desk. It doesn't make sense to have stacks of paper if you can't go to it and get what you want. It's a paper chase.

In the end, Dwayne felt useless. "I had to present a program that is not working for them and you can't really say anything to the people." The government needs to

do something more about what they are giving people for welfare assistance . . . There is no way you can take care of purchasing your personal needs and the needs of a child, pay rent, and be able to live. They wind up getting evicted or put in a shelter. That's why there are so many people in shelters.

After having worked in a bureaucracy that values guidelines and rules over substance, Dwayne is moving to the hospital, as he said, to the other side of the desk, to represent the needy against the system. It is also why, he said, he works on Saturday mornings at the junior high school tutoring and counseling kids.

Working in the welfare office, he felt that he was too often hurting the people who needed him.

Every time I was working on what I could to help the person, they suffered. If my director found out that I was helping this person, say, get their vacation approved or whatever, he would make it difficult for me and the client. I thought that was wrong.

The damage was exacerbated, Dwayne thought, because no one thought about these people as similar to themselves. They lacked empathy. Some of the "people that work in the office have received assistance. And the way they treat some of the people, you wonder to yourself, why do they do that? You were going through the same thing" at one time. "I've had a lot of arguments with people at the office about how to treat people but it got nowhere fast. All it did was make matters worse for me."

Dwayne Franklin knows, however, that it was not only rigid rule-following and lack of empathy that aggravated the situation in the office. He thinks that he may have made matters worse for himself, and for those he wanted to help, because he crossed the boundary between public and private, between personal and professional roles. He could not leave things alone. He was not only writing computer programs and developing systems to make the process more efficient and the office more accountable, he was not only trying to secure benefits for needy people, which he thought was his job, but he took the office's problems home and to the political arena. And, he said, "when you go over authority, you really rock the boat."

> When the director said, "This is how it stands," I wouldn't hesitate to call his boss and see what her opinion is, or call the mayor's office or whatever it involves. Because I don't think the law had stopped right there where I was standing.

From Ewick, Patricia, and Susan S. Silbey. "Dwayne Franklin" in "Before the Law." The Common Place of Law. University of Chicago Press, 1998. 64–74. Copyright 1998. Reprinted by permission of University of Chicago Press through Copyright Clearance Center.

Questions to Consider

1. We hear multiple voices here—Dwayne Franklin's narrative is contextualized by Ewick and Silbey. How might this affect our understanding and perception of Franklin?
2. What were Franklin's negative experiences with the police? Why do you think that despite these incidents, Franklin, an African American, contends that "minorities don't necessarily have a harder time"?
3. What are the different ways in which Franklin learns about the law? In what ways might these views still be limited or inaccurate?
4. As a welfare officer, Franklin noted that he often pursued complaints "because I don't think the law had stopped right there where I was standing." What does he mean by this statement, and what does it suggest about an individual's role in the legal system?
5. Were you surprised by Franklin's many encounters with the law? In what ways have you been involved with or affected by the law or its various agents? How have these experiences shaped your perspectives?

Interview with Captain Mike Gauldin
PBS *FRONTLINE*

This interview is one of a number the PBS program FRONTLINE *completed for the episode "What Jennifer Saw," a reflection on the events in Burlington, North Carolina, in July, 1984, when two women were raped by a man one of them identified as Ronald Cotton. Cotton was convicted in 1984 and retried in 1987; at the second trial, the other woman also identified Cotton as her assailant. Convicted of both rapes, though proclaiming his innocence and accusing fellow prisoner Bobby Poole of the crimes, Cotton was sentenced to life. Ten years after the rapes, with access to DNA-testing capabilities, new attorneys and Innocence Project founders Peter Neufeld and Barry Scheck reopened the case. Although one DNA sample was too degraded to test, the other showed that the rape could not have been committed by Cotton—the DNA belonged to Bobby Poole. Here* Frontline *interviews then-Police Captain Mike Gauldin, who, as detective, led the investigation. Gauldin, who went on to become chief of police and has since retired, has continued to speak out about this case and subsequent improvements in criminal investigative processes that can reduce the likelihood of erroneous convictions. As you read Gauldin's account, consider the points at which witness misidentification and other factors could have led to the defendant's conviction. How and for whom might such reflections encourage change?*

───────── ◆ ─────────

Q: Describe showing the victim, Jennifer, the photo array . . .

GAULDIN: We had received six names of individuals who were said to have resembled the composite drawing of the suspect. And as it turned out, we had arrest photos on all six of those people. We decided to put together a photo array involving those six people to show to our victims, including Jennifer Thompson, to ascertain whether or not our assailant would be among those six people.

And this happened, I think within two days of the assault and Jennifer Thompson met with myself and another detective at the police department, for the purpose of looking at this photo spread. And we made it clear to her that we had a number of photographs that we wanted her to look at, if she would look at them carefully, and determine if her assailant was among those.

But we also made it clear to her that she was not compelled to make an identification, that her assailant may or may not be among those six photographs. And she was given an opportunity to see those six photographs collectively, and after looking at them I think for about five minutes, she was able to make an identification, and she identified Ronald Cotton as her assailant.

Q: And what happened with the other rape victim who was shown the photo array?

A: The second rape victim was also shown the same photo array. It was independent of Jennifer Thompson, at a time prior to Jennifer Thompson actually being able to see the line up. And the second rape victim was not able to make an identification.

Q: What is happening in terms of the investigation between you as the investigator, her as the victim? Is there a kind of teamwork that comes into play there?

GAULDIN: Sure, there is a bond that tends to develop between the victim and the police who are involved in the investigation, because there has to be a close working relationship in order to accomplish what it is you're trying to accomplish, and that is simply to identify the perpetrator of the crime. I don't know how else to answer that.

She, the victim of a sexual assault, is essentially the person who is best able to tell you all the circumstances surrounding the incident itself, who is the person best able to work with you in an effort to try to determine who the perpetrator is. So you do have to develop a good working relationship with your victim in an effort to hopefully solve the case.

Q: And how did she come across?

GAULDIN: I found that Jennifer Thompson was a very unusual victim in that she made it very clear at the onset that she had studied in detail her assailant purposefully to be able to identify him at a later time if she ever saw him again. And bear in mind that this was all taking place at the time of the sexual assault. She had enough presence of mind to do that, which I think is somewhat unusual based on my experience. A lot of victims, which is fairly common, are so traumatized, so overcome with fear during the course of the sexual assault itself, that it is unusual to find somebody who is capable of having that presence of mind.

I found Jennifer Thompson to be a very determined person who believed without a doubt that if she saw her assailant again that she would be able to identify him.

Q: At what point did you conclude that Ronald Cotton was guilty?

GAULDIN: It became apparent to me after having conducted the interview, after having discovered that his alibi statement was essentially a lie, and after having found the shoe evidence, the flashlight evidence under his bed that we felt like linked him to both rapes, not only Jennifer Thompson's rape through the foam rubber that was found in her apartment, but through the flashlight linking him to the second rape that was perpetrated the same night. Of course, we had Jennifer Thompson who identified him initially as her assailant. I felt very strongly after all of that, that he was the perpetrator in both cases.

Q: The physical line up follows.

GAULDIN: A week after Ronald Cotton's arrest, we were able to do a physical line up in which both victims were able to see Ronald Cotton, among six other black males. This line up was undertaken at our police department in an administrative conference room. We didn't have the facility that we have now with the one-way mirror that affords the victims a great deal more privacy. In fact, both victims were allowed to go into this conference room in which the seven black males who were part of the line up stood directly across from them in the room.

Ronald Cotton was number five in the line up. Both victims were allowed to go in and view the line up participants. They did this independent of each other. The line up participants were instructed to stand shoulder to shoulder and then on command step forward, make a complete turn 360 degrees, back facing the line up viewer. And then repeat certain words that were said during the course of both sexual assaults.

Jennifer Thompson viewed this procedure involving those seven people with Ronald Cotton as number five. Initially she turned to me, I was conducting the line up and said that it was between four and five. I asked her if she wanted that procedure repeated. She said that she did. After the procedure was repeated, she identified Ronald Cotton as her assailant.

The second victim, after having seen the same line up procedure independent of the first victim wrote down the number four, indicating that number four, who stood in the line up, Kenneth Watkins, was her assailant. And we followed that up with an interview with the second victim and was able to determine that she was picking him out solely because in physical build she felt he resembled her assailant.

I should point out too that Ronald Cotton was the only suspect in the physical line up. That the other six participants, including Kenneth Watkins, were actually city employees who were standing in the line up at our request, and were not suspects of any crime.

Q: Explain briefly the relationship between who was in the photo array and who was in the actual line up, the physical line up.

GAULDIN: The photo array that was used early on in this investigation including six photographs of persons who we had received names of who were said to resemble the composite of the perpetrator, of which Ronald Cotton was one of those six.

The physical line up involved only Ronald Cotton as a suspect in this case. It was after he had been identified in the photo array. The other six participants in the physical line up were not suspects in this case. In fact, they were all city employees, I think, who we had asked to participate in the line up.

The common denominator among the photo array and the physical line up was Ronald Cotton. He was the only person in both.

Q: And what about the concern that a defense lawyer would have that Jennifer as a victim goes to a line up trying to identify somebody and has seen his photo before?

GAULDIN: Of course, the defense attorneys raise the issue that Ronald Cotton was the only person found to exist in both line ups and that might have, in some way, persuaded Jennifer Thompson to identify him as her assailant for that reason and that reason alone. But I think it's important to know that Jennifer was told prior to the line up she would see seven black males. And that she was not compelled to identify anybody. If she saw her assailant, the person who committed this crime against her, to indicate who that person was. And as I said, she identified Ronald Cotton.

I was very confident of her ability to identify her assailant. Because of not only how well she was able to describe him, the lighting situation, I felt like was sufficient in her apartment for her to see him. She made it clear to me that she had studied him extremely well. Knew that she would be capable of identifying him. So I felt very confident that were he her assailant, that she could identify him.

Q: What else did the attorneys at the trial really object to about the identifications?

GAULDIN: Also at issue during the trial regarding the identification procedure was the fact that the second victim identified somebody else during the course of the line up, that she actually picked out number four, who was Kenneth Watkins, who was a city employee and not suspected of any crime. Of course, we made it clear that we conducted an interview with the second victim after the line up procedure, and she explained to us that she was just so upset, so frightened from having to go into the room and being confronted by potential rape suspect that she just picked out a person, wrote down the number, that person wasn't the person who raped her.

Q: How did that first trial go?

GAULDIN: I think the first trial went extremely well. I think that we were able to put on our evidence and make our case. I think the defense attorneys represented Ronald Cotton very well. They did raise issue with the fact that the second victim was not able to make an identification, and in fact, had picked out somebody other than Ronald Cotton, but the judge ruled during the course of the trial that evidence not be included in trial. And it did not surprise me, when it was all said and done, that Ronald Cotton was convicted the first time around.

Q: Was that fair that the judge didn't allow that other stuff in?

GAULDIN: At the time, I thought that it was fair that the judge did not allow the second victim's inability to make an identification in that trial, because this particular trial exclusively dealt with the first victim who was Jennifer Thompson who had been able to make an identification, and I felt like it was the right decision at the time. . . .

Q: After the first verdict and Ron Cotton is in jail, you come across an arrest of Bobby Poole. What happens? Do you ever tie that back to Cotton somehow?

GAULDIN: Bobby Poole was arrested in April of 1985, three months after Ronald Cotton's conviction in the Jennifer Thompson case. He was arrested for two attempted second-degree sexual assaults that occurred the same night. Shortly after his arrest we also connected him with two other rape cases, one dating back to January of 1984. After having gone through the trial with Ronald Cotton, after having prosecuted him and the jury finding him guilty of the Jennifer Thompson case, we felt like we had a strong case there and didn't see any need to . . . and was not compelled to look at Bobby Poole in the Jennifer Thompson case.

Q: Then there's going to be a second trial and Elizabeth, the second victim comes forward. . .

GAULDIN: There was a second trial ordered in the Ronald Cotton case in 1987, two years after his original conviction. As a result of the second victim not being allowed to testify about her misidentification. In a pre-trial conference in October of 1987 with the second victim, the second victim declared that she knew all along that Ronald Cotton was her assailant, that she actually knew it at the time of the physical lineup, that she was just too frightened to come forward with that information, and this was made to the district attorney in the second case who was Octaves White.

Q: Two years later, how did that strike you?

GAULDIN: I was surprised two years later by the second victim's declaration. As I have said before, I was surprised that she was able to make an identification because she had not been able to identify in a photo array nor in the physical lineup, but after having been told that she was very frightened, extremely upset during the course of the physical lineup and that was the reason why she didn't come forward, she was frightened of Ronald Cotton I came to understand it better.

Q: With these two rape charges now being drawn together into one case, what did it allow you to do in terms of your evidence . . .

GAULDIN: As a result of the second victim being able to now say that Ronald Cotton was her assailant, Ronald Cotton was indicted for that particular offense as well, and of course, that changed the complexion of the second prosecution in that it allowed us to bring in all of the evidence associated with the second trial, which not only included being able to use the second victim as a witness, who I think did a very good job in presenting her testimony, and I think it was believable by the jury.

But in addition to that, it allowed us to use the flashlight that we had originally recovered from underneath Ronald Cotton's bed and when we searched his apartment. I thought that the flashlight was one of the most compelling pieces of evidence initially in that not only did it match conclusively the one that was described by the second victim, but when we did the background it was the same make and so forth, so we were able to use that and the second victim which changed the second prosecution. . . .

Q: What are your overall thoughts on this case?

GAULDIN: One of the things that I've always been concerned about in being a police officer is that I've always hoped that I would never work on a case that would falsely imprison somebody, and of course, now I know that I have. I've been part of a case . . . led to Ronald Cotton being in prison for 11 years for something that he didn't do.

But in all candor, I've done a lot of soul searching and we've looked at the files; I've reread them time and time again. There's nothing that I would have done differently.

If DNA had existed in 1984 and in 1987 we would have used it. When this was brought forward in 1995, we didn't object to this evidence being subjected to DNA testing. We wholeheartedly supported it. We voluntarily yielded for that reason, and when the DNA showed that there was a different perpetrator other than Ronald Cotton, we pursued Bobby Poole.

I'm very sorry that Ronald Cotton was imprisoned for 11 years and that has caused me to do a lot of soul searching and thinking about his situation, but I can't see what would have been done differently in 1984 and 1987.

Q: And your thoughts on DNA?

GAULDIN: It is the critical piece of evidence that ultimately exonerated Ronald Cotton, and incriminated Bobby Poole.

Q: So it worked two jobs.

GAULDIN: In this particular case, the DNA evidence not only excluded somebody—namely, Ronald Cotton—but it included somebody—namely, Bobby Poole. And I think it was a first in the state that has ever happened.

For those who speculate about (DNA's) usefulness, its importance—this case is a shining example of how important it is. Not only did it exclude Cotton, but it included another assailant who ultimately confessed to both cases. It's very critical evidence. Of course, it all hinges on how well it's tested, how well it's been collected and maintained which is at sometimes an issue.

Q: And, you are using the Cotton case now in teaching?

GAULDIN: I recently used this case in teaching entry-level police officers in our academy how important the process of criminal investigation is. To show how important it is to do everything, or try to do everything right, because in this case, I honestly believe that we did everything that we could do at the time in 1984 and in 1987. . .

I used this case to illustrate to them that even when you have a very good case, even when you do everything right, that this case serves as an example of what can happen to somebody. They can be imprisoned for a crime that they didn't commit; and ultimately I led to the point that imagine what would happen if you conducted an investigation that was not conducted properly of what could happen.

Q: Did you watch the Larry King Live Show when Ronald Cotton appeared on it?

GAULDIN: I was very interested in watching the Larry King Live Show when I found out that Ronald Cotton was going to appear on it. I wanted to see Ronald Cotton and to hear what Ronald Cotton had to say because I had not had an opportunity to see him before then, and I was very surprised and actually taken back a bit by Ronald Cotton's demeanor because it really surprised me that he seemed not to hold any animosity toward the system, toward the prosecution, toward the police, toward the victims, and it really astounded me that he didn't.

From WGBH Boston, "Interviews: Captain Mike Gauldin" in "What Jennifer Saw." FRONTLINE at PBS, February 1997. Online at www.pbs.org/wgbh/pages/frontline/shows/dna/interviews/gauldin. html. Copyright © 1995–2011 by WGBH Educational Foundation. Reprinted by permission of FRONTLINE.

NOTE: More information—including other interviews, photographs of the suspects, and an essay on appropriate police procedure—can be found at the FRONTLINE website regarding this case, www.pbs.org/wgbh/pages/frontline/ shows/dna/.

Questions to Consider

1. Consider Gauldin's first response about Jennifer Thompson's identification of the suspect. How do the interviewer's follow-up questions help make more specific, and problematic, the process of identification?
2. The bond Gauldin describes that developed between investigator and victim and his confidence in Jennifer seem admirable—responses a victim would appreciate. In what ways could they be problematic?
3. Note that the interviewer moves between questions that take Gauldin back to the scene ("Then there's going to be a second trial . . . ") and those that ask for a retrospective approach ("Two years later, how did that strike you?"). What are the purposes of these different strategies?
4. In other interviews and facts of the case, it is noted that Cotton and Poole were misidentified by others, such as fellow inmates. If misidentification is possible no matter how scrupulous the process of identification, how should the legal system respond?
5. Gauldin says that he can't see what he would have done differently in 1984 and 1987. What does this statement suggest about the limitations of retrospective analysis? In what ways is it still useful?

Making Connections

1. Bobby DeLaughter argued that jurors in the Evers case needed to convict the defendant because this offense "is something that every decent human being should absolutely be sickened by." Such outrage and emotional appeals can help sway a jury and are applauded when we agree with the verdict. How can we be sure, however, that decisions are not based solely on our emotional and empathic reaction to issues and events?

2. In the address by Dennis Barrie, he calls on his audience to make a stand. What issues do the other readings raise about which we could make a stand? To whom would we address our concerns?

3. At any given time, factors such as the level of technological advancement and cultural perceptions of right and wrong can make it difficult for a defendant to get what we would later call a fair trial. How are concerns like these exhibited in the cases in this chapter, and how can we try to avoid the negative implications of these limitations?

4. The Innocence Project, responsible for clearing many wrongfully accused, is dedicated to "reforming the criminal justice system to prevent further injustice" (see their website at www.innocenceproject.org). One way is to avoid "junk science"—testimony of purportedly scientific evidence that hasn't been proven reliable. How difficult do you find understanding scientific information, and what problems do you think a jury would face in judging such testimony?

5. How would you characterize the different attitudes toward the law that these different speakers represent? To what do you attribute these differences?

6. What kinds of recurring or intransigent problems in our legal system are evident in these texts? How might they be lessened or avoided?

7. Community standards are used in law to help determine what materials should be considered obscene. Community standards can be problematic, however; consider a community's decision to discriminate or ban books. For what reasons might community standards be useful? What qualifications on their use might be justified?

8. In what ways do these texts address the issue of empathy, and why is this seen as important within legal systems? Can it be employed fairly?

9. What are the different purposes for each speaker's comments? How might these differences affect our understanding of the issues involved?

10. Each of these speakers presents one side of an issue. Look up other views on these subjects. Who are other stakeholders, and what are their concerns? How does knowledge of these other viewpoints modify your perspective on the subject?

When Law Comes to Campus

I disapprove of what you say, but I will defend to the death your right to say it.

Voltaire

If asked to name the most important right guaranteed by the U.S. Constitution, many Americans would name freedom of speech. Yet like other constitutionally guaranteed rights, it is not absolute. The First Amendment prohibits only Congress (and by extension, the states) from "abridging the freedom of speech," and even then some restrictions on content have been deemed acceptable. Courts continue to grapple with what content can be limited and in which situations such limits are appropriate.

The most famously stated limitation on free speech was voiced by Supreme Court Justice Oliver Wendell Holmes in *Schenck v. United States* (1919); he argued that "the most stringent protection of free speech would not protect a man falsely shouting fire in a theater and causing a panic." Note his careful use of this example. It's not just "shouting fire"; it's "falsely" shouting fire. And it's not just shouting without a result; it's a shout inducing panic that could cause harm. Preventing serious harm has come to be known as a "compelling state interest" that can supersede free speech; such an interest is a high bar to hurdle. Even then, laws are required to be tailored as narrowly as possible. With these limitations come additional questions of interpretation: What is a compelling state interest, and how narrowly tailored is narrow enough?

Further questions exist regarding who has the right to limit speech and what exemptions to these limitations might be warranted. Imagine talking back to your parents; your parents might prohibit such speech, but this isn't an abridgment of your First Amendment rights. Your parents' household rules are not government restrictions; such "laws," therefore, don't rise to the level of constitutional consideration (though not everything in the family is off-limits to constitutional scrutiny). What happens, however, when the entity prohibiting speech is a place of employment, a local organization, or a school? Generally, the more private the entity, the more courts consider it like your family; the more public or the more reliant on public funds, the more courts consider it akin to government. Public schools have typically been held to constitutional constraints.

Even though the free exchange of ideas is considered by many to be a crucial element in educational settings, whether and to what extent constitutionally protected freedom of speech should be recognized in these venues is vigorously debated. The readings in this chapter reflect some of these concerns. In a case commonly referred to as "Bong Hits 4 Jesus" because of the banner a student held up outside his high school, the Supreme Court was faced with whether or not this representation of speech should be protected. In oral arguments by the attorneys in this case, in a review of the case in an article from *Education Week*, and in an analysis of the case by legal scholar Stanley Fish, we see various perspectives on whether this, or similar speech, should be permissible.

Wendy Kaminer argues that exposure to all kinds of speech and ideas is crucial in learning environments, especially college campuses. An interview with her by Brendan O'Neill provides examples of campuses around the world where speech limitations have been put into place; in contrast, Kevin Hoffman details an instance of hate crimes on a Wisconsin campus that were met not with limitations on speech, but with encouragement for speech—including some types you might find surprising. An example from that campus's website shows how a variety of groups approached the challenge.

Throughout these readings, consider how they represent the rights, and also the responsibilities, of individuals and society. Hateful speech and illegal behavior can cause harm beyond a single victim, but what should our responses be, and who should respond? You may not arrive at any simple answers. Instead, you will need to define terms, consider whose interests are affected, and try to determine guidelines based on significance. Such close analysis, rather than a blanket response, is what the courts are called upon to do everyday.

Oral Argument Before the Supreme Court of the United States in *Deborah Morse, et al., Petitioners v. Joseph Frederick*

Eighteen-year-old high school student Joseph Frederick, late to school, unfurled a fourteen-foot banner in Juneau, Alaska, just as TV cameras were about to film the street on which he stood, opposite the school. Along the street where the Olympic torch would soon travel, cheerleaders and band members were ready to perform, and other students already waited, although whether they had to return to school afterwards was in dispute. Teachers and high school principal Deborah Morse were also present. Morse told Frederick to take down the banner that read "Bong Hits 4 Jesus." She saw it as encouraging drug use, whereas Frederick said he just wanted to be on TV. When Frederick refused to take the banner down, Morse suspended him for ten days. A suit ensued that ended up on appeal in the Supreme Court. You will read portions of the oral arguments presented to that court by Kenneth Starr, the lawyer for Morse and other petitioners, and by Douglas Mertz on behalf of Frederick, the respondent. As you read, note other cases brought up by the lawyers and some of the justices, including Tinker v. Des Moines *(1969), in which the Supreme Court ruled that high school students' wearing of black armbands in opposition to the Vietnam conflict was symbolic protected speech;* Bethel School District v. Fraser *(1986), in which a student's suspension for a speech riddled with sexual innuendo was not considered a violation of the student's First Amendment rights; and* Hazelwood v. Kuhlmeier *(1988), in which the Court ruled that a school could censor a school-sponsored newspaper for "legitimate pedagogical" reasons. Notice also that unlike the closing arguments that you might have seen lawyers make in television dramas in which they talk uninterrupted to a jury, in these arguments to the justices, the attorneys barely begin to speak before they are peppered with questions. Whose arguments—and what arguments—do these become?*

———————— ✦ ————————

IN THE SUPREME COURT OF THE UNITED STATES

CHIEF JUSTICE ROBERTS	The Court will hear argument first today in case 06-278, Morse vs. Frederick. Mr. Starr.

ORAL ARGUMENT OF KENNETH W. STARR
ON BEHALF OF THE PETITIONERS

MR. STARR	Mr. Chief Justice, and may it please the Court: Illegal drugs and the glorification of the drug culture are profoundly serious problems for our nation. Congress has so recognized, as has this Court, time and again. The magnitude of the problem is captured in the amicus brief, the Court has a number of amicus briefs before it: . . . the amicus brief of General McCaffrey, Secretary Bennett, and a number of organizations. And particularly, pages 5 to 9 of that brief, the nature and the scope of the problem are well-captured.
JUSTICE KENNEDY	Well, is this case limited to signs about drugs? What is the rule that you want us to adopt for deciding this case?
MR. STARR	The rule the Court—that it articulated in Tinker. The rule of the Court as articulated in Tinker is that there is, in fact, a right to political speech subject to disruption, requirements that the speech not be disruptive.
JUSTICE KENNEDY	Disruptive of what? Disruptive of the classroom order? There was no classroom here.
MR. STARR	Including but not limited to. This was a school authorized event, this was education outside of the classroom. It was essentially a school simply out of doors. It was essentially—
JUSTICE SOUTER	Well, I can understand if they unfurled the banner in a classroom that it would be disruptive, but what did it disrupt on the sidewalk?
MR. STARR	The educational mission of the school. . . .
JUSTICE KENNEDY	Well, suppose you have—suppose you have a mission to have a global school. Can they ban American flags on lapel pins?
MR. STARR	Absolutely not, because under Tinker that is political expression. Let me be very specific. This case is ultimately about drugs and other illegal substances.

JUSTICE GINSBURG   So if the sign had been "Bong Stinks for Jesus," that would be, and Morse had the same reaction, that this was demeaning to the Olympics and it was unruly conduct, that there would be a protected right under Tinker because the message was not promoting drugs?

MR. STARR   She stated in her answers to interrogatories that she may very well not have interfered with the banner had it in fact said legalize marijuana. Under our theory, we think she could have interfered with that because it was disruptive to the event, it was disorderly to the event itself. . . .

MR. STARR   . . . what we are also urging the Court to consider is its gloss on Tinker and Frazier, and also what this Court said in Kuhlmeier. And in Frazier, the Court was very clear, the first three paragraphs in part three of the opinion, in talking about the habits and manners of civility, and inculcating the values of citizenship. That, in fact, is what is happening here. There is an effort of the—to prevent a message that is inconsistent with a fundamental message of the schools, which is the use of illegal drugs is simply verboten, and we believe that is permitted under Tinker—. . . .

JUSTICE STEVENS   It's also critical here to your case that it was a school event. If it, if this had . . . been two blocks down the street there would have been no objection.

MR. STARR   If Mr. Frederick had seen fit to go down Glacier Avenue to J and J's, a popular hangout, there would have been no high school jurisdiction. There may have been elementary school—but yes. He could have gone, Justice Stevens, to the State capital or anywhere along the ten mile route.

JUSTICE GINSBURG   Suppose it were Saturday instead of a weekday.

MR. STARR	I beg your pardon.
JUSTICE GINSBURG	Suppose it were Saturday, not a school day. And the school children were not required to show up at the Olympic event but were encouraged to and the same thing happened. Would it make a difference that it wasn't in the course of a regular school day?
MR. STARR	No. I think it still, under your hypothetical would be school sponsored. But there might be a more difficult showing of disruption or inconsistency with the educational mission. That is what this Court articulated in Frazier and again in Kuhlmeier that the school is able under our policies of federalism and value of federalism and democratic theory to fashion its educational mission subject to constitutional safeguards. And that mission of preventing the schools from being infected with pro-drug messages continues wherever there is school jurisdiction, and that would include on a Saturday field trip or other kind of activity and I think that—. . . .
JUSTICE SOUTER	. . . in response to Justice Scalia's question you said certainly that the school has got the right to have a policy that forbids violating the law and calling for violations of the law. Accepting that as a premise, don't we need, before the school may suppress the speech, don't we need at least a statement which is clearly inconsistent with that policy? And if that is so, is Bong Hits 4 Jesus inconsistent with it? It sounds like just a kid's provocative statement to me.
MR. STARR	Your Honor, with all due respect, the key is to allow the school official to interpret the message as long as that interpretation is reasonable. You might disagree with that just as Justice Brennan disagreed with whether Matt Frazier's

speech was all that terrible. But he said even though it wasn't all that terrible I nonetheless defer to the interpretation of school officials. That's what our educational system is about. . . .

ORAL ARGUMENT OF DOUGLAS K. MERTZ, ESQ.
ON BEHALF OF THE RESPONDENT

MR. MERTZ	Mr. Chief Justice and may it please the Court: This is a case about free speech. It is not a case about drugs.
CHIEF JUSTICE ROBERTS	It's a case about money. Your client wants money from the principal personally for her actions in this case.
MR. MERTZ	He does have a damages claim against the school district and the principal, but that's by no means his chief object here. The overwhelming object is to assert his free speech—
JUSTICE KENNEDY	Well, would you waive damages against this principal who has devoted her life to the school, and you're seeking damages for her for this sophomoric sign that was held up?
MR. MERTZ	We are certainly willing to negotiate a minimum settlement of damages. That is not the object here.
CHIEF JUSTICE ROBERTS	But there's a broader issue of whether principals and teachers around the country have to fear that they're going to have to pay out of their personal pocket whenever they take actions pursuant to established board policies that they think are necessary to promote the school's educational mission.
MR. MERTZ	That is indeed a legitimate fear, Your Honor, and we believe the existing law takes care of it by requiring before qualified immunity can be breached that there be a demonstration that under the existing law at the time available to her—
CHIEF JUSTICE ROBERTS	And you think it was clearly established that she had to allow a student at a

school-supervised function to hold a 15-foot banner saying "Bong Hits 4 Jesus"?

MR. MERTZ

I think it was clearly established at the time, Your Honor, that a principal could not engage in viewpoint censorship of a nondisruptive expression, under both Ninth Circuit law and this Court's law. The case had—

JUSTICE SOUTER

Does that, does that general statement that you just made apply to all circumstances in which a student-teacher relationship might be involved? For example, in the course of teaching a class in Shakespeare would your rule prevail?

MR. MERTZ

The rule on qualified immunity?

JUSTICE SOUTER

Yes, the general rule which the teacher is supposed clearly to have known here. For example, in the Shakespeare class, kid doesn't, doesn't say anything. He doesn't yell or scream or even raise his hand. He just holds a little sign in the Shakespeare class that says "Bong Hits 4 Jesus." As I understood the general rule that you said the teacher was bound to know here, the teacher I suppose would be required or the school would be required to tolerate that sign in the Shakespeare class; is that correct?

MR. MERTZ

I believe the analysis would be the Tinker analysis in terms of substantial disruption of the lesson.

JUSTICE SOUTER

Well, would there be a substantial disruption?

MR. MERTZ

It would all depend on the circumstances. My guess is that if it were simply passively—

JUSTICE SOUTER

If the kids look around and they say, well, so and so has got his bong sign again—
(Laughter.)

JUSTICE SOUTER

—they then return, they then return to MacBeth. Does the—does the, does the teacher have to, does the school have to tolerate that sign in the Shakespeare class?

MR. MERTZ	I believe that in circumstances where it is a substantial distraction—
JUSTICE GINSBURG	Can't it just say no signs when you're supposed to be learning?
MR. MERTZ	Your Honor, I think the answer is yes if they had a content-neutral rule prohibiting signs in school. I believe that would be—
CHIEF JUSTICE ROBERTS	But can't the school decide that it's part of its mission to try to prevent its student from engaging in drug use and so that it's going to have a viewpoint on drug use and that viewpoint is going to be that it's opposed to it and so that it takes a particular view with respect to signs that in their view seem to encourage drug use?
MR. MERTZ	Certainly it is within the school's mission to discourage drug use. Certainly it has many tools to allow it to get its own viewpoint—certainly it can—it does not need to provide a forum in the school itself for students with a contrary viewpoint. But when a student is basically on his own time, whether it's outside of school—
CHIEF JUSTICE ROBERTS	So your position would be different if this were in the student gym and they were having a discussion. There was a program to discourage drug use and he held up his sign; you would say it would be all right to take down the sign inside the school gym?
MR. MERTZ	No, I'm not so sure.
CHIEF JUSTICE ROBERTS	So it doesn't matter that this is outside. It matters on the content of the sign, not the location?
MR. MERTZ	Well, what matters is whether there is a substantial disruption of what the school is trying to achieve legitimately, whether it's a classroom lesson or a lesson on drug use.
JUSTICE SCALIA	Well, but the school has—the school has a program, an anti-drug program that shows movies, it brings in policemen and social workers to preach against drug use and you're saying that—never mind

unfurling a banner. You're saying that it has to let students contradict this message it's trying to teach, to walk around, you know, with a button that says "Smoke Pot, It's Fun." . . .

MR. MERTZ
I believe, Your Honor, that a nondisruptive pin, badge, whatever you want to call it, would have to be tolerated. However, they would not have to tolerate a student who interrupts a anti-drug presentation.

JUSTICE SCALIA
But the school, even though it is trying to teach one point of view, can allow students to come in and undermine that point of view, assuming that it's legitimate to teach that point of view? It can allow students to come in and undermine what it's trying to teach? . . .

MR. MERTZ
I think they cannot prevent presentation of a contrary viewpoint as long as it is done in such a way that it doesn't interfere with the school's own presentation of its viewpoint.

JUSTICE KENNEDY
Can the student be allowed to wear a button that says "Rape Is Fun"?

MR. MERTZ
No, I don't think so—

JUSTICE KENNEDY
Why?

MR. MERTZ
There is a distinction there.

JUSTICE KENNEDY
Why?

MR. MERTZ
Because when you're talking about hate speech, speech that advocates violence, then you're in another category of speech. There has been general recognition—

JUSTICE SCALIA
Nonviolent crimes are okay, it's only violent crimes that you can't, you can not promote, right? Right?

MR. MERTZ
I think there is a—

JUSTICE SCALIA
"Extortion Is Profitable," that's okay?

MR. MERTZ
Well—

JUSTICE SCALIA
This is a very, very, with all respect, ridiculous line. . . .

JUSTICE SCALIA	I think we're using disruption in two different senses here and we should probably separate the two. One sense is disrupting the class so that whatever is being taught can't be taught. But you're also using it in the sense of undermining a general message that the school is trying to get across: Obey the law, don't use drugs, whatever. Maybe we should have a different word for—the first is disruption. Disruption is a, is a funny word for the second. Let's called it undermining instead.

Now, you think both of them, however, are bad and both of them can be a basis for suppressing the speech? |
MR. MERTZ	If I understand your question correctly, the second of them might better be called allowing competing viewpoints.
JUSTICE SCALIA	So you think undermining is perfectly okay? You would never consider undermining to be disruption and therefore bad?
MR. MERTZ	I think undermining in the sense of preventing impeding the school from delivering its own message—
JUSTICE SCALIA	Okay, but only that.
MR. MERTZ	—would be substantial disruption.
JUSTICE SCALIA	Right after a class on drugs, he can be standing there in the hall and say: This class was ridiculous, drugs are good for you, I use them all the time, I urge all of you. That's perfectly okay? That's not undermining?
MR. MERTZ	I believe that is the kind of speech—
JUSTICE SCALIA	That's not disruption?
MR. MERTZ	—that we must tolerate no matter how unwise it is.
JUSTICE GINSBURG	But couldn't the school, couldn't the school board have a time, place, or manner regulation that says you're not going to use the halls to proselytizer for your cause, whatever it may be?

MR. MERTZ	I believe that's correct.
JUSTICE GINSBURG	You could have reasonable rules of decorum for what goes on inside the school building.
MR. MERTZ	Right.
CHIEF JUSTICE ROBERTS	Does the school have to be completely neutral in that respect? Does it have to punish who says that was a good program, I'm not going to use drugs, and you shouldn't either, because he's taking position on a public issue?
MR. MERTZ	I think a content neutral, content neutrality is critical here, and if the school wants to allow anti-drug comments, messages, then it has an outside of the official forum—
CHIEF JUSTICE ROBERTS	Where does that notion that our schools have to be content neutral—I thought we wanted our schools to teach something, including something besides just basic elements, including the character formation and not to use drugs. They have to be neutral on whether you should use drugs or not?
MR. MERTZ	Content neutrality goes to what speech is suppressed or punished. As far as the school delivering its own message, there is no requirement of equal time or that it be neutral. It's got its own viewpoint in the case of drugs, a viewpoint that almost all of us agree with, and it should be able to espouse—
JUSTICE SCALIA	A school isn't an open forum. A school isn't there for everybody to teach the students whatever he wants. It's there for the teachers to instruct. And you're turning it into an open forum. If the school says, addresses one issue, everybody else has to be able to address that issue.
MR. MERTZ	I don't believe that's the case at all, Your Honor.
JUSTICE SCALIA	That's not my vision of what a school is.

MR. MERTZ	In the classroom delivering the prescribed messages, in the school assemblies, when the school wishes to present a particular message, that's one case. However, in the lunchroom, outside in recess, across the street, that is a quintessentially open forum where it would not be proper, I think, to tell students you may not mention this subject, you may not take this position. . . .
CHIEF JUSTICE ROBERTS	Can we get back to what the case is about. You think the law was so clearly established when this happened that the principal, that the instant that the banner was unfurled, snowballs are flying around, the torch is coming, should have said oh, I remember under Tinker I can only take the sign down if it's disruptive. But then under Frazier I can do something if it interferes with the basic mission, and under Kuhlmeier I've got this other thing. So she should have known at that point that she could not take the banner down, and it was so clear that she should have to pay out of her own pocket because of it.
MR. MERTZ	Mr. Chief Justice, there are two different time points we have to talk about. There's the heat of the moment out there on the street, but then later back in the office when she actually decided to levy the punishment after she had talked to him, after she heard why he did it and why he didn't do it, after she had had a chance to consult with the school district's counsel. At that point in the calmness of her office, then she should indeed have known it. And she did testify that she had taken a master's degree course in school law in which she studied Kuhlmeier and Frazier and Tinker. So—
CHIEF JUSTICE ROBERTS	And so it should be perfectly clear to her exactly what she could and couldn't do.
MR. MERTZ	Yes.

JUSTICE SCALIA	As it is to us, right? (Laughter.)
JUSTICE SOUTER	I mean, we have had a debate here for going on 50 minutes about what Tinker means, about the proper characterization of the behavior, the nonspeech behavior. The school's terms in dealing with the kids that morning. The meaning of the, of the statement. We've been debating this in this courtroom for going on an hour, and it seems to me however you come out, there is reasonable debate. Should the teacher have known, even in the, in the calm deliberative atmosphere of the school later, what the correct answer is?
MR. MERTZ	We believe at the very least she should have known that one cannot punish a nondisruptive holding of a sign because it said something you disagreed with. . . .

From Morse v. Frederick. *Transcript of oral argument 19 March 2007. No. 06-278. Supreme Ct. of the US. 25 June 2007.*

NOTE: You will see that the transcript refers to Frazier *rather than* Fraser. *This is just one example of the errors that sometimes persist in court documents that depend on reproducing speech such as court testimony.*

Questions to Consider

1. Since the justices read the parties' written briefs, or arguments, as well as the lower courts' rulings, prior to oral arguments, they already know much of the case. The transcripts reveal that questions still play a large role. Why are questions so crucial to understanding the nature of this, or any, argument?

2. What is the benefit of using, or rejecting the use of, other cases and hypotheticals by analogy? Consider what examples you might call on if you were arguing to your parents that they should help fund your purchase of a car. How would you use examples of your own or others' good past behavior, and how would you defend yourself against your parents' use of negative examples?

3. There is an attempt to define various words and phrases, including *disruption* and *school sponsorship*. What other terms are scrutinized? Is consensus reached?

4. Formal rules govern these arguments, including a typical time limitation of thirty minutes per side. Nevertheless, we see informality as well, such as occasional indications of laughter, Justice Scalia's noting that the line of

questioning was "ridiculous," and multiple interruptions. The transcript also captures unfinished sentences and verbal non sequiturs. Given these various features, how would you describe the tone of these arguments, and what about that tone surprises you?

5. At one point Justice Scalia responds to various descriptions of school and says, "That's not what my vision of what a school is." Why are these views of the justices and lawyers relevant? What is your vision of what a school is and what is appropriate speech in that venue?

Ruling in "Bong Hits" Case Seen as Leaving Protection for Students' Free Speech

MARK WALSH

In this article from Education Week, *a national newspaper covering educational issues affecting grades K–12, the ruling by the Supreme Court in* Morse v. Frederick *is examined. Mark Walsh, a writer who has covered legal issues in education for almost two decades, notes not only the decision, but also some of the potential implications for schools and their administrators. We see how the Court split 6–3 on the ultimate decision and how even the majority was divided on what basis the decision was, or should have been, made. In these separately written majority, concurring, and dissenting opinions, Walsh suggests that we can predict how the Court might decide future cases on this issue. Having read the oral arguments but before reading this article, what do you think the outcome of the Court's deliberation will be? What do you think it should be?*

◆

The U.S. Supreme Court's first major ruling in two decades on student speech was a decisive victory for schools and administrators in the case over a student's display of a "Bong Hits 4 Jesus" banner. But the nuances in the justices' opinions leave significant protection for more serious political and social expression by students.

How the court's June 25 ruling plays out for the latest generation of student-speech disputes, including those stemming from the culture wars over religious expression and gay rights, may take years to figure out, legal experts say. It was only days, though, before lower courts took note of the decision in other student-speech disputes.

"The First Amendment is a little bit wounded right now, but it has survived," Douglas K. Mertz, a cooperating lawyer with the American Civil Liberties Union, said right after the decision.

Mr. Mertz had argued before the Supreme Court on behalf of Joseph Frederick, who was a senior at Juneau-Douglas High School in January 2002 when he and other students unfurled the banner at an Olympic-torch relay outside the school in Juneau, Alaska.

Deborah Morse, then the principal of Juneau-Douglas High, was upset by the banner's reference to drug paraphernalia. Ms. Morse asked Mr. Frederick and the others to drop the banner, according to court papers. When Mr. Frederick refused, he was suspended by the principal for 10 days, an action upheld by administrators and the board of the 5,000-student district.

Francisco M. Negrón Jr., the general counsel of the National School Boards Association, said the decision in *Morse v. Frederick* (Case No. 06-278) showed the court "is really recognizing the realities with which educators are faced."

KEY OPINION BY ALITO

"Educators and principals are happy that they won't have to be second-guessed" in disciplining students over drug-related messages, said Mr. Negrón, whose association had filed a friend-of-the-court brief on the side of the Juneau district and Ms. Morse.

While the judgment in the case was 6-3, a five-justice majority emphasized that schools have the authority to regulate drug-related messages on public school campuses.

"The special characteristics of the school environment, and the governmental interest in stopping student drug abuse . . . allow schools to restrict student expression that they reasonably regard as promoting illegal drug use," Chief Justice John G. Roberts Jr. said in the majority opinion.

The chief justice rejected Mr. Frederick's argument that the case did not involve school speech at all because the banner was displayed on a sidewalk across from Juneau-Douglas High.

He noted that students had been released from class during school hours to see the Olympic-torch relay passing by their school, under the supervision of teachers and administrators.

His opinion was joined by Justices Antonin Scalia, Anthony M. Kennedy, Clarence Thomas, and Samuel A. Alito Jr.

Justice Alito wrote a significant concurring opinion, joined by Justice Kennedy, that helped narrow the majority's holding by stressing the context of the banner's perceived drug message.

Justice Alito said he joined the decision on the understanding that it "provides no support for any restriction of speech that can plausibly be interpreted as commenting on any political or social issue."

Justice Stephen G. Breyer filed an opinion in which he concurred in the outcome. He said he would have ruled for the district purely on the basis of the principal's immunity, and he would have avoided the First Amendment question.

Justice John Paul Stevens, writing a dissent joined by Justices David H. Souter and Ruth Bader Ginsburg, said that while the banner was a "nonsense" message, "the court does serious violence to the First Amendment in upholding—indeed lauding—a school's decision to punish Frederick for expressing a view with which it disagreed."

But Justice Stevens' opinion agreed with the majority that the principal did not deserve to face personal liability in the case, as the appellate court had ruled.

Kenneth W. Starr, the former U.S. solicitor general who represented Ms. Morse and the Juneau school district before the Supreme Court, said he agreed that Justice Alito's concurrence narrowed the decision's free-speech implications.

"Justices Alito and Kennedy expressed very strong pro-student-speech views," Mr. Starr said in an interview. "That means that another [student-speech] case might be decided differently."

Widely disparate groups that had filed friend-of-the-court briefs on Mr. Frederick's side agreed.

"There appears to be a clear majority in favor of student religious speech being protected in schools," said Casey Mattox, a lawyer with the Christian Legal Society, in Springfield, Va., which often fights public school restrictions on student religious expression.

Gay-rights groups had also supported Mr. Morse, and they were in unison with religious-rights groups in welcoming the narrowness of the decision.

"It feels to me like this decision would provide absolutely no justification to limit speech about sexual-orientation issues" in public schools, said Jon W. Davidson, the legal director of the Lambda Legal Defense and Education Fund, in New York City.

TIGGER AND A T-SHIRT

In his majority opinion, Chief Justice Roberts repeated the famous line from the court's 1969 decision in *Tinker v. Des Moines Independent Community School District* that students do not "shed their constitutional rights to freedom of speech or expression at the schoolhouse gate." That case upheld students' right to wear black armbands to protest the Vietnam War as long as school was not substantially disrupted.

Early this month, a state trial judge in California cited the *Morse* decision's "reconfirming" of *Tinker* in a preliminary ruling halting a strict school dress code that had ensnared a young student wearing the Winnie the Pooh character Tigger on her socks, as well as students wearing pink ribbons for breast-cancer awareness and a T-shirt reading "Jesus Freak."

"Certain clothing prohibited by the attire policy . . . did convey a particularized message subject to First Amendment protection," Judge Raymond A. Guadagni said about the Napa Valley Unified School District's policy.

And on June 29, the Supreme Court declined to hear an appeal from school administrators over the discipline of Zachary Guiles, a Vermont student who had worn an anti-President Bush T-shirt to school in 2004. A federal appeals court had sided with the student.

Despite the potential similarities, the justices declined to return the appeal from administrators in *Marineau v. Guiles* (No. 06-757) to the lower court for reconsideration in light of the *Morse* decision.

Walsh, Mark. "Ruling in 'Bong Hits' Case Seen as Leaving Protection for Students' Free Speech." Education Week 18 July 2007: 27–28. Copyright 2007 by Editorial Projects in Education. Reprinted by permission of Education Week.

Questions to Consider

1. Who is the audience for *Education Week*? How does this audience, and the purpose of the newspaper, influence the focus of the coverage in this article?
2. Was the decision a surprise to you? With which of the justices' decisions and rationales do you agree, and why?
3. Walsh notes other cases decided by lower courts in the wake of the *Morse* decision; in one, certain depictions on student clothing were held subject to First Amendment protection, including Winnie the Pooh characters. What arguments could be raised by students, teachers, and administrators in support of or against these kinds of depictions?
4. Friend-of-the-court briefs, also known as *amicus curiae* briefs, are often filed in cases to attempt to inform and influence the decision. Fourteen such briefs were filed, including those by the National School Boards Association, D.A.R.E. America, Students for Sensible Drug Policy, the Christian Legal Society, and Lambda Legal Defense and Education Fund. Why do you think these groups chose to file briefs? Who else could you imagine filing *amicus curiae* briefs?
5. Although it might seem that teachers and administrators have different goals and perspectives than students, for what reasons might you argue that teachers should have the right to censor or discipline students relating to their speech or expression? What factors, including grade level, would impact your answer?

Clarence Thomas Is Right
STANLEY FISH

Lawyer, legal theorist and scholar, dean emeritus, and social critic Stanley Fish has taught at various law schools across the country and is presently the Davidson-Kahn University Professor of Humanities and Law at Florida International University in Miami. A prolific writer on many subjects, from poetry to pedagogy, from politics to the practice of law, he has also edited and contributed to the reader There's No Such Thing as Free Speech, and It's a Good Thing, Too. *In addition, Fish writes a legal blog for* The New York Times, *where this blog entry appeared; over four hundred reader comments expressed a variety of support for and criticism of Fish's opinion. There may be a similar range of views in your classroom regarding Fish's idea—which runs contrary to the view represented by many analysts and the Supreme Court—that students and teachers alike have no First Amendment rights in an educational setting. What kinds of support does he provide for this position, and how convincing is his argument?*

◆

On June 25th the Supreme Court held in *Morse v. Frederick* that it was all right to discipline a high school student because he and some of his friends had unfurled a banner reading "Bong Hits 4 Jesus" at a school-sponsored event.

The facts are not in dispute. When the principal of the school, Deborah Morse, asked the students to take the banner down, one of them, Joseph Frederick, refused. He was suspended and his suspension was upheld by the school superintendent, who cited a board policy prohibiting any form of expression that "advocates the use of substances that are illegal to minors." Mr. Frederick then filed suit, alleging that his First Amendment rights had been violated. A three-judge panel of the United States Court of Appeals for the Ninth Circuit agreed with him, but the Supreme Court reversed by a 5-to-4 vote, and held for Principal Morse.

The Court's discussion unfolds under the shadow of a 1969 case, *Tinker v. Des Moines Independent Community School District*, the key sentence of which declared that students do not "shed their constitutional rights to freedom of speech or expression at the schoolhouse gate." Not that students are free to say or express anything they like. The test, the Court said in *Tinker*, is whether the speech in question can be said to "materially and substantially disrupt the work and discipline of the school." In 1969, students had worn black armbands signifying their opposition to the Vietnam War. Applying the test it had just formulated, the Supreme Court held that since no such disruption was documented, the speech was protected.

The majority opinion in *Frederick*, written by Chief Justice John Roberts, ducks the disruption issue and bases its holding on the school's right and responsibility to educate "students about the dangers of illegal drugs." After all, it reasoned, "*Tinker* is not the only basis for restricting student speech," citing to *Bethel School District v. Fraser*'s declaration that "the constitutional rights of students in public schools are not automatically coextensive with the rights of adults in other settings" (1986).

The minority opinion, written by Justice John Paul Stevens, challenges on two points. By singling out speech about drugs as a proper object of regulation, the majority "invites stark viewpoint discrimination," a constitutionally suspect disfavoring of a message simply because of its content. Moreover, the minority adds, it's not at all clear what the message was or even that there was a message. Mr. Frederick asserted that he wasn't advocating anything; the sign was meaningless; the only thing he intended (or hoped for), he said, was to get himself on television.

The majority ignores Frederick's account of his own intention, and insists that it is enough that the interpretation of his intent by Principal Morse was "a reasonable one." The minority replies that, "The beliefs of third parties, reasonable or otherwise, have never dictated which messages amount to proscribable advocacy."

And so it goes, back and forth.

But Justice Clarence Thomas isn't having any. He concurs with the majority in its holding for Principal Morse, but he rejects the context within which both the majority and the minority make their points. In short, he rejects *Tinker* and the idea that schoolchildren have any First Amendment rights at all. Why? Because "originally understood, the Constitution does not afford students a right to free speech in public schools."

Thomas argues from both history and principle: "In the light of the history of American public education, it cannot seriously be suggested that the First Amendment 'freedom of speech' encompasses a student's right to speak in public schools." Early public schools, Thomas reports, "were not places for freewheeling debates or explorations of competing ideas." Rather, schools were places where teachers "relied on discipline to maintain order."

And this view of what properly goes on in public schools was confirmed in the rulings of state courts in Vermont, Connecticut, Maine, Alabama, Tennessee, Kentucky, Indiana, North Carolina, California and Missouri, among others. It is only since *Tinker*—which, Thomas contends, "effected a sea change" in this area of law—that we have been troubled by talk of students' speech rights. (One suspects that Thomas is uneasy about the expansion of First Amendment rights in general. As recently as 1942, in *Chaplinsky v. New Hampshire*, the Court was able to rehearse a paragraph-long list of forms of speech that did not rise to the level of constitutional notice. That paragraph could not be written today.)

Although Thomas does not make this point explicitly, it seems clear that his approval of an older notion of the norms that govern student behavior stems from a conviction about how education should and should not proceed. When he tells us that it was traditionally understood that "teachers taught and students listened, teachers commanded and students obeyed," he comes across as someone who shares that understanding.

As do I. If I had a criticism of Thomas, it would be that he does not go far enough. Not only do students not have First Amendment rights, they do not have any rights: they don't have the right to express themselves, or have their opinions considered, or have a voice in the evaluation of their teachers, or have their views of what should happen in the classroom taken into account. (And I intend this as a statement about college students as well as high-school students.)

One reason that students (and many others) have come to believe that they have these rights is a confusion between education and democracy. It is in democratic contexts that people have claims to the rights enumerated in the Constitution and other documents at the heart of our political system—the right to free speech, the right to free assembly, the right to determine, by vote, the shape of their futures.

Educational institutions, however, are not democratic contexts (even when the principles of democracy are being taught in them). They are pedagogical contexts and the imperatives that rule them are the imperatives of pedagogy—the mastery of materials and the acquiring of analytical skills. Those imperatives do not recognize the right of free expression or any other right, except the right to competent instruction, that is, the right to be instructed by well-trained, responsible teachers who know their subjects and stick to them and don't believe that it is their right to pronounce on anything and everything.

What this means is that teachers don't have First Amendment rights either, at least while they are performing as teachers. Away from school, they have the same rights as anyone else. In school, they are just like their students, bound to the protocols of the enterprise they have joined. That enterprise is not named democracy and what goes on within it—unless it is abuse or harassment or assault—should not rise to the level of constitutional notice or any other notice except the notice of the professional authorities whose job it is to keep the educational machine running smoothly.

Fish, Stanley. "Clarence Thomas Is Right" in "Opinionator." From The New York Times *online, 8 July 2007. Online at opinionator.blogs.nytimes .com/2007/07/08/clarence-thomas-is-right/. Copyright 2007 by* The New York Times. *All rights reserved. Used by permission and protected by the copyright laws of the United States. The printing, copying, redistribution, or retransmission of this content without express written permission is prohibited.*

Questions to Consider

1. Stanley Fish chooses a slightly misleading title to represent his position, a position that isn't clarified until almost the end of his blog. Even then, he qualifies his agreement with the Court. What exactly is his argument, and what effect do these rhetorical strategies have on his ability to persuade the reader of his viewpoint?

2. Although Fish notes that "the facts are not in dispute," he appears not to include in his consideration certain "facts" that some might see as important, such as whether Frederick was in school at the time of the incident. Who would view this still-open question as needing to be determined, and why? What does such variation in opinion on even the relevancy of information suggest about how perspective and context can be factors in the ultimate outcomes of decisions?

3. Fish points out that the Court "ignores Frederick's account of his own intention" while it believes Morse's interpretation that the banner promoted drug use. Why does Morse's interpretation matter while Frederick's does not? Do you agree that Morse's interpretation was reasonable?

4. Fish includes a one-sentence paragraph: "And so it goes, back and forth." How is this paragraph being used rhetorically to further Fish's argument and his organization of this blog?

5. What does Fish mean when he says that students, including college students, "do not have any rights," including those of speech, expression, giving opinions, and so forth? Does this mean students should not be able to engage in those activities, or that it is not important for the educational process, or something else? Do you agree?

The Left Has Been Infected by the Disease of Intolerance

BRENDAN O'NEILL

Do you ever have a problem arguing the finer points of a position you have held for a long time? That is what Wendy Kaminer expresses in the opening of this article, in which she is asked why academic freedom is important. Kaminer was interviewed in 2006 by Brendan O'Neill, a London-based journalist and editor of spiked online. *In this article O'Neill incorporates Kaminer's views on academic freedom, intolerance, and authoritarianism as exhibited by students and also notes his own concerns, largely based on examples from American and British universities. Kaminer, an American attorney and social critic, has written on a variety of cultural concerns, from pornography and single-sex schools to volunteerism and recovery programs. As Kaminer and O'Neill discuss defending the liberty and responsibility to speak on college campuses, consider the evidence presented. Would you identify yourself or your classmates as "young authoritarians"?*

---- ✦ ----

"Asking why academic freedom is important is like asking why love is important, or why it's important to eat when you're hungry." Wendy Kaminer is momentarily stumped. For her, the need for free thinking and free speech in universities, both on campus and inside the classroom, is so obvious, such a no-brainer, that: "You know what? I'm having trouble articulating a defence of it!"

A social critic and former member of the National Board of the American Civil Liberties Union (ACLU), whose latest book is *Free for All: Defending Liberty in America Today*, Kaminer says it should be apparent to anyone who has ever set foot in a university that "freedom is essential there." Yet today, in some universities on both sides of the Atlantic, academic freedom is in danger of being corroded from within—by academics and administrators intolerant of colleagues who hold unconventional, unpopular views, and students who rush to ban anything that offends their sensitivities, be it right-wing rags, Eminem or Kit-Kats (more of which in a minute).

"Okay, why is academic freedom important? Because in order to think, in order to exercise your freedom, you need to be educated—and in order for people to be educated they need to have the freedom to consider a very wide range of ideas, to have their own preconceptions questioned, and questioned vigorously," says Kaminer. "They have to learn how to tolerate ideas that are really abhorrent to them. They need to learn the difference between ideas and actions. They need to learn that people can have very different ideas, and they can debate them without coming to blows.

"You know, in our world today, one way you can stop people from coming to blows about their conflicting ideas is by teaching them how to argue, and teaching them not to be afraid of argument. There's an important difference between being embarrassed or feeling intellectually or emotionally wounded because you're at the losing end of an argument, and actually being physically assaulted. I think it's incredibly important for students to learn how to argue, and to learn how to appreciate and even enjoy argument."

Kaminer believes that the need for this kind of attitude in universities—where people are encouraged not only to swot up on facts and figures but also to be open-minded, robust, self-critical—goes hand-in-hand with a Uni's traditional role of guarding and imparting knowledge.

"Being exposed to other ideas, being challenged, being put on the spot, being made to examine their own most basic beliefs—for students that is at least as important, if not *more* important than learning the fundamentals of their subject. What good is it to learn facts if you don't learn how to think and how to defend your ideas? John Stuart Mill talks about this. When he talks about freedom of speech and freedom of thought, he talks about the importance of having your ideas tested and learning how to defend them. If you don't know how to defend your ideas, then they can't mean very much to you.". . .

Kaminer's description of a free university, where challenging and even confrontational ideas are batted between and among teachers and students, sounds very appealing—but all too often today, the reality is quite different. She says: "There are still a lot of very good schools and very good teachers, who try to stimulate their students and expose them to different ideas." No doubt that is true. But in some universities there is also a creeping culture of conformism, a sense that certain ideas are beyond the pale and thus must be crushed by the long arm of the censor (often, these days, a university-appointed ethics committee or a self-righteous students' union).

Increasingly, university administrations restrict what academics can talk about. In the US post-9/11, some academics were chastised for speaking out against America's war in Afghanistan. Trustees of the City University of New York made "formal denunciations" of faculty members who criticised US foreign policy at a teach-in, and similar measures were taken against academics at the University of Texas at Austin, MIT, the University of North Carolina at Chapel Hill and the University of Massachusetts at Amherst (2). In both American and British universities there has been a proliferation of ethics committees that judge what are suitable and "appropriate" areas of research for academics, and even advise teachers on the minutiae of how to communicate with their students. Durham University in England recently decreed that lecturers should obtain approval from an ethics committee if they want to give tutorials on difficult or potentially heated topics, such as abortion or euthanasia. Universities even prescribe what kind of language to use. The University of Derby, also in England, has a pretty Orwellian "Code of Practice for Use of Language," which advises teachers that their "use of language should reflect the university's mission and support relationships of mutual respect." As Frank Furedi has argued on *spiked*, such illiberal policies are not "simply the handiwork of a few philistine zealots. [They are] the inexorable consequence of an academic culture that is increasingly prepared to censor itself and others" (3).

Then there are students. Once seen as being among the most progressive, or certainly the most open-minded members of society, today more and more of them are increasingly ban-happy, responding to controversy not by having the argument out—by "questioning things vigorously," as Kaminer puts it—but by demanding censorship, silence, an end to words or images that might potentially upset fragile members of the student body.

In a stinging piece on a "mob of students" at Brown University in Rhode Island, who stormed the offices of the student newspaper *The Brown Daily Herald* and seized its entire print run after it ran an advert paid for by a right-wing politician who denounced reparations for slavery, Kaminer wrote of "the distressing number of young authoritarians" on American campuses. "Self-righteous intolerance of dissent remains distressingly common among supposedly progressive students on liberal campuses," she complained (4).

Such self-righteous intolerance is rampant among British students, too. In recent years, the Sussex University Students' Union has banned the right-leaning tabloid the *Daily Mail* for being "bigoted" (ironic, I know), leading one Sussex student to complain that the union is "treating us like babies and it's offensive." The union at Sheffield University banned the playing of Eminem records at student dos, because the rapper's use of words like "fags" breaks the union's anti-homophobia policies. At the School of Oriental and African Studies in London the union has banned Israeli Embassy representatives from speaking because part of its union policy states that Zionism is racism, and racists should "not be given a platform." Other unions have banned the sale of Coca-Cola and Kit-Kats in protest at the working practises of their parent companies (5).

Far from being a site of free thinking and free exchange of ideas, the university seems to have become a laboratory for new forms of censorship and conformism. "Kids come to college, and for the first couple of weeks of freshman year they're in a sensitivity course, where they're told what they're allowed to say and what they're not allowed to say," says Kaminer. "They are subjected to thought-control programmes the minute they arrive. That is not a very good start."

For Kaminer, this subtle but pernicious stifling of free speech on campus is bad news. Firstly because it helps to alter the way some students and teachers think, tending to make them closed-minded and fearful of challenging arguments—at institutions where openness and free debate are essential. And secondly because it denigrates the quality and level of public debate more broadly. Censorship is not only a bad rap for those who are censored: the right-wing advertisers or the Eminem record-players. It is also a bad rap for the rest of us, in the sense that genuine conflicts of views and interest are never had out and thus never resolved, and certain ideas are given authority not through public interrogation and debate but by being hand-picked and elevated as "correct" by small cliques of student organisers or ethics committees. Censorship therefore encourages ignorance and conformity—a kind of medieval nodding along with the whims of authority—rather than a critical culture where ideas can be thrown around, debated, defeated, improved or pushed further. . . .

How have students become these self-righteous "young authoritarians"? For Kaminer, "it is partly because they have been brought up in today's victimised, intolerant culture." She argues that restrictions on free speech are made not only by the right seeking to quell dissent among their left-leaning or liberal critics, but also by liberals themselves, who have bought into ideas of "hate speech" and "harmful speech."

"One of the saddest trends among people who consider themselves liberal or progressive over the past 10 or 15 years has been this increased intolerance of free speech, and this notion that there is some right, some civil right, not to be offended, which trumps somebody else's right to speak in a way that you find offensive. It is like a disease, an infection, that has taken hold on the left. It is an incredibly regressive notion."

Kaminer traces it back to the American feminist anti-porn movement of the 1980s, to authors such as Catherine MacKinnon and Andrea Dworkin. They, and others, were among the first, says Kaminer, to articulate the idea that "you have a civil right not to be offended or 'arguably harmed,' even metaphorically, by somebody else's speech." Indeed, Kaminer points out that some of these feminist theorists made little distinction between words and actions: they argued that porn *is* violence, that to watch porn is to commit a violent act and that watching porn often directly encourages men to commit violent acts. According to Kaminer, this idea has spread widely, so that many more forms of hate speech—from racist speech to anti-Semitic speech, misogynist speech to xenophobic speech—are now seen as being potentially harmful, as encouraging listeners to hate and act violently towards others.

The same justification is made for clampdowns on both Islamic radicals and fascist groups here in Britain. Apparently if we allow Islamists to propagate their ideas then more young Muslims will be tempted to blow themselves up; and if we don't censor fascists in organisations like the British National Party then their words will stir the white masses to launch pogroms against foreigners.

Kaminer says these arguments are deeply problematic. There is a clear distinction between words and actions, she says, and it is us, the audience, the people who decide whether or not to give words consequences.

"Words have power, of course they do. If they didn't, why be a writer? Why be an activist? But words don't cast spells over people. When feminists argue that giving a man porn is like saying 'kill' to an attack dog, it implies that men are just dogs on short leashes, that they have a Pavlovian response that they cannot control. It ignores the fact that speech is a two-way exchange. The speaker is not Svengali: the audience hears what he says, interprets it, and they make their minds up. The way you combat bad speech is with good speech. You don't combat it with censorship. That just doesn't work, and it demeans debate."

For Kaminer, there is far more at stake here than certain words and images. Free speech is necessary for progress, for improving humanity's lot. "Looking at the history of the US, it is hard to imagine how any of our truly progressive movements could ever have advanced if people were not free to assemble and speak—and in ways that other people often found offensive! One hundred and fifty years ago people thought that women shouldn't speak in public; that was a violation of God's law. It was only by violating God's law—and in the process offending a lot of people—that women's rights were put on the agenda. It is sometimes by being offensive that we push society forward."

In other words, we are always better off in the marketplace of ideas than in the cloistered halls of officially sanctioned and ethically correct speech.

(2) "America: the end of freedom?," Cambridge University mailing list, 2002
(3) See "The new Chief Inquisitor on campus," by Frank Furedi
(4) "Mob rules," Wendy Kaminer, *American Prospect*, March 2001
(5) "Defend free speech, now more than ever," by Mick Hume

From O'Neill, Brendan. "The Left Has Been Infected by the Disease of Intolerance." spiked online. 27 October 2006. Copyright 2006. Reprinted by permission of spiked online.

Questions to Consider

1. Why were Eminem and Kit-Kats considered problematic on some college campuses? In relation to these incidents, Kaminer and O'Neill use the term "self-righteous intolerance." What is meant by this term, and what does Kaminer consider to be the cause of this attitude?

2. What behaviors, groups, speakers, or products are controversial on your campus? What would be the related arguments of various stakeholders? How might such differences be resolved?

3. "Words," Kaminer says, "have power"; that is why writers write and activism continues. Despite such power, O'Neill and Kaminer argue against institutions that employ restraints on speech. Do you agree? Should nothing be off limits?

4. Kaminer suggests that our attitude toward speech often depends on the prevailing culture, which can be unduly oppressive; she mentions, for example, that women once were not permitted to speak in public and that it was only by violating that rule that "women's rights were put on the agenda" and society moved ahead. How can we attempt to identify and act against laws that arise from inappropriate motives such as prejudice?

5. In this article, O'Neill is representing Kaminer's views on speech, but he, too, appears to have a specific perspective on this. Where does O'Neill's perspective show through? What specifically are Kaminer's and O'Neill's arguments about speech, and what rhetorical strategies do they employ to promote these arguments?

Students Say Hate Crimes Created Campus Unity

KEVIN HOFFMAN

Reporter Kevin Hoffman explains, in this article from The Janesville Gazette *online in November 2010, how the administration and students at University of Wisconsin–Whitewater reacted to a series of hate crimes in and around the university community. The responses, including a forum held on campus with various representatives of the campus community, might surprise you. As you read the article and the accompanying notes from the forum, consider what you would want your university to do and what you would be willing to do if something like this happened on your campus. Would this be appropriate as well if the behavior were hateful speech or symbolic speech (for example, nooses hanging in trees) as opposed to assaults?*

--------------- ✦ ---------------

UW-Whitewater has changed, but its message has not.

The university always has billed itself as southeastern Wisconsin's melting pot, pooling students from Milwaukee to China. Its mission to welcome diversity with open arms conflicts with a rash of hate crimes this semester.

It could have been easy for the university to ignore the problem, students said, but it did the opposite.

"I think we got some (bad) press in the last few months, and that's not what we're about—this is what we're about," said music department Chairman Mike Allsen, speaking with visitors Monday following the "Sing Against Hate."

The public choir event lasted about 30 minutes, attracting the attention of students passing through the University Center on their way to lunch.

"There's been a bunch of events like these," he added. "It's not like there was any university-wide, public relations sort of effort. This is just a genuine pouring of feeling of what we're about."

It's been nearly three weeks since three black students reported someone vandalized their cars, spray painting "KKK" on the doors and hood. Two students, perceived to be lesbians, were assaulted in separate incidents earlier this semester.

Still, the university continues to accelerate its efforts to squash hate and intolerance. After students organized a campus-wide rally, administrators followed suit by sponsoring forums, holding public meetings and scheduling various events to promote awareness.

UW-Whitewater this week announced its "We Are All Purple" campaign, distributing more than 3,000 buttons with messages like "United Against Hate." The "Sing Against Hate" brought more than 100 people to the University Center, and the annual diversity week begins Monday.

Junior Bill Simmons, president of the Residence Hall Association, said several of the 4,100 students housed in dormitories were afraid to walk to classes or take part in activities. But they've turned a corner. Vice Chancellor Tom Rios said one student staff member told him people are closer now more than ever. Students greet each other in hallways, and more are becoming involved at residence hall meetings.

"I see a lot of people coming together in general," Simmons said. "At the residence halls people come on board and say, 'We got to stop this.'"

Hate crimes aren't unique to UW-Whitewater. Chancellor Richard Telfer said during a staff meeting last week he spoke to officials at UW-Platteville and UW-Eau Claire that reported similar crimes against students for their perceived sexual orientation or race.

The fact that the spotlight turned directly on UW-Whitewater irked some administrators, but the school hasn't shied away from the issue. E-mails were sent out to students following the crimes, and press releases alerted media.

Campus officials said part of their goal was to be as transparent as possible.

"I believe that (we're singled out)," Rios said. "This is the sixth institution I've worked at and compared to all others, Whitewater seems to be less riddled and have less incidents of intolerance. Even as I interact with students and ask them about their experience, they love this place regardless of what their identities are."

Junior Donvontae Walton, a member of Black Student Union and various other organizations, is among hundreds of students publicly defending the university and the atmosphere it harbors for its diverse population.

One event scheduled during "This Is Our House Diversity Week" is "Ask a Black Dude," gathering a panel of African-American students to answer questions from audience members. "Game of Life" is another social experiment, presenting students with difficult situations to better understand how people react to them.

Walton said he hopes the recent incidents haven't changed outside perceptions of UW-Whitewater, but the people on campus know better.

"It has changed from a media standpoint because a lot of people say, 'Wow, UW-Whitewater has all this hate crime, and it's not the same community as it was,'" he said.

"I know for sure there are different hate crimes at other UW schools. I do feel like Whitewater is picked on a little more because it's a smaller town."

Students said they understand the university wasn't obligated to respond the way it did. The fear around campus and discussion about the incidents is slowly fading, but university officials continue to move forward.

Professors last week said students needed more visible signs of support and assurance that the university takes the issue seriously. A website was launched as a result, offering updates around campus and resources for victims.

That's garnered a lot of support from organizations and students that want UW-Whitewater to be recognized as a safe community.

"I'm incredibly happy with the response," Simmons said. "This little hiccup, blip on the radar, shouldn't affect students' perceptions of the campus."

Hoffman, Kevin. "Students Say Hate Crimes Created Campus Unity." GazetteXtra.com. *28 November 2010. Online at gazettextra.com/news/2010/ nov/28/students-say-hate-crimes-created-campus-unity/. Copyright 2010. Reprinted by permission of the* Janesville Gazette.

NOTE: In the wake of the crimes, the university posted the website "We Are All Purple" with information on the crimes, videos of some of the campus activities noted in Hoffman's article, and links to comments from various university officials. Additionally, the site contains a summary of recommendations from a forum that included faculty, staff, and students. That forum is reproduced here and can be found as a link under Resources, entitled "We Are All Purple Forum Suggestions/Recommendations Summary," at the following website: www.uww.edu/news/we-are-all-purple.

"WE ARE ALL PURPLE" FORUM, DECEMBER 1, 2010, *UNIVERSITY OF WISCONSIN–WHITEWATER*

The following are suggestions/recommendations from the breakout sessions from the "We Are All Purple" Forum, December 1, 2010. The titles of the breakout sessions include: 1) Safety and Personal Safety; 2) Short-Term Strategies; 3) Long-Term Strategies; 4) How to Engage in Difficult Dialogues—Faculty & Staff; and 5) How to Engage in Difficult Dialogues—Students.

Suggestions/Recommendations

- Organize more activities with a focus against hate crimes such as special dancing events, food gatherings to talk about safety and crime preventions, or having dinners with a theme to understand different religious beliefs (e.g., Hindu style, Buddhist).

- Educate students about diversity needs in the classroom, have diversity exercises/assignments that are a required part of the curriculum especially in classes in which the majority of the students are enrolled.
- Provide workshops to train people about differences in society, experiential or otherwise—by experienced facilitators.
- Tie diversity into Residence Life/University Conduct System.
- Have diversity seminars as part of freshman orientation and/or graduation requirements for seniors. Create a diversity day in New Student Seminars.
- Address self-segregation.
- Address diversity issues in faculty training.
- Consider requirements within diversity curriculum, while making the courses relevant.
- Package curricular activities and define learning outcomes for diversity.
- Maintain correspondence with Multicultural Student Organizations.
- Develop dialogue on Human Perspective as a one-credit course.
- Establish a concrete definition on what we consider "Dialogue."
- Pursue initiatives with or without incidents.
- Develop diversity courses tailored to majors.
- Enhance professional orientations using the LEARN Center.
- Recommended steps to engage in difficult dialogues:
  1. Set up guidelines, discuss vocabulary—in general students would like to have respectful conversations but sometimes they don't know how to do it. They are afraid of saying things that may hurt someone.
  2. Depersonalize: focus on issues and decouple from personalizing. Discuss stereotypes, keep the atmosphere inclusive— classrooms should be a safe place for all students; adopt free lines of communication—ensure no one is being marginalized.
  3. Personalize: this should be reserved to the end; use your own identity/life experiences, if any, to discuss difficult topics; professors should bring personal examples to share, discuss ideas on racism, homophobia and fear— address issues from both sides.
  4. Recognize that: students are not comfortable discussing racial discrimination issues.
     a. Approaches will have to be very bold; instructors are supposed to be role models.
     b. We all look at the world through different eyes. How to map those eyes? What are some preconceived perceptions? Has the world defined some groups to be

more superior than others based on class/race/ethnicity and gender?

    c. Instructors are scared by students, possible repercussion. Where and how to begin dialogues in such scenarios? Many times faculty tend to internalize and not speak up.

  5. Provide assignments, rhetoric as a vehicle, explore ways of communication.

  6. Analyze strategies for non-instructional staff. Speak, don't be silent. Silence is passive affirmation.

- Engage in strategic planning activities for campus-wide Inclusive Excellence.
- Build faculty/staff capacity—they would also be excellent resources for activities. A suggestion was made that we have summer workshops with grant funding, and a number of programmatic ideas for how to approach this "training" were discussed. Using the LEARN Center's first year faculty program was also mentioned. We can't really change the educational experience without preparing the faculty.

Suggestions/recommendations that will be done or are in progress

- Security cameras are needed across campus; encourage text messaging to place a tip to the police. Need to do something more to increase security on campus.
- WSG is developing a Whitewater/Warhawk Pride video, developing a "Zumba Dance Against Hate." Students are having dinner with different administrative leaders on campus and difference organizations. Include activities that create a sense of pride.
- Conversations about hate crimes appeared to be limited to some sociology, communication classes, meetings, and forums; there were more discussions after the faculty/staff meeting on November 16th.
- Professors should offer extra credit for students to attend events like the forum and make it a part of the curriculum. Interactive activities are helpful to get students more involved.
- Rallies, forums, campaigns (pens, T-shirts), news media
  - Not really addressing how we can stop these things from happening
- Being aware instead of focusing on fear of what might happen
- Many people are starting to open up (i.e., new student seminar classes).
- People are making sure they are keeping tabs on each other.
- The outreach is helping people to build a closer community.

- Need to do something to get the issues out and educate people.
- How do we change mindsets and reach the people who don't go to the programs, forums, and other activities?
- Change needs to be addressed in the curriculum. Some professors fear discussing diversity. Need multiple directions on ways of addressing the issues.
- Keep doing what we are doing. Whitewater is doing something.
- Individually reach out of their groups.

Suggestions/recommendations already done

- Personal safety escorts coordinated by the UW-Whitewater Police Department
- Multi-agency training
- Care team weekly meetings about concerns, intervention strategies
- Involve students more in their residence halls
- A proactive approach to responding to the hate crimes. The students appreciate the Chancellor's immediate responses.
- The Campus media and "We Are All Purple" Website and Forum are powerful, and positive.

"We Are All Purple Forum Suggestions/Recommendations Summary." From University of Wisconsin Whitewater: We Are All Purple. *1 December 2010. Online at www.uww.edu/news/we-are-all-purple. Copyright 2010. Reprinted by permission of the University of Wisconsin–Whitewater.*

Questions to Consider

1. In his article, Kevin Hoffman states that one student, Donvontae Wilson, "defends the university." Why would he or other students need to defend the university? Should they?
2. Who would benefit from such events as the "Sing Against Hate" and "Game of Life"?
3. Note that the forum described consisted of five breakout sections. Why do you think the breakout separated faculty and staff from students in considering "How to Engage in Difficult Dialogues"? Why are dialogues about race, gender, sexual orientation, and hate crimes so difficult to engage in? What suggestions would you add to the discussion about how to make these conversations easier?
4. What activities does your university engage in to promote diversity and acceptance of diversity? How effective do you think these are? What else could be done?
5. Some might argue that the next step for this university is to consider rules against hateful speech since such speech might lead to more criminal incidents. What would your response to this argument be?

Making Connections

1. Stanley Fish and Wendy Kaminer seem diametrically opposed in their viewpoints on freedom of speech on college campuses. On what could you imagine they might agree, and where and under what circumstances would their viewpoints diverge?

2. On the *GazettXtra.com* site where Hoffman's article was published, rules were in place regarding postings of comments to blogs, including no "racism, sexism, or any other sort of –ism that degrades another person." Social network sites like Facebook ask for feedback on potentially offensive postings. According to Kaminer, should these kinds of limitations on speech exist? Are derogatory comments more or less likely to be acceptable off campus?

3. Who should be responsible for dangerous language? Consider recent cases in the news, such as those of Megan Meier, who was harassed through MySpace, or Kristin Helms, who met an older man on that site; lawsuits alleged that the site promoted situations resulting in each girl's suicide. What guidelines would you draft to describe the responsibility of users and of the publishers of a site like Facebook?

4. The texts in this section are very diverse, including a transcript of an oral argument, a blog, and a news article. How would you characterize the differences among these genres in terms of form, rhetorical strategies, and purpose?

5. Given what Stanley Fish argued about students' freedoms and what the administration at the University of Wisconsin–Whitewater encouraged its students to do, what unstated attitudes about college students and the role of the university do these positions reflect?

6. The attitude of a college or university toward some of the issues discussed in this chapter can be found by looking at its mission statement and the code of conduct to which students are held. Where does your school draw the line between acceptable and unacceptable speech and conduct? What rationale about learning is implicit in these lines?

7. Stanley Fish considers university students as having a lack of freedom comparable to that of high school students. What freedoms have you experienced in college that you weren't allowed to have in high school, in terms of both your school experience and your overall life experience? In what ways might these freedoms be useful now and in the future, and which freedoms come with a potential price?

8. The controversies in this chapter regarding speech and expression are discussed mainly in relation to educational contexts. What similar controversies are you aware of that take place outside education, such as in political, religious, and entertainment spheres? Are the outcomes and considerations similar? Why or why not? In what ways does context matter?

9. Note that Fish's blog describes the decision by the Supreme Court in *Morse* as 5–4, whereas Walsh's article from *Education Week* calls it a 6–3 decision. Each view depends on Justice Breyer's opinion, in which he concurs in part with the majority but also dissents in part, making it unclear to some legal scholars where to situate his decision. Given the practice of looking at previous cases and opinions as precedents, how do you think this ambiguity could be used by the parties and the judges in future cases that are similar to *Morse*?

Can My Avatar Serve My Sentence? Real Laws in a Virtual World

Reality is merely an illusion, although a very persistent one.
                                                    Albert Einstein

What do a Monty Python skit and a canned meat product have in common? Both are rumored to be responsible for the origin of a word that we often use now to denote unwanted, widespread, and repetitive email: spam. Ironically, two attorneys were responsible for the first recognized commercial use of spam email. In 1994, law partners Lawrence Canter and Martha Siegel used a wide delivery of unsolicited email to draw attention to their services as immigration attorneys. They received business from some, but also the ire of many, recipients; the angry responses raised the question, as do more serious practices that have become evident since then, of how we should govern matters in a virtual world.

In Chapter 1 we read Sandra Day O'Connor's argument that modern warfare may demand a reassessment of whether our existing laws are sufficient to provide guidance and to reflect our governing principles in new situations. The same could be said of the technological world. Lawrence Lessig considers this in "The Path of Cyberlaw," written in the early stages of Internet usage. As Lessig suggests, whether we need new laws may depend on how flexible our language can be in describing new behaviors as variations of the old ones. Even so, Lessig points out the dual concerns of privacy within the Internet—the danger of private information becoming known and the danger of users hiding behind the curtain of anonymity that the Internet can, at least partially, provide.

This duality is represented in an article about Google's activities. "To Google" has become synonymous with finding endless information on almost any subject imaginable; the flip side, as evidenced in the news release from the Office of the Privacy Commissioner of Canada, is Google's collection of massive amounts of highly personal information on computer users—including Internet usage beyond their Google searches. The more relevant question may not be whether anyone is watching our activity on the Internet, but who is watching the watchers.

Like the Privacy Commissioner, some of those watching are monitoring illegal behavior. Kevin Cogill found that out when, within hours of uploading a prerelease album by Guns N' Roses, the band's attorneys were sending Cogill a letter to cease and desist. An article on this case by David Kravets and the accompanying court documents help us see how information about Cogill, as well as about those who accessed Cogill's download, was part of the case against him. Similarly, when an avatar named Volkov Catteneo jeered at Kevin Alderman to "go ahead and sue," Alderman did just that, claiming that Catteneo had illegally shared a device Alderman had created and marketed within Second Life. Subpoenas during the legal proceedings allowed Alderman to find the man behind the avatar, despite his efforts to hide his electronic tracks. In both cases, governing principles were also called into question: What are the limits of privacy? How do we measure virtual damages? Does copyright protection still exist in a virtual world, and should it?

In the last reading, Daniel J. Solove looks at how far the Internet has come since Lessig's early predictions, and he considers how our new perspective may color what we view as reasonable legal responses. Many students, unlike many professors and writers such as Solove and Lessig, are digital natives—born into a new culture whose language and behavior might be shaping a completely different outlook on concepts such as privacy and copyright. With which writers and situations do you find yourself in agreement? How would you use laws to govern this virtual world?

The Path of Cyberlaw

LAWRENCE LESSIG

Much of Lawrence Lessig's career has dealt with issues of technology and the law. Prior to his current position as professor of law at Harvard Law School, Lessig was professor of law at Stanford Law School, where he founded its Center for Internet and Society. In this article, published in the Yale Law Journal *in the 1994–95 issue, Lessig asks what cyberspace is and how its practices should be governed. To provide you with some temporal perspective, attorney and writer Jere Webb noted in 1996 in "Trademarks, Cyberspace, and the Internet" that "as little as two years ago the word 'Internet' was an unknown or vague concept to most Americans. Now everyone is clamoring to get on the Net." Given that our society was just on the brink of embarking into this wired territory, Lessig's article provides a prescient introduction. His use of analogies, common examples, references to court cases, and his overall cautionary tone serve to help navigate what was then a new area, all without the benefit of hindsight. What does this suggest about the role law should play when concepts and contexts are new?*

◆

If you're not a cyberspace maven, but mill around a bit among those who talk about this cyberspace stuff—if you surf, as it is said, the information superhighway—there are two questions that you might ask about how this new space will get regulated.

The first question goes roughly like this: Should this new space, cyberspace, be regulated by analogy to the regulation of other space, not quite cyber, or should we give up analogy and start anew?[1] In Bruce Ackerman's terms, should we muddle into this new space as ordinary observers, just applying our old ways of thinking, or should we enter this world as scientific policymakers, armed with a comprehensive view, structuring the environment of this world to fit with this comprehensive view?[2] . . .

---

[1]*See, e.g.,* I. Trotter Hardy, *The Proper Legal Regime for "Cyberspace"*, 55 U. PITT L. REV. 993. 994 (1994) (discussing view that "old analogies just don't cut it").

[2]This schema is set out in BRUCE A. ACKERMAN, PRIVATE PROPERTY AND THE CONSTITUTION 10–15 (1977), as the product of two dimensions of opposition. The first dimension ranges between an ordinary versus scientific perspective on legal discourse and the second between an observer versus policymaking perspective. In the former, the ordinary perspective believes "legal language cannot be understood unless its roots in the ordinary talk of non-lawyers are

Consider the first question first: Will we regulate by analogy, or by something else? It should take just a second to see the strangeness in such a question. For just how could cyberspace be regulated except by analogy? Just what is it—cyberspace— apart from what we can describe by analogy? This is not a space that we know, in the sense of a space that we have inhabited. Indeed, in one sense, it is just a pattern of electrons skimming a net of computers, a construct that describes a location where a collection of activity occurs.[3] But described like this, the space could not be understood, or at least it could not be understood by us. It is understood by us only when we put things into it, when we carry into it our own language, when we colonize it, when we domesticate it. It is no accident that we speak of *e-mail,* or that we describe postings on *"electronic bulletin boards"* or that we wonder about the dynamics of real-time discussions in *"CB-chat"* areas. We have no choice but to take control of this space at first with our ordinary terms, if indeed we are to understand it. And it is through a practice of analogy that this occupation occurs.

The same point focuses the second question as well—whether there is really anything new here. For if we will understand this new realm at first by importing the old, then one way to under- stand the "new" is just that which does not fit old ways of speak-

constantly kept in mind" while the scientific believes that "the distinctive con- stituents of legal discourse (are) a set of technical concepts whose meanings are set in relation to one another by clear definitions without continuing reliance upon the way similar-sounding concepts are deployed in nonlegal talk." *Id.* at 10–11. By contrast, in the latter approach the observer believes "the test of a sound legal rule is the extent to which it vindicates the practices and expectations embedded in, and generated by, dominant social institu- tions" while the policymaker believes that the legal system contains "a rela- tively small number of general principles describing the abstract ideals which the legal system is understood to further." *Id.* at 11–12. The two dimensions together make four possible approaches—the ordinary observer, the ordinary policymaker, the scientific observer, and the scientific policymaker. Acker- man's focus in *Private Property* is on the two extreme ideal types of this matrix, the ordinary observer and the scientific policymaker. But as I suggest here, what is interesting about cyberspace regulation is the progression that it sug- gests through these four possibilities before one gets to the option of choosing between Ackerman's two types. One might, that is, need (epistemically) to pass through the ordinary observer stage to build a world within which scientific policymaking is possible. Or so I suggest here.
[3]Its contours are actually far more complex. For an introduction to various conceptions of cyberspace, see Michael Benedikt, *Introduction* to Cyberspace: First Steps 1,1-3 (Michael Benedikt ed., 1991).

ing. The new will be that which we have to construct to describe—
the gap between our old language and new experiences; the place
where the ordinary observer's language gives out. We will discover
what is new by applying, and failing to apply well, what is ordinary or old to this new space. . . .

The same technology that will make possible this experiment in humanity can also, if allowed, destroy the very essence
of what now defines individuality. I report here a conversation
with the computer system administrator at a major university
concerning information available to users about what other
users at the university are doing on the computer system. As one
can imagine, 7000 students and faculty members, plugged into
the Net as they have been for a while, have begun to discover
something of the potential that this world promises; they have
begun to practice some of the forms of association I have just
described. Most of this interaction is done through a UNIX-
based machine.[14] UNIX offers users (ordinary users—I am not
speaking of hackers) an extremely powerful ability to monitor
just what others are doing. At any time, any user can type the
command "w" at his or her (mainly his[15]) console, and the system will report what every other user of the system is doing at
just that moment. On this listing, conveniently displayed for all
to see, is an indication of, for example, with whom others are e-
mailing, or with whom they are "chatting," or, more amazingly,
what newsgroups they are reading. Hit the "w" command, and
the system will report to you that user 123C is reading alt.poli-
tics.radical-left, or alt.sex.foot.fetish. And once you discover
what 123C is reading, you can then use the "finger" function to
discover who 123C is in real life, and then, using a phone book
function, find out what 123C does, where 123C lives, and even
when his or her birthday is.

If one can do this once, one can do it repeatedly. So that one
could write a simple UNIX routine to scan the system every five
minutes, and collect a profile of just what everyone is reading, to
whom everyone is talking, and what everyone is thinking. . . .

---

[14]"UNIX" refers to the operating system of the machine, like DOS refers to the
operating system of a primitive IBM PC, or Windows to the operating system
of the more recent (and futile) efforts of Microsoft to mimic the Apple Macin-
tosh. *Cf.* Andrew S. Rappaport & Shmuel Halovi, *The Computerless Computer
Company,* HARV. BUS. REV., July–Aug, 1991, at 69, 71 (chronicling
Apple/Microsoft competition).

[15]Peter H. Lewis, *Exploring New Soapboxes for Political Animals,* N.Y. TIMES,
Jan, 10, 1995, at C6 (asserting most Internet users are male).

I report this here—among lawyers, among people who for example have read *NAACP v. Alabama*[17]—because I trust this should be quite striking. Striking since no doubt very few of the users on the system actually realize that what they read, or with whom they speak, can so easily be monitored. And striking because the potential for abuse here, especially for vulnerable groups, is so great. Perhaps more surprising, however, was that the administrator with whom I spoke just couldn't understand the problem. I was, he said, the first person who had ever questioned the fact that this information was available to anyone and everyone. And the first person he had ever spoken to who even raised the possibility that there may be privacy issues at stake here.

The "techies" understand the potential of these forms of association, but it is as if they imagine associations of just techies—extremely smart, inquisitive, a bit counterculture, but deep down not such a bad lot.[18] They have known cyberspace longer than we have, but they imagine cyberspace populated by people other than us. The systems they have given us have extraordinary potential, but they were not designed to protect individuals against this extraordinary potential for others to abuse. The invasion of the "w" command is just one example of a more general problem[19]—the same technology that makes cyberspace possible also makes it extremely easy to monitor an increasingly large scope of individuals' lives.

The same technology, of course, can also help restore the privacy otherwise stolen. Two techniques in particular—in essence the same technique—allow users some ability to repurchase their privacy. One is the technique of anonymity, which enables individuals to control what about themselves is known by those with whom they interact—control, for example, whether others know a user's name or association or, more generally, any feature of that individual. The other is the technique of encryption, with which users are able, in effect, to speak a language that only intended

---

[17]357 U.S. 449 (1958) (striking down statute requiring disclosure of membership lists as violative of Due Process Clause of Fourteenth Amendment and its protection of right to privacy of association). Of course the activity of the university in disclosing such information is not proscribed by *NAACP*. My claim is just that the interests that motivate *NAACP* should carry over to the university context.

[18]*But see* Gary Chapman, *Barbed Wired*, NEW REPUBLIC, Jan. 9 & 16, 1995, at 19 (describing antisocial, elitist attitude of techie culture).

[19]I don't mean to suggest that the function of the "w" command is necessarily problematic. In a world where people are not using machines for personal use, the command is legitimately useful. The problems begin once the machines enter aspects of life in which privacy is critical.

recipients can understand. Both techniques are the same, for both are simply ways that the user can control what about him or her is knowable by others on the system, whether it be the user's identity, or the meaning of the words spoken. Both techniques give users the ability to recreate something of the privacy that the technology would otherwise have taken away.

The techniques of anonymity and cryptography themselves, however, have given rise to an extraordinary debate among legaloids. For both are getting to be far too good. Begin with anonymity. Given the range of associations that I have just surveyed (i.e., newsgroups, chat groups, and MUDs), we can see many good reasons why someone would want to remain anonymous or pseudonymous. One wants to contribute to a political discussion without suffering the cost of unpopular views; one wants to find information without revealing that one needs that information; one wants to assume a role in a certain discussion group to explore an alternative identity. All of these are relatively harmless (to society) uses of anonymity.

Not all anonymity, however, is so benign. Perfect anonymity makes perfect crime possible. The ability to appear invisibly on a network and slander, or harass or assault, certainly will increase the incidence of those on the network who slander, or harass or assault. Thus those who police worry that there may be real reason to prevent or regulate this technologically granted anonymity—to license it, or register it, to control how much about oneself one may not say.[20]

The same problem is raised by cryptography. As I have described it, cryptography is the ability not so much to hide who you are, but to hide what you say, by encoding it in a way that no one except intended readers can understand.[21] With public key encryption, it becomes extremely simple to make one's words truly private.[22] Then only with the proper key could someone unlock these thoughts.

---

[20]See, e.g., the proposal by Connecticut State Representative Pat Dillon "that would virtually eliminate anonymity on-line." Beverly Galge, *The Babe File*, NEW HAVEN ADVOCATE, Feb. 9, 1995, at 7; *see also* A. Michael Froomkin, *The Metaphor Is the Key: Cryptography, the Clipper Chip and the Constitution*, 143 U. PA, L. REV. 709, 742–43 (1995) (discussing government positions on encryption).

[21]For an extraordinarily complete account of this debate, see Froomkin, *supra* note 20.

[22]With public key encryption, messages require two keys to be decrypted, one public key, and one private key. With the public key, a user can encrypt a message that then can be read only by the holder of the private key. *See* EDWARD A. CAVAZOS & GAVINO MORIN, CYBERSPACE AND THE LAW 30 (1994); BENJAMIN WRIGHT, THE LAW OF ELECTRONIC COMMERCE 17 (1991). So, for

The value of some encryption is the same as the value of some anonymity; indeed, it may be more pressing: a lawyer speaking to her client; two lovers on a public network; a purchaser sending credit card information over the Net. But the costs of encryption are also the same as the costs of anonymity: For just as there are perfectly good reasons why someone would want to hide her or his words from unwanted eyes, there are perfectly evil reasons why someone would want to do so. Again, encryption makes possible criminal activity (a conspiracy) without any possibility of the government tracking it down.

One should not exaggerate the government's or society's loss here. No doubt it has always been possible for people to find places where their words can be understood only by the intended recipient. An encrypted conversation is just the 1990's version of a walk in the park, or a chat on the subway. But even unexaggerated, the government's fear here is real: With perfect encryption or perfect anonymity, the return to crime certainly does increase. And this increase certainly does justify the government's interest in finding ways to regulate both. . . .

With both, a constitutional balance will have to be drawn between these increasingly important interests in privacy, and the competing interest in collective security. Already the extremes are well staked out, with some arguing that no regulation of either should be permitted, and others arguing that only with regulation should either be allowed.[24]

My point, however, is not about what the balance should be.[25] My point is about timing—when the balance should be drawn. There are many who now see the extraordinary expressive and associational potential that cyberspace offers. Most, however, do not. If the many prove correct, the most will eventually see the same—as the space becomes more common, as their children become transformed by it, as life takes root within it. But this seeing will take time. It will require that individuals gain an experience with this new space that gives them the sense of what this

example, a hitman could advertise his willingness to commit some crime, and publish the ad with his public key. Then, someone could accept the offer, encrypting the acceptance with the public key, and be assured that only the hitman could read the acceptance. A separate problem, however, is whether the offeree can tell if the offeror is who he says he is.

[24]See the collection of positions in 1994 CRYPTOGRAPHY AND PRIVACY SOURCEBOOK (David Banisar ed., 1994).

[25]Of course, I have my own view. I can see nothing wrong with requiring that all systems attach encrypted fingerprints on all transactions, such that it is always possible, with a key, to trace a transaction back to a particular individual, though impossible, without the key, to decrypt the fingerprint to identify that person.

new space is. Only when this experience is common should we expect to be in a position to understand its significance. When the technology, when the experience, when the life in cyberspace presses us, only then should we expect law to understand enough to resolve these questions rightly.

To meet this point about timing, I have suggested that we follow the meandering development of the common law. Let me end by returning to this theme in the specific context of the First Amendment, to ask how, just now, First Amendment doctrine should respond.

My suggestion is that it shouldn't. Or at least it shouldn't just now. Or at least it should do everything it can to stand back from deciding these conflicts until the nature of these conflicts is well mapped, well constructed, well understood. A prudent Court—Supreme Court, that is—would find ways to let these questions simmer for a while, to let the transition into this new space advance, before venturing too boldly into its regulation. Not that no court should decide these issues—for again, there is a great value and an important need for lower courts to wrestle with these questions, if only to create a body of legal material from which others may draw in considering these questions. But no court should purport to decide these questions finally or even firmly. Here especially should be the beginning of a dialogue, which perhaps more than others is meant to construct its subject more than reflect it. And since it is easier to correct lower court mistakes, or second-guess lower court intuitions, it is at this lower level that the dialogue should occur. Constitutional law is fundamentally concerned with who should decide what constitutional questions when. My suggestion here is that we rely for the moment on lower court judges, to give the law the material with which to understand this new realm.

From Lessig, Lawrence. "The Path of Cyberlaw." Yale Law Journal *104: 7 (1995): 1743–55. Copyright 1995. Reprinted by permission of the* Yale Law Journal *through Copyright Clearance Center.*

Questions to Consider

1. Law journals are written mainly for the legal profession and often contain many footnotes that not only cite sources but provide further and more detailed information. What do these footnotes add, and why doesn't the author choose to include the information in the text?

2. This article's tone is rather casual. Point to specific examples that help create Lessig's tone. How does this tone help balance the technical nature of this article?

3. Lessig asks the question "How could cyberspace be regulated except by analogy?" What does he mean, and which analogies does he subsequently use? In what ways are these helpful, especially in this new arena?

4. When classifying types of associations available on the Web, Lessig relies on some unstated assumptions about how people act when they are unseen or anonymous as opposed to interacting face-to-face. What are these assumptions? In your experience, have they been borne out in the online environments that have since been created?

5. What exactly is Lessig's argument? Note his varying points of support and how he limits those points. Why is he so cautious?

Google Contravened Canadian Privacy Law, Investigation Finds

OFFICE OF THE PRIVACY COMMISSIONER OF CANADA

Google Street View allows a user to view street-level photographs of places of interest—and in some cases, the view captures people and cars, revealing minutiae that have concerned some whose lives have been caught for all to see. Just how minute is the information gathered may not be clear from the photographs; personal information including complete emails was also captured as Google sought to identify area [Wi-Fi] locations. In this news release about an investigation conducted by the Office of the Privacy Commissioner of Canada, recommendations are made to prevent disclosure of this information. To what extent do these recommendations seem effective and reasonable?

------------------------- ✦ -------------------------

NEWS RELEASE

OTTAWA, October 19, 2010—Google Inc. contravened Canadian privacy law when it inappropriately collected personal information from unsecured wireless networks in neighbourhoods across the country, an investigation has found.

The Privacy Commissioner's investigation also concluded that the incident was the result of an engineer's careless error as well as a lack of controls to ensure that necessary procedures to protect privacy were followed.

"Our investigation shows that Google did capture personal information—and, in some cases, highly sensitive personal information such as complete e-mails. This incident was a serious violation of Canadians' privacy rights," says Privacy Commissioner Jennifer Stoddart.

"The impact of new and rapidly evolving technologies on modern life is undeniably exciting. However, the consequences for people can be grave if the potential privacy implications aren't properly considered at the development stage of these new technologies."

The personal information collected included complete e-mails, e-mail addresses, usernames and passwords, names and residential telephone numbers and addresses. Some of the captured information was very sensitive, such as a list that provided the names of people suffering from certain medical conditions, along with their telephone numbers and addresses.

It is likely that thousands of Canadians were affected by the incident.

Technical experts from the Office of the Privacy Commissioner travelled to the company's offices in Mountain View, Calif. in order to perform an on-site examination of the data that was collected. They conducted an automated search for data that appeared to constitute personal information.

To protect privacy, the experts manually examined only a small sample of data flagged by the automated search. Therefore, it's not possible to say how much personal information was collected from unencrypted wireless networks.

The Privacy Commissioner launched an investigation under the federal private-sector privacy law, the *Personal Information Protection and Electronic Documents Act*, or PIPEDA, after Google revealed that its cars—which were photographing neighbourhoods for its Street View map service—had inadvertently collected data transmitted over wireless networks installed in homes and businesses across Canada and around the world over a period of several years. The networks were not password protected or encrypted.

Google collected the personal information because of a particular code integrated into the software used to collect [Wi-Fi] signals. The code was developed in 2006 by a Google engineer who was taking advantage of Google's policy of allowing its engineers to use 20 per cent of their time to work on projects of interest to them. He developed the code to sample all categories of publicly broadcast [Wi-Fi] data and included lines that allowed for the collection of "payload data," which refers to the content of the communications.

The code wound up being used in the Google Street View cars when the company decided to collect information about location of publicly broadcast [Wi-Fi] radio signals in order to feed this information into its location-based services database.

When the decision to use the code was taken, the engineer who created it did identify "superficial privacy implications." Those implications were never assessed by other Google officials because the engineer failed to forward his code design documents to the Google lawyer responsible for reviewing the legal implications of the [Wi-Fi] project—contrary to company policy.

Google asserts that it was completely unaware of the presence of the payload data collection code when it began using the software for its location-based services. While the code was reviewed before being installed on Street View cars, the review was only to ensure that the code did not interfere with the Street View operations.

"This incident was the result of a careless error—one that could easily have been avoided," says Commissioner Stoddart.

In light of her investigation, the Privacy Commissioner recommended that Google ensure it has a governance model in place to comply with privacy laws. The model should include controls to ensure that necessary procedures to protect privacy are duly followed before products are launched.

The Commissioner has also recommended that Google enhance privacy training to foster compliance amongst all employees. As well, she called on Google to designate an individual or individuals responsible for privacy issues and for complying with the organization's privacy obligations—a requirement under Canadian privacy law.

She also recommended that Google delete the Canadian payload data it collected, to the extent that the company does not have any outstanding obligations under Canadian and American laws preventing it from doing so, such as preserving evidence related to legal proceedings. If the Canadian payload data cannot immediately be deleted, it needs to be secured and access to it must be restricted.

The Privacy Commissioner will consider the matter resolved upon receiving, by February 1, 2011, confirmation from Google that it has implemented her recommendations.

The Privacy Commissioner of Canada is mandated by Parliament to act as an ombudsman, advocate and guardian of privacy and the protection of personal information rights of Canadians.

"Google Contravened Canadian Privacy Law, Investigation Finds." Office of the Privacy Commissioner of Canada *19 October 2010. Online at www. priv.gc.ca/media/nr-c/2010/nr-c_101019_e.cfm. Copyright 2010. Reprinted by permission of the Office of the Privacy Commissioner.*

Questions to Consider

1. The Commissioner works independently of other government sectors in Canada regarding privacy and personal information rights. Why is this independence important in upholding this mandate?
2. The news release sets out a variety of causes for the inappropriate collection of data. What are these, and how do the Commissioner's recommendations address these?
3. To what extent does this news release, aside from the investigation itself, also serve to protect the public interest?
4. The Commissioner is identified as acting as "an ombudsman, advocate and guardian"—what are the distinctions among these roles, and in what ways do you see this incident and report as reflecting these various roles?

5. Advocates on behalf of U.S. citizens include the Electronic Privacy Information Center (EPIC), which has contacted the Federal Communications Commission to investigate similar concerns about Google here in the United States. EPIC identifies itself as a public-interest research center dependent on donations; information can be found at www.epic.org. In what ways does this type of organization differ from the Canadian Commissioner's office, and what do you see as the advantages and disadvantages of each?

Feds Demand Prison for Guns N' Roses Uploader

DAVID KRAVETS

*Kevin Cogill admitted that he had illegally uploaded copyrighted
materials; his actions were not so much in dispute as was the
penalty that he should incur for those actions. Cogill was initially
threatened with prison and thousands of dollars in restitution. In the
following article by David Kravets, writing for* Wired Online, *Kravets
outlines the sentencing options facing Kevin Cogill. As you read
Kravets's report, consider what questions were still to be answered at
this point in March 2009; note that Cogill had already pled guilty.
This article is one of many Kravets has written about the intersection
of technology and law in the* Wired *blog "Threat Level: Privacy,
Crime and Security Online." Other articles include questions of limitations on cell phone wiretapping, the appropriate limits on government use of identity theft legislation, and online murder threats.
How do we weigh the threats presented in a case such as Cogill's?*

---- ◆ ----

Federal prosecutors in Los Angeles are pursuing a 6-month prison
term for a Los Angeles man who pleaded guilty in December to
one misdemeanor count of uploading pre-release Guns N' Roses
tracks, according to court documents.

Kevin Cogill was arrested last summer at gunpoint and
charged with uploading nine tracks of the *Chinese Democracy*
album to his music site—antiquiet.com. The album, which cost
millions and took 17 years to complete, was released November
23 and reached No. 3 in the charts.

The sentence being sought—including the calculation of damages based on the illegal activity of as many as 1,310 websites that
disseminated the music after Cogill released it—underscores how
serious the government is about punishing those for uploading
pre-release material.

"Making a pre-release work available to the worldwide public
over the internet where it can be copied without limit is arguably
one of the more insidious forms of copyright infringement," prosecutor Craig H. Missakian wrote in court documents. "That is
because once released it is virtually impossible to prevent unlimited dissemination of the work."

As part of the 28-year-old Cogill's guilty plea, he informed the
authorities that he received the music online and unsolicited—a

confession Missakian said might pave the way for more "targets" to be prosecuted.

"Needless to say, artists like the band Guns N' Roses put their blood, sweat, toil and tears into the creative process," Missakian said. "And this country has seen fit to protect their rights—and in doing so foster and encourage the creative process by which all of society benefits."

The government claimed the amount of infringement equaled $371,622. The higher the number the larger the potential prison term. The government said it produced a "reasonable estimate" and gave the defendant the "benefit of the doubt" in its calculations, which were based on each infringement being worth 99 cents on iTunes.

The Recording Industry Association of America, however, told the judge overseeing the case that the defendant's conduct resulted in more than a $2.2 million loss based on a "$6.39 legitimate wholesale value" for the nine tracks the RIAA claims . . . were downloaded about 350,000 times.

Regardless of the phantom figures, the numbers floated by the government and the RIAA assume that the music would have been purchased had it not been downloaded for free.

Here's how the feds concluded the $371,622 in damages:

They said the music was streamed from Cogill's site 1,123 times to 801 IP addresses over a two-hour period. The authorities, based on a "conservative estimate," concluded nearly 400,000 downloads.

"This number is based on a sample of 30 out of 1,310 unauthorized web sites that offered the leaked songs to the public between June 19, 2008 and November 21, 2008," Missakian wrote. . . . "Of the 1,310 web sites identified as having unauthorized copies of the music that defendant streamed, 30 of those contained information showing the number of downloads from their sites."

Of those 30 sites, the government said there were 16,976 downloads of *Chinese Democracy*.

"It is most likely that this number represents the number of downloads of the group of 9 leaked songs, for a total of 152,784 downloads of individual songs (16,976 × 9)," Missakian wrote. "It is, however, not possible to say at this time whether the figure represents the group of 9 songs or individual songs. Giving the defendant the benefit of the doubt, the government will assume that the 16,976 figure represents downloads of individual songs."

But wait, the prosecution wrote more:

In addition to the above number, the Court should also add an additional number for the number of downloads from the remaining 1,200-plus web sites that offered the songs for download. The average number of downloads from the 30 sites for which actual data exists is 565. Again, giving the defendant the benefit of the doubt, the Court could reduce that number by one half and estimate that each other site accounted for 280 individual downloads, or a total of 358,400 (1,310 − 30 × 280), during the relevant period. By taking the total number of downloads of 375,376 (16,976 + 358,400) and multiplying that number by $.99 per song downloaded, the infringement about becomes $371,622.

According to court records, Cogill uploaded nine songs from the 14-track album on June 18. Court records show he confessed to the FBI. The case was cracked by an investigator with the Recording Industry Association of America, according to court records.

Cogill's attorney, David Kaloyanides, told the court that no jail time was warranted. . . . He added that, "There is no way to determine how many downloads were made."

Sentencing is set for May 4.

By the way, the RIAA said it would be willing to accept $30,000, instead of $2.2 million in restitution, if Cogill "was willing to participate in a public service announcement designed to educate the public that music piracy is illegal."

Kravets, David. "Feds Demand Prison for Guns N' Roses Uploader." Wired.com *13 March 2009. Online at www.wired.com/threatlevel/2009/03/ feds-demand-6-m/. Copyright © 2009 by Condé Nast Publications. All rights reserved. Originally published in* Wired.com. *Reprinted by permission.*

NOTE: The following are documents filed with the court and provided by hyperlinks within the article by David Kravets. As you read through them, consider what these documents on behalf of the parties to the case add to Kravets's article. Note that the motion by the government (also referred to as plaintiff, since the government brought the initial action against Kevin Cogill) and the defendant's motion (i.e., the motion on behalf of Kevin Cogill) establish their own arguments in support of their sentencing positions and provide rebuttal to each other's positions. The documents also comment on the presentence report and recommendation (PSR), which is not included. Based on these arguments, what sentence would you recommend for Cogill?

GOVERNMENT'S POSITION RE PRESENTENCE REPORT AND SENTENCING FOR DEFENDANT IN *UNITED STATES OF AMERICA, PLAINTIFF V. KEVIN COGILL, AKA "SKWERL," DEFENDANT*

Plaintiff United States of America ("plaintiff" or "the government") hereby respectfully submits its position regarding sentencing of defendant Kevin Cogill ("defendant").

INTRODUCTION

The United States Probation Department's (the "USPO" or "Probation") recommended sentence of probation fails to account for key factors set forth in 18 U.S.C. § 3553(a) ("Section 3553(a)"). In particular, the recommendation does not reflect—or discuss— the gravity of the offense and will do nothing to deter other would-be leakers in this rapidly expanding threat to the music industry. To the contrary, far from attempting to analyze the nature of the offense, the PSR appears more concerned with the circumstances surrounding defendant's arrest—mentioning not once but twice that agents arrested defendant "at gun point"—a factor not identified anywhere in Section 3553(a), the United States Sentencing Guidelines ("guidelines" or "USSG") or in any case that the government has found. Nevertheless, one cannot deny Congress has recognized that leaking pre-release works over the Internet constitutes a serious and growing commercial threat demanding more of a punishment than a slap on the wrist. As such, in the government's view a short custodial sentence is appropriate and satisfies Section 3553(a). . . .

B. GOVERNMENT'S POSITION RE SENTENCING

1. THE INFRINGEMENT AMOUNT

. . . With respect to the number of downloads from the third-party sites that obtained the songs as a result of defendant's violation, a conservative estimate is over 300,000 downloads. . . .

By taking the total number of downloads of 375,376 (16,976 + 358,400) and multiplying that number by $.99 per song downloaded, the infringement [amount] becomes $371,622. (Linares Decl., ¶ 2). Under Section 2B1.1, that would translate into an additional 12-level increase in defendant's total offense level, or a level 21, for a sentencing range of 37 to 46 months. Taking an additional 4 levels off under Section 5K1.1, reduces that range to 27 to 33 months.

2. SECTION 3553(a) FACTORS

The factors identified in Section 3553(a) militate in favor of a sentence that is more than probation. First, a probationary sentence does not reflect the seriousness of the offense. The PSR goes to unusual lengths to downplay the gravity of this crime while at the same time failing to analyze the nature of the harm. The PSR does so first by referring to the offense as a mere "error in judgment" and then by concluding that "it is clear that this offense is not a typical copyright piracy case in which the defendant's motivation was to profit from the distribution of a copyrighted work."

The PSR is correct that this is not a typical copyright infringement case; in reality, it is more serious than the typical case. Making a pre-release work available to the worldwide public over the Internet where it can [be] copied without limit is arguably one of the more insidious forms of copyright infringement. That is because once released it is virtually impossible to prevent unlimited dissemination of the work. As the international music trade group IFPI explained in 2007:

> Pre-release leaks are one of the most damaging forms of internet piracy that is currently eroding legitimate sales of music across the world. Recorded music sales fell by more than a third internationally in the last six years, and independent studies show that a major factor in this decline has been internet users accessing peer-to-peer networks to steal music online. Pre-release piracy is particularly damaging to sales as it leads to early mixes and unfinished versions of artists' recordings circulating on the internet months ahead of the release.

See Article, "British and Dutch police raids shut down world's largest pre-release pirate music site," IFPI (Oct. 23, 2007), online at, http://www.ifpi.org/content/section_news/20071023.html. The PSR, however, does not discuss this significant and growing problem.

The PSR also minimizes the seriousness of the conduct in two other ways, first by noting that defendant only streamed the music and, second, by noting that he did so for only a short time. Both points, even if true, demonstrate a misunderstanding of the nature and circumstances of the offense. Whether the music was streamed—as opposed to being made available for download—is irrelevant. So-called "stream rippers"—software add-ons that enable users to copy the streamed content—are commonplace. As such, for all practical purposes, defendant made these songs available for copying. And, in fact, that is exactly what happened. We know that users made copies because those copies ended up on third party web sites where they were then downloaded by the thousands.

Similarly, the fact that the streamed content was available on defendant's site for only a short time is also irrelevant since on the Internet seconds are sometimes all it takes. The reason for that is obvious. The power to copy and disseminate material over the Internet is free, easy, and virtually impossible to control. And, again, that is exactly what occurred here. Notwithstanding the fact that defendant's site crashed soon after he posted the songs, that was long enough for copies of the songs to be made and uploaded to numerous other sites where they were downloaded by the thousands.

Beyond the financial loss resulting from such an offense, the PSR also fails to consider the potential damage caused to the creative process by such conduct. Needless to say, artists like the band Guns N' Roses put their blood, sweat, toil and tears into the creative process. And this country has seen fit to protect their rights—and in so doing foster and encourage the creative process by which all society benefits. Minimizing the importance of those protections by characterizing the present conduct as merely a lapse in judgment, ignores this important goal. In short, this is a far more serious offense than the PSR suggests.

Nor would a probationary sentence promote respect for the law or afford adequate deterrence to criminal conduct, two equally important considerations under Section 3553(a). One of the primary motives behind sentencing decisions is general deterrence—i.e., the value in sending a strong message that makes other would-be criminals think twice about committing the same crime. *See United States v. Barker,* 771 F.2d 1362 (9th Cir. 1985) ("desire to 'send a message' through sentencing [not] inappropriate" and "[i]ndeed, perhaps paramount among purposes of punishment is the desire to deter similar misconduct by others"). Deterrence takes on even greater importance in cases like the present where stopping the crime before it happens is key; since trying to un-ring the bell is virtually impossible. A probationary sentence, by comparison, sends exactly the wrong message by suggesting to other would be offenders that a slap on the wrist is all that awaits.

The government does not dispute that the remaining Section 3553(a) factors—such as specific deterrence—militate in defendant's favor. Moreover, as discussed below, the government does not deny that defendant has cooperated fully and deserves consideration for doing so. Rather, the government maintains that a subjective view about the gravity of the offense does not alone justify a departure from the guidelines under Section 3553(a).

C. MOTION UNDER § 5K1.1

The government recommends that defendant receive an additional 4-level reduction in his total offense level under U.S.S.G. § 5K1.1 for substantial assistance. Defendant's substantial assistance consisted of attending proffer sessions with government investigators where he provided substantial information about the crime in which he was involved, including information about new potential targets. In the government's view, the information defendant provided amounts to substantial assistance within the meaning of § 5K1.1. The government views the information that defendant provided as complete, truthful, and reliable. The information provided and the offer of additional further assistance was also timely, coming at a point early enough in the investigation to be useful to the government. Based on the nature of defendant's cooperation, the government believes that a 4-level reduction is appropriate.

D. GOVERNMENT'S POSITION RE SENTENCING

With a 4-level reduction in defendant's guidelines calculation pursuant to § 5K1.1, his adjusted offense level would become 17 with a corresponding sentencing range of 27 to 33 months. Since this range exceeds the statutory maximum of one year, the government believes a 6-month sentence satisfies the dictates of the relevant provisions of 18 U.S.C. § 3553(a).

Restitution is also mandatory in the case. The RIAA estimates that defendant's conduct resulted in a loss of approximately $2 million. (See Declaration of Craig H. Missakian, Ex. A . . .). The RIAA would also be willing to accept, in lieu of this amount, the lesser sum of $30,000 in restitution if defendant was willing to participate in a public service announcement designed to educate the public that music piracy is illegal.

From US v. Cogill. *Government's Brief re Sentencing. CR No. 08-01222 PLA. US Dst Ct CA, 2009.*

DEFENDANT'S POSITION RE SENTENCING IN *UNITED STATES OF AMERICA, PLAINTIFF V. KEVIN COGILL, DEFENDANT*

I. INTRODUCTION

The Court should adopt the recommendation of the Presentence Report and Recommendation ("PSR") and impose a sentence of one-year probation under the terms and conditions set forth in the PSR, waive all fines, and order no restitution in this case as the government has not provided any "victim" information from which restitution could be determined and because under the facts of this case, a determination of actual loss to any purported victim is not reasonably quantifiable.

II. FACTUAL BACKGROUND

1. Procedural Posture

On or about June 18, 2008, defendant received unauthorized copies of songs purporting to be nine musical tracks from the album "Chinese Democracy" performed by the rock ban[d] Guns N' Roses. A valid United States Copyright existed on each of the nine songs of the "Chinese Democracy" album, which on June 18, 2008, had not yet been released but was being prepared for commercial release by Guns N' Roses and Universal Music Group's Interscope-Geffen-A&M records (the record label).

Within minutes of receiving the unauthorized tracks, Mr. Cogill uploaded the tracks to his Internet website Antiquiet.com. The tracks were not made available for downloading but only for listening in real time by a streaming player. At the time, Mr. Cogill was aware that the musical tracks were protected under United States copyright laws, and he was aware that he did not have authorization to upload the songs over the Internet and that to do so was illegal.

Mr. Cogill cooperated with federal law enforcement officers throughout their investigation. He provided them with his computers both at home and work. He met with or spoke to the agents several times. Finally, the agents wanted to speak with Mr. Cogill about the case again at which time Mr. Cogill told them he was in the process of retaining counsel. He informed the agents that as soon as he had hired his lawyer, he would be happy to continue cooperating in the investigation.

The following morning, Mr. Cogill was arrested at gun point by five FBI agents. He was initially charged in a felony complaint.

On October 16, 2008, Mr. Cogill entered a cooperation plea agreement. The government agreed to file misdemeanor charge[s] only in exchange for Mr. Cogill's assistance in identifying the source of the leaked tracks. On December 15, 2008, the Court accepted his change of plea.

Pursuant to the terms of Mr. Cogill's plea agreement, he provided timely and complete information relating to how he acquired the tracks from the Chinese Democracy album.

2. History Of The Copyrighted Work

Mr. Cogill created his website Antiquiet.com as a musical commentary and review website, or "blog". The term "blog" is a contraction of the term "Web log" and is a website usually maintained by an individual with regular entries of commentary, descriptions of events, or other material such as graphics or video. Many blogs provide commentary or news on a particular subject. The ability for readers to leave comments in an interactive format is an important part of many blogs.[1]

Mr. Cogill created and maintains Antiquiet.com as a music journalism blog. Mr. Cogill and others review music, conduct

---

[1]Wikipedia, *Blog*, accessed February 10, 2009, http://en.wikipedia.org/wiki/Blog.

interviews with artists and discuss a variety of aspects of music and entertainment industry news. The creation of Antiquiet.com is the result of his passion for music. He is a particularly dedicated fan of the band Guns N' Roses.

The album "Chinese Democracy" began its creation with a former variation of the band Guns N' Roses. The former band began writing and recording tracks for the album in 1994. However, as a result of in-fighting among band members, three of the four members left the band in 1996 leaving lead singer Axl Rose to recreate the band anew without the album or most of its tracks having been completed.[2] Rose was the only original band member to continue working on the album while the Guns N' Roses band underwent additional artist changes, three different studio affiliations, and four band managers.[3]

Work on the album was sporadic. Rose and the Guns N' Roses band of the moment continued to lay new tracks, record different tracks, mix different tracks, to the point where it is estimated that Rose had a personal library of "potential" Chinese Democracy songs numbering over 1,000 tracks or variations and mixes of tracks.[4] By 2005 it was estimated that various labels having involvement with the album had sunk over $13 million into its creation—a record amount of investment for any album of its type.[5]

In 1999, Rose invited the music magazine *Rolling Stone* to preview some of the tracks for the album. The magazine published an article indicating that there might be a release date in 2000. But the album still did not appear.[6]

Several other feints at a release of Chinese [D]emocracy took place over the next few years. Finally, in 2004, Geffen Records (one of the record label divisions of Universal Music Group, or "UMG")

---

[2]Wikipedia, *The History of Chinese Democracy*, accessed February 10, 2009, http://en.wikipedia.org/wiki/History_of_Chinese_Democracy. Guns N' Roses has traditionally had four primary band members with three other associated members who play with the band regularly, but who are not usually counted as the core artists. *See id.*

[3]Leeds, Jeff. *The Most Expensive Album Never Made*, March 6, 2005, The New York Times, http://www.nytimes.com/2005/03/06/arts/music/06leed.html? Rose is, in effect, Guns N' Roses, and is the copyright holder for the band's music. It is unclear what rights or interest UMG, or any of the former Guns N' Roses band members have in the copyright of Chinese Democracy. The government has not produced any such information in discovery in this case.

[4]*Id.*

[5]*Id.*

[6]*Id.*

shut down all funding for the album.[7] The label wrote to Rose informing him that . . . the band had exceeded all budgeted and approved recording costs for the album and that the label considered it Rose's obligation to fund and complete the album. The label had effectively shut down the band even going so far as to lock up the band's instruments and recording equipment.[8] [T]he label released a "greatest-hits" compilation, over Rose's objection, in an attempt to recoup some of its investment in Chinese Democracy.[9]

Throughout 2004 and 2005 rumors of the album's release continued. . . .

The album was not released until November 23, 2008.

According to industry insiders, the label had entered an exclusive retail sales contract with Best Buy in which the retailer paid for 1.3 million copies of the album up front. Although the album's United States sales in the first week of release were approximately 261,000 copies, as of February 6, 2009, the total U.S. [s]ales of the album had only reached 537,000. But the label had already been paid for the 1.3 million copies through its contract with Best Buy.[13]

Industry executives have blamed the album's poor sales on Rose himself for failing to promote the album through videos, tours and interviews. Other insiders have attributed it to Best Buy, arguing that the retailer did little to promote its exclusive rights to sell the album.[14] Rose has pointed the finger at Interscope Records and its CEO, Jimmy Iovine, for not putting enough support behind the album's production and marketing. In an interview with the music news magazine Billboard, Rose expressed his opinion that Interscope and UMG had not approached the album seriously and did nothing to promote the album prior to its release.[15]

---

[7]Universal Music Group controls over twenty different record labels for music recording and publishing in the United States. One of these labels is the trilable of Interscope-Geffen-A&M Records. UMG estimates that it controls nearly 98% of the recording industry in the United States. Universal Music Group. *Company Overview*, accessed February 16, 2009, http://new.umusic.com/overview.aspx.

[8]*Id.*

[9]*Id.*

[13]Cohen, Johnathan *The Billboard Q&A: Axl Rose*, February 6, 2009, http://www.billboard.com/bbcom/feature/the-billboard-q-a-axl-rose-103939032.story.

[14]Cohen, Johnathan *The Billboard Q&A: Axl Rose*, February 6, 2009, http://www.billboard.com/bbcom/feature/the-billboard-q-a-axl-rose-103939032.story

[15]*Id.*

Notably absent from any public discussion of the possible reasons for the album's poor showing is any mention of the numerous leaks of the Chinese Democracy tracks either by Mr. Cogill or any of the other leaks throughout the years.[16] To the contrary, in the same Billboard interview, Axl Rose expressed that he did not believe that the album's sales were harmed at all by Mr. Cogill's actions.[17]

And it is unlikely that Axl Rose, Interscope, or UMG could prove with any certainty the cause of the lackluster sales of the album. Numerous tracks on the final album had been leaked throughout the years. Industry insider and journalist Mick Wall (author of numerous books on Guns N' Roses including *W.A.R. The Unauthorized Biography of William Axl Rose*) stated that in 2006–2007 time frame he obtained nine of the 14 tracks appearing on the released version of Chinese Democracy—long before Mr. Cogill uploaded any of the tracks to Antiquiet.com.[18] And apparently people associated with the album have also freely distributed or played various tracks from the album at various times.[19]

Moreover, recording industry veterans have acknowledged that there is no loss suffered from pre-release leaks of music. In fact, many insiders acknowledge that pre-release leaks help promote an album by creating interest and discussion among fans and critics and, therefore, actually boost sales.[20] This idea finds support when examining sales figures for albums that had significant pre-release leaks. For example, in 2007, three of the top six

[16]At present, the entire album is available for free on-line streaming and, with the appropriate software, burning to CD, at the social network site Imeem.com. http://www.imeem.com/gunsnroses/music/ZDPzX2B2/guns_n_roses_chinese_democracy/.

[17]Cohen, Johnathan *The Billboard Q&A: Axl Rose*, February 6, 2009, http://www.billboard.com/bbcom/feature/the-billboard-q-a-axl-rose-103939032.story

[18]Van Buskirk, Eliot. *Full Interview: Mick Wall on Axl Rose*, November 25, 2008, Wired.com, http://blog.wired.com/music/2008/11/mick-wall-takes.html.

[19]Versions of the album had been circulating since 2001. In his interview with Wired.com, Mr. Wall described a "record company executive" who held private listening sessions for journalists in London in 2007 playing finished tracks of the version of the album he received while working on the project in 2001. *Id.* As early as September 2003, a New York radio DJ Eddie Trunk played one of the tracks from Chinese Democracy that had been brought to the radio station by Mets baseball player Mike Piazza, who had apparently received the CD in the mail from an unknown source. D'Angelo, Joe, *New GN'R Tune Leaked By . . . Mets Cather Mike Piazza?!* February 9, 2003, MTV, http://www.mtv.com/news/articles/1477813/20030902/runs_n_roses.jhtml.

[20]Crosley, Hillary, *Music Industry Insiders Find Upside in Album Leaks*, July 11, 2008, Reuters, http://www.reuters.com/article/musicNews/idUSN1126044820080712?

debut sales weeks included three major releases that had been leaked. One of these albums, Lil Wayne's "Tha Carter III", reached one million albums sold in the first week even though Universal Music Group estimates that one million people downloaded the album illegally prior to its release.[21]

The industry has also taken advantage of pre-release leaks for market research. By monitoring traffic on peer-to-peer networks to gauge unauthorized leaks, the label is able to develop information to help in product promotion. Specifically, the monitoring permits the label to identify age, gender, and location of those downloading the tracks, as well as identify which songs are the most popular.[22]

3. The Infringement Activity

Mr. Cogill received the tracks via the Internet through a "chat" feature. The tracks were unexpected and unsolicited by Mr. Cogill. In fact, Mr. Cogill did not even know what it was he was receiving until he started to listen to the tracks. When Mr. Cogill realized what he had received, as a music journalist he believed it was necessary to share the tracks. He also saw this as an opportunity to promote the Antiquiet.com website as a music industry news blog and make a name for himself.

It took approximately 20 minutes to prepare the website in order to upload the tracks and prepare the streaming software. The tracks were not made available for downloading. Mr. Cogill intentionally limited the format for accessing the files so that the tracks would be available through Antiquiet.com for visitors to listen to the tracks in real-time. However, with the appropriate software, it is possible to "rip" the files from Antiquiet's server for downloading.[23] But, other than tracking the number of "hits" or site visits, Mr. Cogill had no way of tracking how many site visitors were actually listening to the tracks. Nor did he have any means of knowing who might be using software to rip the files for downloading.

Within 20 minutes of uploading the tracks, the Antiquiet site crashed and visitors could no longer access the website or the tracks. Before Mr. Cogill could correct the problem, he received a

---

[21]*Id.*
[22]*Id.*
[23]Some of this software that permits the user to "rip" files from streaming media is restricted to downloading the files as they play. In other words, the capturing software must "record" the streaming media as it is played in real time. Other software can rip the files faster than they are streamed. There is no way to track whether software is ripping streaming files or whether the files are being ripped in real time or not. It is also impossible to determine whether or not files are being ripped at all.

call from a Guns N' Roses representative instructing him to take the songs down. He informed them that the site had crashed and that he would not post the songs again. Approximately one hour later, Mr. Cogill received a cease and desist letter emailed from Axl Rose's attorney. Mr. Cogill never posted the songs again.

In total, the tracks Mr. Cogill had received were available for streaming for approximately 20 minutes. Of the "hits" or visits to the site, there is no way to determine how many visitors listened to the tracks, how many tracks were played, whether anyone ripped the files from the streaming player, and if so, how many tracks were in fact downloaded.[24]

III. DISCUSSION

A. Objections to Presentence Report and Recommendation

Mr. Cogill has no objections to the factual statements and findings of the Presentence Report and Recommendation ("PSR"). The only additional information Mr. Cogill submits is that recently, following the disclosure of the PSR, he was laid off by his employer. He is currently unemployed but trying to do contract project work. Although the information provided by his employer was that he was laid off for "no cause", he was the only person at the company to be laid off and there was some indication that his employer's decision was motivated in part because of Mr. Cogill's conviction in this case. . . .

I. CONCLUSION

As fully set forth above, the Court should adopt the recommendation of the Probation Office as set for[th] in the PSR and sentence Mr. Cogill according to that recommendation.

From US v. Cogill. *Defendant's Brief re Sentencing. CR No. 08-01222 PLA. US Dst Ct CA, 2009.*

Questions to Consider

(*Spoiler alert:* The last question provides the sentencing outcome. Be sure to consider the other questions beforehand.)

1. Kravets necessarily provides only limited information from the court documents. In considering the texts provided, how does Kravets present a balanced picture of the controversy and the opponents' arguments, as opposed to presenting an argument of his own?

[24]The full running time for the album is over 71 minutes.

2. How do the motions differ from Kravets's article in purpose, tone, and rhetorical strategies? How do these factors relate to the different audiences of the three texts?

3. In its motion, the government explains why Cogill's action deserves a longer sentence (up to three years) even though the government argues for a six-month sentence (partly because of the limits imposed by the plea agreement). The government also repeats that it will give "the defendant the benefit of the doubt." Why are these strategies used?

4. Do the numbers in Kravets's quotes from excerpted portions of the government's motion make your head spin? Note that the alleged monetary loss is only one of the reasons the government argues for a strong sentence; what are the others?

5. The defendant's motion notes that Cogill was served with a "cease and desist" letter. Look up those words; why are they both used? In what other ways do the two motions reflect a legal nomenclature?

6. In the defendant's motion, much of the history of Guns N' Roses is explained. What is the purpose of this history, and how would you evaluate its usefulness in supporting the defendant's argument?

7. Cogill's actions in this case and personal information are presented in the defendant's motion. He is described as "a particularly dedicated fan of the band Guns N' Roses" and as being laid off by his former employer. What is the intent of including this information? Should it have an impact on the decision maker?

8. On July 14, 2009, David Kravets reported that Cogill was sentenced to one year of probation and two months of home confinement. Part of the sentencing included Cogill's willingness to create an anti-piracy message. What would you expect such anti-piracy messages from a convicted "pirate" to include? What would convince you not to engage in illegal downloading or sharing of material?

Second Life Avatar Sued Over Virtual Sex Device

PHIL DAVIS

*Entrepreneur Kevin Alderman knows that avatars not only popu-
late Second Life, but they can engage in rather intimate behaviors;
he should know, because he's responsible for creating SexGen, a
device that allows users to animate their avatars in ways that might
be rated X were they on the movie screen with real actors. In this
Associated Press article that appeared in* USA Today, *freelance
reporter Phil Davis explains that Second Life has had its share of
real-life legal issues. In this case, Alderman accuses an avatar of
illegally copying and distributing his program in violation of copyright and trademark laws. In virtual reality, what constitutes
crimes and criminals?*

◆

Kevin Alderman didn't bring sex to *Second Life*. He just made
it better.

The 46-year-old entrepreneur recognized four years ago that
people would pay to equip their online selves—which start out
with the smooth anatomy of a Barbie or Ken doll—with realistic
genitalia and even more to add some sexy moves.

Business at Eros, Alderman's company, has been brisk. One of
his creations, the SexGen Platinum, has gotten so popular that
he's now had to hire lawyers to track down the flesh-and-blood
person behind the online identity, or avatar, that he says illegally
copied and sold it.

The $45 SexGen animates amorous avatars in erotic posi-
tions. It is software code, written in the scripting language of
Second Life, and placed in virtual furniture and other objects.
Avatars click on the object and choose from a menu of animated
sex acts.

Alderman filed a civil lawsuit in U.S. District Court in Tampa,
last month alleging an avatar named Volkov Catteneo broke the
program's copy protection and sold unauthorized copies. Alderman, who runs his business from home in a Tampa suburb,
allows users to transfer his products, but prohibits copying.

"We confronted him about it and his basic response was,
'What are you going to do? Sue me?'" Alderman said. "I guess the
mentality is that because you're an avatar . . . that you are
untouchable. The purpose of this suit is not only to protect our

income and our product, but also to show, yes, you can be prosecuted and brought to justice."

Catherine Smith, director of marketing for *Second Life*-creator Linden Lab, said she knew of no other real-world legal fight between two avatars.

However, Linden Labs itself has been sued more than once by subscribers over seizures of virtual property. In 2005, Japanese media reported that a Chinese exchange student was arrested for stealing virtual items from other players in an online game, "Lineage II."

"Second Life" isn't a game. There are no dragons to slay or other traditional game objectives. San Francisco-based Linden Lab describes it as "an online digital world imagined, created & owned by its residents."

Linden Lab provides a free basic avatar, a 3-D virtual representation of the user in male or female form. Everything else costs real money. A 16-acre virtual island costs $1,675 plus monthly maintenance fees of $295. Virtual money, called Lindens, can be exchanged with real dollars at an average rate of about 270 Lindens to the dollar.

Avatars can be equipped with flowing gowns and tiny tattoos, and users with programming and Photoshop skills can reshape themselves into a virtual Greta Garbo or just about any shape imaginable. With a little cash, users can also have people like Alderman transform the avatars for them.

At Alderman's virtual storefront in *Second Life*, shoppers can try out a dragon bed powered by one of his SexGen engines. Along with programmers and designers, he employs a sales staff who hang around the shop like real salespeople to pitch the perfect sex toys. He is investing in a $25,000 motion-capture suit, a low-end version of one used to create digital characters in movies, to create more realistic sex moves for *Second Life* avatars.

As customers demand more real life in *Second Life*, though, these virtual creations can collide with reality.

"Virtually every aspect of real life is getting duplicated, and all the laws that can be applied to the real world are being applied in *Second Life*," said Jorge Contreras Jr., an intellectual-property attorney in Washington, D.C.

Last year, *Second Life* was rocked by a scandal over users who had modified their avatars to look like children and simulated pedophilia. Last month, Linden Lab shut down gambling in *Second Life* after concerns arose that virtual games of chance might violate U.S. gambling laws when members cashed in Lindens for real money.

Now comes Alderman's SexGen suit, which was filed July 3 and seeks unspecified damages. It accuses the unknown owner of the Catteneo avatar of violating copyright and trademark protections by copying, distributing and selling copies of Alderman's software.

Alderman's attorney, Francis X. Taney Jr. of Philadelphia, said the lawsuit has gotten a lot of attention because it involves sex, but is fundamentally about long-established law.

"It's a piece of software and software is copyrightable," Taney said. "It's also expressed in graphics, which also are copyrightable. There is some sizzle. People like to say it's really far out there, but at the end of the day I equate it to basic intellectual property principles."

Unlike many popular online worlds, such as *World of Warcraft*, Linden Lab grants its users broad rights to create and sell content with few restrictions. Users can install copy protection and seek U.S. copyright and trademark protections, all of which Alderman did for the SexGen software.

"Whenever you create a situation where people are buying and selling things and potentially misappropriating them from their rightful owners, it is only a matter of time before the legal system gets called in," said Fred von Lohmann, a senior staff attorney at the Electronic Frontier Foundation in San Francisco. "This seems like a relatively straightforward case. It sounds like there is a real copyright issue."

Taney believes he knows who Catteneo is in real life, but is confirming it through subpoenas of records of eBay's PayPal payment service as well as chat logs and trade history in *Second Life*. He said Linden Lab and PayPal turned over their records, and he is preparing another round of subpoenas.

"We're proceeding carefully," Taney said. "This guy has claimed the information he gave to Linden was bogus. We are looking for ways to cross check and corroborate the information." Catteneo, who did not respond to several interview requests sent through the *Second Life* messaging system, will likely have a hard time hiding.

"There is a whole lot less anonymity online than people think," von Lohmann said. "There are over 20,000 people who have been sued for downloading music. They may have felt anonymous, but [they] weren't."

Alderman is unlikely to be the last to drag an avatar into court as the designers in *Second Life* try to protect their creations in the same way clothing designers such as Gucci try to eliminate realistic knockoffs.

In recognition of the growing legal issues *Second Life* is likely to generate, the country of Portugal recently set up an arbitration center in the virtual world, though it has no power to enforce its decisions.

The legal issues may be similar offline and online, but von Lohmann said the trials could be a lot more interesting.

"In a virtual world, you have the ability to gather evidence you don't have in the real world," he said. "Everything that happens in *Second Life* is reflected on computer servers. Depending on how long they keep the records, you could actually replay the event as it happens."

Davis, Phil. "'Second Life' Avatar Sued over Virtual Sex Device." USA Today 10 August 2007. Online at www.usatoday.com/tech/webguide/internetlife/2007-08-10-virtual-sex-lawsuit_N.htm?csp=34. Copyright 2007. Reprinted by permission of the YGS Group.

Questions to Consider

1. The lawyers quoted in this article suggest that this situation is just like real life. What do you see as different from real life in the examples of the scandals noted in this article, such as the allegations of pedophilia, theft, and gambling by users and/or their avatars?

2. One way Second Life experiences are like those in real life is that items cost money. What would you "spend" to inhabit a virtual world? Consider real money, but also intangible expenses, such as time, energy, imagination, and time away from other activities. What are some advantages and disadvantages of such expenses?

3. We don't hear in this article from Volkov Catteneo, the avatar being sued. What argument do you think he would make in justifying his actions? Would you find the argument persuasive?

4. Kevin Alderman's job is a controversial one; elsewhere he has called his own avatar, Stroker Serpentine, "a pornographic mogul." In the real world, this occupation would be a controversial one. Should it be controversial as a virtual occupation? Where should the line be drawn as to what should be subject to legal or moral sanctions?

5. What rhetorical strategies reflect Davis's informative purpose for an audience who might not know what this virtual world is like?

The End of Privacy?

DANIEL J. SOLOVE

Tag—you're it! The relatively innocent game of tag that we played as children becomes a much more questionable game on the Internet. Imagine an embarrassing picture that someone else has tagged with your name and that suddenly surfaces twenty years from now when you're a vice president of a local business. This isn't the stuff of imagination, but of reality. Daniel J. Solove, an internationally known expert in the area of privacy law, addresses such realities in this article for Scientific American. *Solove describes the future that Lessig imagined—our present reality—and provides examples of how material once thought of as private is now routinely placed on the Internet in videos and blogs and on social networking sites belonging to us and others. Solove, the John Marshall Harlan Research Professor of Law at George Washington University Law School, is the author of numerous articles and books tackling what implications such widespread dissemination of information may have and whether regulation of this arena is the answer. As you read, ask yourself where you would draw the line between private and public and between the freely available and the protected.*

◆

Young people share the most intimate details of personal life on social-networking Web sites, portending a realignment of the public and the private.

He has a name, but most people just know him as "the Star Wars Kid." In fact, he is known around the world by tens of millions of people. Unfortunately, his notoriety is for one of the most embarrassing moments in his life.

In 2002, as a 15-year-old, the Star Wars Kid videotaped himself waving around a golf-ball retriever while pretending it was a lightsaber. Without the help of the expert choreographers working on the Star Wars movies, he stumbled around awkwardly in the video.

The video was found by some of the boy's tormentors, who uploaded it to an Internet video site. It became an instant hit with a multitude of fans. All across the blogosphere, people started mocking the boy, making fun of him for being pudgy, awkward and nerdy.

Several remixed videos of the Star Wars Kid started popping up, adorned with special effects. People edited the video to make the golf-ball retriever glow like a lightsaber. They added Star Wars music to the video. Others mashed it up with other movies. Dozens of embellished versions were created. The Star Wars Kid appeared in a video game and on the television shows Family Guy and South Park. It is one thing to be teased by classmates in school, but imagine being ridiculed by masses the world over. The teenager dropped out of school and had to seek counseling. What happened to the Star Wars Kid can happen to anyone, and it can happen in an instant. Today collecting personal information has become second nature. More and more people have cell phone cameras, digital audio recorders, Web cameras and other recording technologies that readily capture details about their lives.

For the first time in history nearly anybody can disseminate information around the world. People do not need to be famous enough to be interviewed by the mainstream media. With the Internet, anybody can reach a global audience.

Technology has led to a generational divide. On one side are high school and college students whose lives virtually revolve around social-networking sites and blogs. On the other side are their parents, for whom recollection of the past often remains locked in fading memories or, at best, in books, photographs and videos. For the current generation, the past is preserved on the Internet, potentially forever. And this change raises the question of how much privacy people can expect—or even desire—in an age of ubiquitous networking.

GENERATION GOOGLE

The number of young people using social-networking Web sites such as Facebook and MySpace is staggering. At most college campuses, more than 90 percent of students maintain their own sites. I call the people growing up today "Generation Google." For them, many fragments of personal information will reside on the Internet forever, accessible to this and future generations through a simple Google search.

That openness is both good and bad. People can now spread their ideas everywhere without reliance on publishers, broadcasters or other traditional gatekeepers. But that transformation also creates profound threats to privacy and reputations. *The New York Times* is not likely to care about the latest gossip at Dubuque Senior High School or Oregon State University. Bloggers and others communicating online may care a great deal. For them, stories and rumors about friends, enemies, family members, bosses, co-workers and others are all prime fodder for Internet postings.

Before the Internet, gossip would spread by word of mouth and remain within the boundaries of that social circle. Private details would be confined to diaries and kept locked in a desk drawer. Social networking spawned by the Internet allows communities worldwide to revert to the close-knit culture of preindustrial society, in which nearly every member of a tribe or a farming hamlet knew everything about the neighbors. Except that now the "villagers" span the globe.

College students have begun to share salacious details about their schoolmates. A Web site called Juicy Campus serves as an electronic bulletin board that allows students nationwide to post anonymously and without verification a sordid array of tidbits about sex, drugs and drunkenness. Another site, Don't Date Him Girl, invites women to post complaints about the men they have dated, along with real names and actual photographs.

Social-networking sites and blogs are not the only threat to privacy. As several articles in this issue of *Scientific American* have already made clear, companies collect and use our personal information at every turn. Your credit-card company has a record of your purchases. If you shop online, merchants keep tabs on every item you have bought. Your Internet service provider has information about how you surf the Internet. Your cable company has data about which television shows you watch.

The government also compromises privacy by assembling vast databases that can be searched for suspicious patterns of behavior. The National Security Agency listens and examines the records of millions of telephone conversations. Other agencies analyze financial transactions. Thousands of government bodies at the federal and state level have records of personal information, chronicling births, marriages, employment, property ownership and more. The information is often stored in public records, making it readily accessible to anyone—and the trend toward more accessible personal data continues to grow as more records become electronic.

THE FUTURE OF REPUTATION

Broad-based exposure of personal information diminishes the ability to protect reputation by shaping the image that is presented to others. Reputation plays an important role in society, and preserving private details of one's life is essential to it. We look to people's reputations to decide whether to make friends, go on a date, hire a new employee or undertake a prospective business deal.

Some would argue that the decline of privacy might allow people to be less inhibited and more honest. But when everybody's transgressions are exposed, people may not judge one another less harshly. Having your personal information may fail to improve my judgment of you. It may, in fact, increase the likelihood that I will hastily condemn you. Moreover, the loss of privacy might inhibit freedom. Elevated visibility that comes with living in a transparent online world means you may never overcome past mistakes.

People want to have the option of "starting over," of reinventing themselves throughout their lives. As American philosopher John Dewey once said, a person is not "something complete, perfect, [or] finished," but is "something moving, changing, discrete, and above all initiating instead of final." In the past, episodes of youthful experimentation and foolishness were eventually forgotten, giving us an opportunity to start anew, to change and to grow. But with so much information online, it is harder to make these moments forgettable. People must now live with the digital baggage of their pasts.

This openness means that the opportunities for members of Generation Google might be limited because of something they did years ago as wild teenagers. Their intimate secrets may be revealed by other people they know. Or they might become the unwitting victim of a false rumor. Like it or not, many people are beginning to get used to having a lot more of their personal information online.

WHAT IS TO BE DONE?

Can we prevent a future in which so much information about people's private lives circulates beyond their control? Some technologists and legal scholars flatly say no. Privacy, they maintain, is just not compatible with a world in which information flows so freely. As Scott McNealy of Sun Microsystems once famously declared: "You already have zero privacy. Get over it." Countless books and articles have heralded the "end," "death" and "destruction" of privacy.

Those proclamations are wrongheaded at best. It is still possible to protect privacy, but doing so requires that we rethink outdated understandings of the concept. One such view holds that privacy requires total secrecy: once information is revealed to others, it is no longer private. This notion of privacy is unsuited to an online world. The generation of people growing up today understands privacy in a more nuanced way. They know that personal information is routinely shared with countless others, and they also know that they leave a trail of data wherever they go. The more subtle understanding of privacy embraced by Generation Google recognizes that a person should retain some control over personal information that becomes publicly available. This generation wants a say in how private details of their lives are disseminated.

The issue of control over personal information came to the fore in 2006, when Facebook launched a feature called News

Feeds, which sent a notice to people's friends registered with the service when their profile was changed or updated. But to the great surprise of those who run Facebook, many of its users reacted with outrage. Nearly 700,000 of them complained. At first blush, the outcry over News Feeds seems baffling. Many of the users who protested had profiles completely accessible to the public. So why did they think it was a privacy violation to alert their friends to changes in their profiles?

Instead of viewing privacy as secrets hidden away in a dark closet, they considered the issue as a matter of accessibility. They figured that most people would not scrutinize their profiles carefully enough to notice minor changes and updates. They could make changes inconspicuously. But Facebook's News Feeds made information more widely noticeable. The privacy objection, then, was not about secrecy; it was about accessibility.

In 2007 Facebook again encountered another privacy outcry when it launched an advertising system with two parts, called Social Ads and Beacon. With Social Ads, whenever users wrote something positive about a product or a movie, Facebook would use their names, images and words in advertisements sent to friends in the hope that an endorsement would induce other users to purchase a product more than an advertisement might. With Beacon, Facebook made data-sharing deals with a variety of other commercial Web sites. If a person bought a movie ticket on Fandango or an item on another site, that information would pop up in that person's public profile.

Facebook rolled out these programs without adequately informing its users. People unwittingly found themselves shilling products on their friends' Web sites. And some people were shocked to see their private purchases on other Web sites suddenly displayed to the public as part of their profiles that appeared on the Facebook site.

The outcry and an ensuing online petition called for Facebook to reform its practices—a document that quickly attracted tens of thousands of signatures and that ultimately led to several changes. As witnessed in these instances, privacy does not always involve sharing of secrets. Facebook users did not want their identities used to endorse products with Social Ads. It is one thing to write about how much one enjoys a movie or CD; it is another to be used on a billboard to pitch products to others.

CHANGING THE LAW

Canada and most European countries have more stringent privacy statutes than the U.S., which has resisted enacting all-encompassing legislation. Privacy laws elsewhere recognize that revealing information to others does not extinguish one's right to privacy. Increasing accessibility of personal information, however, means that U.S. law also should begin recognizing the need to safeguard a degree of privacy in the public realm.

In some areas, U.S. law has a well-developed system of controlling information. Copyright recognizes strong rights for public information, protecting a wide range of works, from movies to software. Procuring copyright protection does not require locking a work of intellect behind closed doors. You can read a copyrighted magazine, make a duplicate for your own use and lend it to others. But you cannot do whatever you want: for instance, photocopying it from cover to cover or selling bootleg copies in the street. Copyright law tries to achieve a balance between freedom and control, even though it still must wrestle with the ongoing controversies in a digital age.

The closest U.S. privacy law comes to a legal doctrine akin to copyright is the appropriation tort, which prevents the use of someone else's name or likeness for financial benefit. Unfortunately, the law has developed in a way that is often ineffective against the type of privacy threats now cropping up. Copyright primarily functions as a form of property right, protecting works of self-expression, such as a song or painting. To cope with increased threats to privacy, the scope of the appropriation tort should be expanded. The broadening might actually embody the original early 20th-century interpretation of this principle of common law, which conceived of privacy as more than a means to protect property: "The right to withdraw from the public gaze at such times as a person may see fit . . . is embraced within the right of personal liberty," declared the Georgia Supreme Court in 1905. Today, however, the tort does not apply when a person's name or image appears in news, art, literature, or on social-networking sites. At the same time the appropriation tort protects against using someone's name or picture without consent to advertise products, it allows these representations to be used in a news story. This limitation is fairly significant. It means that the tort would rarely apply to Internet-related postings.

Any widening of the scope of the appropriation tort must be balanced against the competing need to allow legitimate news gathering and dissemination of public information. The tort should probably apply only when photographs and other personal information are used in ways that are not of public concern—a criterion that will inevitably be subject to ongoing judicial deliberation.

Appropriation is not the only common-law privacy tort that needs an overhaul to become more relevant in an era of networked digital communications. We already have many legal tools to protect privacy, but they are currently crippled by conceptions of privacy that prevent them from working effectively. A broader development of the law should take into account problematic uses of personal information illustrated by the Star Wars Kid or Facebook's Beacon service.

It would be best if these disputes could be resolved without recourse to the courts, but the broad reach of electronic networking will probably necessitate changes in common law. The threats to privacy are formidable, and people are starting to realize how strongly they regard privacy as a basic right. Toward this goal, society must develop a new and more nuanced understanding of public and private life—one that acknowledges that more personal information is going to be available yet also protects some choice over how that information is shared and distributed.

Solove, Daniel J. "The End of Privacy?" Scientific American. 299:3 (September 2008): 100–106. Copyright © 2008 by Scientific American, a division of Nature America, Inc. Reproduced with permission. All rights reserved.

Questions to Consider

1. What different perspectives would older and younger generations have on privacy and other terms or behaviors that may have changed with the use of the Internet? In what ways might your present perspective change as you get older, and why?

2. Since Solove wrote this article in 2008, there have been even more concerns about privacy issues relating to identity theft, predators, bullies, and other problems. With what cases and events are you familiar, and how do you protect yourself online?

3. Solove argues that we need to have a balance between freedom and control. Where would Solove strike this balance? Where would you?

4. Solove is also concerned about users of social network sites being exploited for commercial purposes—if you like a movie, why not have Facebook let others know? Why is this a problem if it reflects only what you've stated in a semi-public forum?

5. At the end of his essay, Solove states that "society must develop a new and more nuanced understanding of public and private life." What does he mean, and has he convinced you that social networking sites have made this imperative?

Making Connections

1. Where would Lessig and Solove agree and disagree about what kinds of legislation might be necessary to respond to privacy concerns on the Internet?

2. Music from an online digital source can be compared to property in Second Life in that both are intangible works of the imagination. What kinds of rules could you design for the appropriate and inappropriate ways to acquire both? In what ways would you differentiate between these and other materials easily available on the Internet in regard to which should be protected?

3. Some of Lessig's predictions about privacy concerns have been borne out. What are comparable predictions about current nascent technology, such as genetic profiling? Has legislation been promoted in those areas? Why or why not?

4. A number of the readings suggest that new technology changes our understanding of concepts such as privacy and property. Consider other concepts—including information gathering, entertainment, and relationships—that have changed since the middle of the twentieth century because of technology. What advantages or problems do these changes present?

5. Alderman's suit and some of the lawsuits against Linden Lab regarding property rights were settled out of court. In these situations, the parties generally agree not to reveal why the case was settled, so we may never know exactly what the facts were or what the court might decide in the future. There is still time to make a case about whether the virtual world should be treated the same as the real world. What would you argue?

6. Kevin Alderman sold Amsterdam, his virtual world, on eBay for $50,000. Should the willingness of others to buy something suggest that it should be treated with all the laws applicable to any transaction? Why or why not?

7. Many of the cases and events referred to in the readings of this chapter are worth looking up and reading about more extensively to provide further context and different perspectives than are provided here. For example, as of 2010 Kevin Cogill had still not made an anti-piracy message, and it was unclear that he ever would. Does the additional information that you learn about lead you to view these cases any differently? Explain.

8. Juicy Campus was one of the many sites that post information by students about other students at universities; this often includes real names and comments or pictures that have the potential to be embarrassing and possibly harmful. To what extent do you think universities should try to respond to these websites? What can or should students do?

9. What do these cases suggest are the prices we pay for the benefit of laws that promote control and order? Are all groups affected equally in terms of being provided protection or of bearing the negative consequences of such laws? Explain.

10. In what ways are the legal documents that you have been reading challenging to understand? What purpose might be served by legal rhetoric that might be difficult for a nonlawyer to comprehend?

Reconsidering Laws:
In Search of Global Values

Right knows no boundaries, and justice no frontiers.
Judge Learned Hand, "A Pledge of Allegiance" (1945)

Laws, in large measure, are an attempt to impart order to society. Although the absence of laws can negatively impact a society's ability to function well or fairly, the mere presence of laws is not sufficient. Remember Rex in Lon Fuller's text from Chapter 1: laws can fail in many ways, including being unclear, unreasonable, unequally enforced, or not enforced at all. We don't have to go far to find real-life examples of government abuse of laws to promote oppression; witness, for example, fugitive slave laws in the United States or the Nuremberg laws in Germany. During the McCarthy era, many wondered if our right to freedom of expression was being ignored.

The opening readings in this chapter reflect the disorder and the concerns about a nation's health that can result from the lack of a well-functioning legal system or from perceived inequities in even a relatively healthy system. The nonprofit organization Fund for Peace compiles an annual Failed States Index, which identifies countries so besieged by economic, political, social, and sometimes natural disasters that total disintegration is possible. Of the twelve most serious indicators noted by the Fund for Peace, a significant number list law-related concerns, including human rights violations, illegitimate governments, gapingly wide inequality, grievances that may encompass government persecution, and the presence of nongovernmental security forces. The article "Why Things Fall Apart" suggests how these factors contribute to dangerously unstable nations. Even though the Fund for Peace profile of the United States shows relative health as of 2007, serious concerns are noted regarding observed legal inequities in the U.S. judicial system.

Other factors that contribute to a nation's instability, such as poverty or a lack of public services, are not always viewed as legal concerns. Anna Dolidze, human rights researcher and attorney from the Republic of Georgia, suggests in "Burger, without Spies, Please" that the United States should consider problems such as hunger and lack of housing as violations of rights that the law should protect, in the same way that it protects freedom of speech and religion. The Universal Declaration of Human Rights already recognizes these as rights worthy of protection; to what extent should we follow suit?

On the other side of the spectrum, according to Philip Howard we might want to consider *Life without Lawyers*, or so his book's title might suggest. More specifically, Howard contends that law needs to allow reasonable risk to balance the inhibiting nature of the law. Whereas the earlier readings in this chapter point to the possibility of national chaos or human rights violations without sufficient law, Howard asks us to consider whether too much law might inhibit our freedom. Finally, whatever laws do exist, the editors of *Tikkun Magazine* ask us to consider a new way of looking at what the law should offer. We should, the editors argue, look to Dr. Martin Luther King Jr.'s prescription for justice—"Love correcting that which revolts against love." Empathy and compassion, say these editors, need to be an integral part of the law.

The readings in this book express a variety of opinions on the status of laws in this country and reflect a right of expression that does not exist in all countries, and that some would argue is not always protected in the United States either. As you analyze the readings in this final chapter, consider that they not only ask us whether to aspire to more law, less law, or different kinds of law, but also suggest the importance of offering these questions for open debate within society. Not only does the right exist to express these concerns, but so, too, does the responsibility. Such are the rights and responsibilities created by a body of laws that we, the people, continue to shape even as they shape us.

Failing Nations: Why Things Fall Apart

ROBERT DRAPER

Robert Draper, a freelance journalist and author of Dead Certain: The Presidency of George W. Bush, *began his writing career as a journalist for the* Daily Texan, *the newspaper for the University of Texas at Austin. In this article for* National Geographic, *Draper moves beyond the U.S. borders and considers the state of nation-states: how states fail but also how, from failure, success can develop. Draper references the Failed State Index, the barometer developed by the Fund for Peace that highlights troubled countries. As you read this article and the accompanying profile of the United States by the Fund for Peace, consider the monumental task for a country to build and maintain a structure that protects all its citizens. What are your country's successes and failures? How has law contributed to that status?*

───────────── ◆ ─────────────

It can happen after one fateful event—a civil war, natural disaster, or brutal takeover—or insinuate itself gradually, like a cancer that eats away at a country for decades. But when a nation is failing, you see it in the eyes of its people.

Over a billion people live in countries in danger of collapse. Some leaders lose control over their territory and cling to their capitals while warlords rule the provinces. Many governments are unable or unwilling to provide the most basic of services. Most are hobbled by corruption and environmental degradation. Such unstable states are dangers not just to themselves but also to the whole world. They incubate terrorism, criminal organizations, and political extremism—because when your country is falling apart around you, any way out can seem like a good way out.

Geography can make a country more vulnerable to instability. Just finding itself in a bad neighborhood puts a country at risk; the war in Iraq, for instance, sent a flood of refugees into neighboring Syria. Crowded nations with huge populations, like Bangladesh, face special challenges. But so do vast countries like Chad, whose very size defeats infrastructure. Landlocked nations with poor soil and little water struggle for self-sufficiency. Yet countries rich in natural resources, such as the Democratic Republic of the Congo, don't always come out ahead. In what is called the resource curse, abundant oil or diamonds can breed competition among elites for control of those lucrative assets.

Historical and cultural tensions can dog nations as well. Nowhere is this more evident than in Africa, home to the top five countries in this year's Failed States Index, compiled annually by the Fund for Peace. "The colonial drawing of arbitrary borders across ethnic and even topographic lines created artificial states," says the Fund's president, Pauline H. Baker. Such regimes often devote more energy to consolidating authority than to fostering national identities and robust government institutions.

One African country that has prevailed over its colonial legacy is Senegal. "It's benefited from enlightened leadership," says Baker. Indeed, the most important factor for ensuring a state's stability is good governance, says Davidson College political scientist Ken Menkhaus. Establishing the rule of law, with institutions to support it, "allows for a predictable investment climate and discourages the rise of armed insurgencies."

Assistance from organizations like the World Bank and United Nations has a mixed record of staving off failure. The most dramatic success stories are countries like India and South Africa that reformed themselves from within. As the United States' recent experiences in "nation building" illustrate, promoting political stability with outside military intervention is far from easy. Iraq and Afghanistan currently rank as the sixth and seventh most precarious states on the planet.

Then there is Somalia, a country whose geography, history, and clan dynamics give it the grim distinction of topping the index for two years in a row. Beyond Somalia, there's little agreement on what a high score on the index really means for a country's future. Colombia, for example, lacks control over parts of its territory. So, has Colombia failed? The bloody aftermath of Kenya's 2007 elections caused the country to go from 26th to 14th in this year's index. But does this backslide foretell failure for Kenya, with its vibrant entrepreneurial class?

Scholars caution against judgment. University of Hawaii professor Tarcisius Kabutaulaka says it's easy to forget that many countries have had troubled histories. "The United States was built out of chaos, out of civil war. And now we expect the rest of the world to adopt our institutions but do it without violence in a short period of time."

In the end, the question of whether a country is failing may best be answered by its own people. If their eyes say "we have been deserted," the verdict has been rendered.

NOTE: Several sources routinely measure the progress of countries around the globe. One is the World Bank at www.worldbank.org, and another is the Fund for Peace, referenced in this article, at www.fundfor-peace.org. Both have websites worth reviewing to get a more complete picture of the relative status of countries and the nuanced measurements that provide overall rankings. The 2007 profile of the United States from the Fund for Peace is included here; as this book was going to print, the Fund for Peace was in the process of updating its country profiles.

UNITED STATES COUNTRY PROFILE, 2007
FUND FOR PEACE

OVERVIEW

Located on the North American continent, the United States of America is bordered by Canada in the North, Mexico in the South, the North Atlantic Ocean in the East, and the North Pacific Ocean in the West. In 1776, Britain's thirteen American colonies declared their independence. With French aid, the colonies won the ensuing war against Britain and were recognized as the United States of America following the Treaty of Paris in 1783. The U.S. Constitution was signed on September 17, 1787 and went into effect on March 4, 1789. The U.S. currently consists of 50 states, which include the Hawaiian Islands in the Pacific Ocean, and Alaska, on the northwestern coast of Canada. The population of the U.S. currently numbers around 303 million and is comprised of 81.7% white, 12.9% black, 4.2% Asian, 1% Amerindian and Alaska native, and 0.2% native Hawaiian and other Pacific Islander. Religiously, the U.S. is 52% Protestant, 24% Roman Catholic, 2% Mormon, 1% Jewish, 1% Muslim, 10% other, and 10% unaffiliated. There is no official national language, but the following languages are spoken: 82.1% English, 10.7% Spanish, 3.8% other Indo-European, 2.7% Asian and Pacific Islander, and 0.7% other. In the state of Hawaii, Hawaiian is the official language. The GDP per capita is $44,000.

SOCIAL INDICATORS

Demographic pressures decreased in the [Failed State Index (FSI)] 2007 to 3.5. In the previous year, the devastating consequences of Hurricane Katrina in southern states caused the score to spike at 5.0. Although 314 people died in 2006 in a spate of natural disasters, such as floods, wild fires, and heat waves, none of these disasters put the kind of pressure on the state that Katrina

USA

	Indicators											
	Total Score	Social					Economic		Political/Military			
		Demographic Pressures	Refugees & Displaced Persons	Group Grievance	Human Flight	Uneven Development	Economy	Legitimacy of the State	Public Services	Human Rights	Security Apparatus	Factionalized Elites	External Influence
2006	34.5	5.0	6.0	3.0	1.0	6.0	1.5	2.5	1.0	5.0	1.0	1.5	1.0
2007	33.6	3.5	5.5	3.2	1.0	5.8	1.8	2.8	1.4	4.6	1.3	1.7	1.0
Point Change	−0.9	−1.5	−0.5	+0.2	0	−0.2	+0.3	+0.3	+0.4	−0.4	+0.3	+0.2	0
Pct Change	−0.7%	−15%	−5%	+2%	0%	−2%	+3%	+3%	+4%	−4%	+3%	+2%	0%

had the year before. However, the effects of Katrina continued to be felt in 2006, as displaced families remained without permanent housing. The HIV/AIDS prevalence rate was about 0.6%. The infant mortality rate was 6.37 per 1,000 live births. The U.S. has a population growth rate of 0.894% and a stable age structure, with 20.2% of the population under the age of 15 and 12.6% of the population age 65 or older. Population density is 84 people per square mile. The U.S. admits tens of thousands of refugees every year. In the fiscal year 2005/2006, the U.S. admitted 62,643 refugees, including 10,586 from Somalia, 8,549 from Laos, 6,666 from Russia, 6,479 from Cuba, 3,100 from Haiti, and 2,136 from Iran. These refugees are often integrated into American society as legal immigrants. Illegal immigrants are controversial and often discriminated against. Although they are usually able to find work, they are paid less and work in worse conditions than U.S. citizens and legal immigrants. The U.S. is currently constructing a barrier along its border with Mexico to keep illegal immigrants out. Group grievance is relatively low in the United States, despite lingering racial inequalities. Human flight is very low since the United States attracts and retains skilled workers with its strong economy.

ECONOMIC INDICATORS

For a developed country, uneven development in the U.S. is relatively high. As of 1997, the lowest 10% of households earn 1.8% of the national income while the highest 10% earn 30.5%. This is because of the lack of skills and education among inner city communities and some minority populations, the highly liberalized economy, and tax policies of recent governments. The macroeconomic indicators, however, are comparatively strong. Unemployment was 4.8%. Inflation was 2.5%. The U.S. has a large GDP of $13.13 trillion and a GDP growth rate of 3.2%. However, the U.S. also has a high public debt that is 64.7% of GDP, and 12% of the population lives below the poverty line. Agriculture employs 0.7% of the 151.4 million-person labor force and generates 0.9% of the GDP. In contrast, the industry sector employs 20.4% of the labor force and generates 22.9% of the GDP, while the services sector employs 78.6% of the labor force and generates 76.4% of the GDP.

POLITICAL/MILITARY INDICATORS

The legitimacy of the state was rated 2.8 in the FSI 2007. The government is somewhat unpopular due to the unpopularity of the war in Iraq and corruption scandals among government officials. However, the strength of the state institutions mitigates unpopularity, despite disappointment with specific individuals or administrations. Most people have access to clean water and improved sanitation. The adult literacy rate is very high at 99%. Public transportation and health care are not as good as in some other developed countries. The infant mortality rate is low at 6.37 deaths per 1,000 live births, and life expectancy is high at 78 years. However, not all U.S. citizens have health insurance, and health care is very expensive, which limits access to health care. Human rights in the U.S. are relatively good. There is, however, increasing criticism of the U.S. human rights record in regards to capital punishment and, more recently, in regards to the erosion of civil liberties in the war on terrorism; particularly controversial issues are Guantanamo prison in Cuba, the suspension of habeas corpus for those accused of terrorist acts, accusations of the use of torture, and extraordinary rendition, in which suspected terrorists are sent to external secret prisons. The security apparatus is civilian-led, highly disciplined, and professional. Elites have become slightly more factionalized since the FSI 2006. Two main political parties dominate the political arena: the Republican Party and the Democrat Party.

CORE FIVE STATE INSTITUTIONS

The U.S. has very highly developed state institutions, which give the state legitimacy rather than legitimacy resting with individual leaders or administrations. Except for incidents of disputed electoral counts which can be highly controversial (e.g., 2000 presidential election dispute in Florida), elections are largely viewed as free and fair, and citizens usually trust their elected representatives to make and vote for policies that will benefit them. Dissatisfaction with particular leaders can be expressed through regular elections with political figures limited to fixed terms and other electoral mechanisms: recalls, referenda, local and state elections; the press which is lively and free; and constitutional checks and balances among the three branches of government.

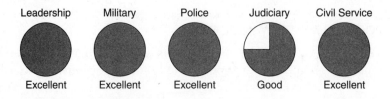

Leadership	Military	Police	Judiciary	Civil Service
Excellent	Excellent	Excellent	Good	Excellent

The U.S. military is strong. Military expenditures equal 4.06% of the GDP. The President is the chief of state and the commander-in-chief; thus, the military is under civilian control and generally accountable to the people. The military budget must be approved by Congress.

The police force is also widely viewed as protecting the people. There is no central police; state and local governments control their own forces. Police are accountable for their actions and police brutality is investigated and punished.

The judiciary is independent and federalized. Defendants have a right to legal counsel and a jury of their peers. Supreme Court Justices are appointed for life by the President, but must be approved by the Senate. There are accusations that African-Americans and other minorities do not get equal justice, however, and the prisons are [disproportionately] filled with minority offenders. Capital punishment is legal and controlled by the states. Controversy also exists over new legal procedures applied to suspected terrorists, who are not subject to either the civilian or military systems of justice. [This] represents a parallel justice system created [for] reasons of national security. In addition, Congress has investigated partisan firing of federal attorneys, undermining the morale and structure of the U.S. Department of Justice.

The civil service is professional, and jobs are based on merit-based tests, well compensated, and offer good benefits.

PROGNOSIS

The U.S. has a strong economy, though it is vulnerable to downturns at times. Its state institutions are sound and supported by constitutional foundations widely accepted by its citizens. However, the U.S. should work to decrease its national debt and create more jobs and better job security. The U.S. should also implement policies that decrease income inequality and uneven access to social services, such as health care. Its human rights policies in the fight against terrorism are controversial and have raised questions about the country's adherence to international norms, treaties [and] policies it helped create. However, while there is a domestic debate on civic rights issues, the general public has not felt that their liberties have been violated or compromised much by government measures taken in the name of national security.

"Fund for Peace Country Profiles: Unites States, 2007" in "Failed States Index." The Fund for Peace. www.fundforpeace.org. Copyright 2008. Reprinted by permission of the Fund for Peace.

Questions to Consider

1. Draper frames his article by using the image of what is reflected in the eyes of the people in failing states. What is the purpose of distinguishing the people from the country of which they are a part?

2. Look at the progress of Draper's article by his use of topic sentences. How would you describe the method of organization that leads him to the penultimate paragraph beginning "Then there is Somalia"? Why, despite this progress, does he end that paragraph by noting that "scholars caution against judgment"? If not judgment, what are we to take away from Draper's article?

3. Draper refers to the Failed State Index, in which the lower the score, the better; Somalia, for example, listed as first in the 2011 Failed Nations list, has a score of 113.4, whereas the United States has a score of 34.8. Eighteen countries, however, have even lower scores, including Portugal, Japan, and Canada; Finland comes in last at 19.7. Some have questioned the accuracy of rankings such as these and have criticized their negative impressions of struggling countries, noting that even the title, "Failed States" (the World Bank refers to "Fragile and Conflict-Affected Countries"), may appear judgmental. What are the challenges of creating these kinds of comparative indices?

4. In what ways, and with what specific language, do the creators of the U.S. profile support their ranking of the United States? How does this profile help put the country in a new and useful perspective for you? What language or information would you want to examine more closely in order to corroborate the analysis, and why? Note that other nations' profiles can be found under the Failed State Index at the Fund for Peace website.

5. For what audience and purpose does it appear these profiles have been created? What does the Fund for Peace website indicate its purpose to be? With what other kind of information and by what other strategies does the Fund for Peace pursue its purposes?

Burger, without Spies, Please: Notes from a Human Rights Researcher
ANNA DOLIDZE

How often do you worry about someone spying on you when you sit down to eat in a fast food restaurant? Anna Dolidze explains how she and those she has interviewed regarding human rights violations have experienced this concern. In her essay, Dolidze poses questions you might not have considered before: Is it more important to have religious freedom or to be free from hunger? How does being free from hunger allow us to better exercise our religious freedom? Dolidze is from the Republic of Georgia, where she has worked as a human rights lawyer and activist, encouraging legal reform and government transparency. Though she continues to return to Georgia to work in a legal capacity, Dolidze moved in order to avoid what she described as intimidation and persecution because of her criticism of that government's human rights record. Upon moving to the United States, Dolidze was accepted as a research fellow to pursue a doctor of the science of law degree (JSD) at Cornell University Law School. In what ways do you see her experiences as informing the arguments that she is making in this article?

◆

Every time I go to a restaurant with my friends, they have to remind me that I have complete freedom of choice in deciding where I would like to be seated. It's because since I have been doing human rights fact-finding in countries where the phrase "human rights" itself causes shivers, frightened glances, and widened eyes, I got used to only sitting in restaurants with my back against the wall, facing the room. One can hardly expect to learn restaurant etiquette when doing human rights fact-finding. However, it's true that restaurant behavior is one of the first things you learn if you start working to document human rights abuses in countries whose governments are hostile to the concept.

When choosing a place to sit, you have to sit with your back to the wall, facing the room, to see if someone has followed you and is now eavesdropping on your conversation. Then, even if no one followed and you are alone with your source—be it a witness or a victim of a human rights violation ready to give a first-hand story—food is the last thing on your mind. As a professional researcher you are bound to take many precautionary measures to maintain the security of those who have shown courage in talking to you. After all, sooner or later you are most likely to complete the mission and leave the country; but those people who agreed to publicize information damaging to the reputation of their authoritarian government will be left behind. They will remain vulnerable to harassment, pressure, and retribution from the repressive machine of the government.

So when I come back to a lovely and quiet place like Ithaca, I have trouble forgoing the habit of sitting with my back to the wall in restaurants. But not only that, when I eat my burger and criticize [the] US government's most recent policy, I am reminded that the people I met during my trip, and have left behind, will probably never enjoy either the meal we are having or the opportunity to raise their critical voice publicly without fear of retribution. Basic civil, political, as well as economic and social rights as described by the *International Bill of Rights* continue to remain luxurious exceptions as opposed to minimum standards of living for the majority of people on the planet.

In Uzbekistan, where I just completed my most recent trip, one can have a delicious meal with shish-kebabs, home baked bread, cheese and fresh produce with tea for only $3, and even this is only affordable to those employed in the capital. Per capita average annual income in the country is $2,389, compared to $48,000 in the United States. However, freedom of expression is just as unaffordable as a decent meal at a restaurant. The government of Uzbekistan has been recognized by most international organizations as one of the most repressive in the world, alongside regimes in Saudi Arabia, North Korea and Myanmar. Those that publicly criticize government activity face the immediate risk of retribution. And the case of Uzbekistan, where fundamental political, as well as social and economic rights are a luxury, is more of a rule than an exception in [the] contemporary world.

As the 2008 democracy index of *The Economist* attests, one third of the world population lives under authoritarian rule—meaning a form of government where state authority permeates throughout almost every part of life and severely curtails freedom of expression to sustain its power. On the other hand, The World Bank 2008 Development Indicators suggest that around 1.4 billion people, every fifth person in the world, lives on less than $1.25 a day. These millions of people will probably never experience things that make up our daily lives. Your most recent restaurant bill might have sustained a whole family for a month in many least-developed countries in the world.

There is substantive disagreement among countries and lawyers, however, if the right to have a normal meal stands on the same footing with the right to say one's own opinion, i.e., if civil and political rights enjoy the same importance as economic, social and cultural rights.

The International Covenant on Civil and Political Rights and *The International Covenant on Economic, Social and Cultural Rights* were adopted at the same time in 1966 and today (along with the *Universal Declaration of Human Rights*) comprise *The International Bill of Human Rights*, a codification of the most fundamental international human rights norms. It's true, however, that the two Covenants contain different language regarding states' obligations on implementation of these rights. *The International Covenant on Civil and Political Rights* speaks of the obligation of each state "to respect and to ensure to all individuals within its territory and subject to its jurisdiction the rights recognized in the present Covenant."

On the other hand, *The International Covenant on Economic, Social and Cultural Rights*, which embodies such rights as a right to adequate housing, right to social security, and right to health, indicates that each state should "take steps [. . .] to the maximum of its available resources, with a view to achieving progressively the full realization of the rights recognized in the present Covenant by all appropriate means [. . . .]" However, many countries, including the United States, have made economic and social rights nonjusticiable, depriving individuals of the possibility of defending their rights through legal means. Although the United Nations itself has been pushing for the idea of indivisibility of human rights, many states through their human rights policies have been encouraging the understanding that economic and social rights are of a secondhand nature. The United States itself has been pursuing this understanding domestically as well as internationally, regarding the implementation of economic, social and cultural rights as a matter of development but not of entitlement.

This way of thinking is flawed both in theory and in practice. In theory, if one agrees that the origin of the concept of human rights lies in the concept of inalienable human dignity, which is the philosophical foundation of current international human rights law, it becomes hard to argue that the right to be free from hunger is less important than the right to be free from torture. Hunger is, in terms of its effect on human psychology and physiology, a form of human degradation and torture. Not surprisingly, deprivation of food, or starvation, has been used as [a] means of torture and has been regarded as such in human rights law. As one of the greatest thinkers, Fyodor Dostoevsky writes in *Crime and Punishment*, "In poverty you may still retain your innate nobility of soul, but in beggary—never—no one. For beggary a man is not chased out of human society with a stick, he is swept out with a broom, so as to make it as humiliating as possible; and quite right, too, forasmuch as in beggary I am ready to be the first to humiliate myself."

Furthermore, it's hard to prove that the possibility to pray freely without government interference is more important to human dignity than the feeling of security brought by a roof over one's head. It is impossible to weigh if deprivation of the right to assembly brings more affront to human dignity than an urgency to sell some of one's organs, which many people in least-developed countries do.

The argument is strengthened in the experience of a human rights researcher. As I have often spoken with witnesses and victims of human rights violations, I have often realized that they lack basic means of transportation, sometimes 15 cents to get to our agreed location. Often when I have spoken to family members of the unjustly arrested and tortured, one of the first concerns I have heard was fear of hunger because the arrested person was the family's breadwinner. I particularly remember a conversation with a father persecuted for his religious beliefs, whose three year old daughter worked in a circus. Numerous examples like this, that one can hear daily in human rights fact-finding missions in developing countries, are the most persuasive and vivid examples that neither set of rights should be singled out and made prevalent over the other. All human beings have an equal entitlement to adequate food as well as the right to freely express their opinion. We are accustomed to the fact that we have the right to enjoy our meal and conversations without government interference. Everyone else in the world too has the right to have a burger, without spies.

Questions to Consider

1. Why do you think Dolidze chooses to frame this essay with the image of sitting in a restaurant ordering burgers? Who is her audience, and how else does she write her essay with them in mind?

2. Though Dolidze starts out in the first person, she moves in the second paragraph to the second person. Why does Dolidze employ this strategy?

3. What precisely is Dolidze's argument, and how does she support it? Note that she uses a wide range of evidence, from economics to literary quotations; which do you consider most effective, and why?

4. What do you find important on a day-to-day basis in order to get to school, do your work, and be a productive citizen? In what ways could you argue that these requirements are important enough—to you and society—to be protected legally?

5. What kinds of legal or social services are available in your community for the poor, the homeless, and the hungry? Who provides these services, and what are the advantages and limitations of such services?

Universal Declaration of Human Rights

In 1948 the Universal Declaration of Human Rights (UDHR) was adopted by the United Nations (UN) General Assembly. It was seen as more comprehensive than the UN Charter and a necessary response to conditions such as those that arose in Nazi Germany during WWII. Canadian John Peters Humphrey was primarily responsible for the first draft, with subsequent drafters including Eleanor Roosevelt from the United States and representatives from Lebanon, China, France, and other countries. The declaration creates consistent language, such as "fundamental freedoms" and "human rights," intended to be applied universally. Although not binding international law, it is seen as useful in applying moral and diplomatic pressure on governments to comply with the enumerated objectives and is widely cited in judicial tribunals around the globe. Which of the enumerated rights do you see as already protected in your country? Which rights are the subject of controversy?

———————— ✦ ————————

PREAMBLE

Whereas recognition of the inherent dignity and of the equal and inalienable rights of all members of the human family is the foundation of freedom, justice and peace in the world,

Whereas disregard and contempt for human rights have resulted in barbarous acts which have outraged the conscience of mankind, and the advent of a world in which human beings shall enjoy freedom of speech and belief and freedom from fear and want has been proclaimed as the highest aspiration of the common people,

Whereas it is essential, if man is not to be compelled to have recourse, as a last resort, to rebellion against tyranny and oppression, that human rights should be protected by the rule of law,

Whereas it is essential to promote the development of friendly relations between nations,

Whereas the peoples of the United Nations have in the Charter reaffirmed their faith in fundamental human rights, in the dignity and worth of the human person and in the equal rights of men and women and have determined to promote social progress and better standards of life in larger freedom,

Whereas Member States have pledged themselves to achieve, in cooperation with the United Nations, the promotion of universal respect for and observance of human rights and fundamental freedoms,

Whereas a common understanding of these rights and freedoms is of the greatest importance for the full realization of this pledge,

Now, therefore,

The General Assembly,

Proclaims this Universal Declaration of Human Rights as a common standard of achievement for all peoples and all nations, to the end that every individual and every organ of society, keeping this Declaration constantly in mind, shall strive by teaching and education to promote respect for these rights and freedoms and by progressive measures, national and international, to secure their universal and effective recognition and observance, both among the peoples of Member States themselves and among the peoples of territories under their jurisdiction.

Article 1

All human beings are born free and equal in dignity and rights. They are endowed with reason and conscience and should act towards one another in a spirit of brotherhood.

Article 2

Everyone is entitled to all the rights and freedoms set forth in this Declaration, without distinction of any kind, such as race, colour, sex, language, religion, political or other opinion, national or social origin, property, birth or other status. Furthermore, no distinction shall be made on the basis of the political, jurisdictional or international status of the country or territory to which a person belongs, whether it be independent, trust, non-self-governing or under any other limitation of sovereignty.

Article 3

Everyone has the right to life, liberty and security of person.

Article 4

No one shall be held in slavery or servitude; slavery and the slave trade shall be prohibited in all their forms.

Article 5

No one shall be subjected to torture or to cruel, inhuman or degrading treatment or punishment.

Article 6

Everyone has the right to recognition everywhere as a person before the law.

Article 7

All are equal before the law and are entitled without any discrimination to equal protection of the law. All are entitled to equal protection against any discrimination in violation of this Declaration and against any incitement to such discrimination.

Article 8

Everyone has the right to an effective remedy by the competent national tribunals for acts violating the fundamental rights granted him by the constitution or by law.

Article 9

No one shall be subjected to arbitrary arrest, detention or exile.

Article 10

Everyone is entitled in full equality to a fair and public hearing by an independent and impartial tribunal, in the determination of his rights and obligations and of any criminal charge against him.

Article 11

1. Everyone charged with a penal offence has the right to be presumed innocent until proved guilty according to law in a public trial at which he has had all the guarantees necessary for his defence.
2. No one shall be held guilty of any penal offence on account of any act or omission which did not constitute a penal offence, under national or international law, at the time when it was committed. Nor shall a heavier penalty be imposed than the one that was applicable at the time the penal offence was committed.

Article 12

No one shall be subjected to arbitrary interference with his privacy, family, home or correspondence, nor to attacks upon his honour and reputation. Everyone has the right to the protection of the law against such interference or attacks.

Article 13

1. Everyone has the right to freedom of movement and residence within the borders of each State.
2. Everyone has the right to leave any country, including his own, and to return to his country.

Article 14

1. Everyone has the right to seek and to enjoy in other countries asylum from persecution.
2. This right may not be invoked in the case of prosecutions genuinely arising from non-political crimes or from acts contrary to the purposes and principles of the United Nations.

Article 15

1. Everyone has the right to a nationality.
2. No one shall be arbitrarily deprived of his nationality nor denied the right to change his nationality.

Article 16

1. Men and women of full age, without any limitation due to race, nationality or religion, have the right to marry and to found a family. They are entitled to equal rights as to marriage, during marriage and at its dissolution.
2. Marriage shall be entered into only with the free and full consent of the intending spouses.
3. The family is the natural and fundamental group unit of society and is entitled to protection by society and the State.

Article 17

1. Everyone has the right to own property alone as well as in association with others.
2. No one shall be arbitrarily deprived of his property.

Article 18

Everyone has the right to freedom of thought, conscience and religion; this right includes freedom to change his religion or belief, and freedom, either alone or in community with others and in public or private, to manifest his religion or belief in teaching, practice, worship and observance.

Article 19

Everyone has the right to freedom of opinion and expression; this right includes freedom to hold opinions without interference and to seek, receive and impart information and ideas through any media and regardless of frontiers.

Article 20

1. Everyone has the right to freedom of peaceful assembly and association.
2. No one may be compelled to belong to an association.

Article 21

1. Everyone has the right to take part in the government of his country, directly or through freely chosen representatives.
2. Everyone has the right to equal access to public service in his country.
3. The will of the people shall be the basis of the authority of government; this will shall be expressed in periodic and genuine elections which shall be by universal and equal suffrage and shall be held by secret vote or by equivalent free voting procedures.

Article 22

Everyone, as a member of society, has the right to social security and is entitled to realization, through national effort and international co-operation and in accordance with the organization and resources of each State, of the economic, social and cultural rights indispensable for his dignity and the free development of his personality.

Article 23

1. Everyone has the right to work, to free choice of employment, to just and favourable conditions of work and to protection against unemployment.
2. Everyone, without any discrimination, has the right to equal pay for equal work.

3. Everyone who works has the right to just and favourable remuneration ensuring for himself and his family an existence worthy of human dignity, and supplemented, if necessary, by other means of social protection.
4. Everyone has the right to form and to join trade unions for the protection of his interests.

Article 24

Everyone has the right to rest and leisure, including reasonable limitation of working hours and periodic holidays with pay.

Article 25

1. Everyone has the right to a standard of living adequate for the health and well-being of himself and of his family, including food, clothing, housing and medical care and necessary social services, and the right to security in the event of unemployment, sickness, disability, widowhood, old age or other lack of livelihood in circumstances beyond his control.
2. Motherhood and childhood are entitled to special care and assistance. All children, whether born in or out of wedlock, shall enjoy the same social protection.

Article 26

1. Everyone has the right to education. Education shall be free, at least in the elementary and fundamental stages. Elementary education shall be compulsory. Technical and professional education shall be made generally available and higher education shall be equally accessible to all on the basis of merit.
2. Education shall be directed to the full development of the human personality and to the strengthening of respect for human rights and fundamental freedoms. It shall promote understanding, tolerance and friendship among all nations, racial or religious groups, and shall further the activities of the United Nations for the maintenance of peace.
3. Parents have a prior right to choose the kind of education that shall be given to their children.

Article 27

1. Everyone has the right freely to participate in the cultural life of the community, to enjoy the arts and to share in scientific advancement and its benefits.

2. Everyone has the right to the protection of the moral and material interests resulting from any scientific, literary or artistic production of which he is the author.

Article 28

Everyone is entitled to a social and international order in which the rights and freedoms set forth in this Declaration can be fully realized.

Article 29

1. Everyone has duties to the community in which alone the free and full development of his personality is possible.
2. In the exercise of his rights and freedoms, everyone shall be subject only to such limitations as are determined by law solely for the purpose of securing due recognition and respect for the rights and freedoms of others and of meeting the just requirements of morality, public order and the general welfare in a democratic society.
3. These rights and freedoms may in no case be exercised contrary to the purposes and principles of the United Nations.

Article 30

Nothing in this Declaration may be interpreted as implying for any State, group or person any right to engage in any activity or to perform any act aimed at the destruction of any of the rights and freedoms set forth herein.

NOTE: The Declaration of Human Rights can be found in English at the United Nations Human Rights website, www.un.org/en/documents/udhr/. The declaration has been translated into more than three hundred languages; a brief excerpt of the translation into Mandarin Chinese follows. This and other languages can be found at: www.ohchr.org/EN/UDHR/Pages/SearchByLang.aspx

CHINESE (MANDARIN) TRANSLATION (Excerpt)

世界人权宣言

联合国大会一九四八年十二月十日第217A(III)号决议通过并颁布

1948 年 12 月 10 日，联合国大会通过并颁布《世界人权宣言》。这一具有历史意义的《宣言》颁布后，大会要求所有会员国广为宣传，并且"不分国家或领土的政治地位，主要在各级学校和其他教育机构加以传播、展示、阅读和阐述。"《宣言》全文如下：

序言

鉴于对人类家庭所有成员的固有尊严及其平等的和不移的权利的承认，乃是世界自由、正义与和平的基础，

鉴于对人权的无视和侮蔑已发展为野蛮暴行，这些暴行玷污了人类的良心，而一个人人享有言论和信仰自由并免予恐惧和匮乏的世界的来临，已被宣布为普通人民的最高愿望，

鉴于为使人类不致迫不得已铤而走险对暴政和压迫进行反叛，有必要使人权受法治的保护，

鉴于有必要促进各国间友好关系的发展，

鉴于各联合国国家的人民已在联合国宪章中重申他们对基本人权、人格尊严和价值以及男女平等权利的信念，并决心促成较大自由中的社会进步和生活水平的改善，

鉴于各会员国业已誓愿同联合国合作以促进对人权和基本自由的普遍尊重和遵行，

鉴于对这些权利和自由的普遍了解对于这个誓愿的充分实现具有很大的重要性，

因此现在，大会，发布这一世界人权宣言，作为所有人民和所有国家努力实现的共同标准，以期每一个人和社会机构经常铭念本宣言，努力通过教诲和教育促进对权利和自由的尊重，并通过国家的和国际的渐进措施，使这些权利和自由在各会员国本身人民及在其管辖下领土的人民中得到普遍和有效的承认和遵行；

Questions to Consider

1. To what extent can you see, especially in the preamble, a response to the events of WWII?

2. As you read the "whereas" clauses, consider whether you agree that these are givens; for example, is this document "essential to promote the development of friendly relations between nations"? Do you think these are considered by the framers to be proven ideas or arguments in themselves?

3. The rights set out in the UDHR were defined in more detail in two distinct covenants—one on civil and political rights and the other on economic, social, and cultural rights—which came into effect in 1976. The United States ratified the first covenant, though not the protocol allowing U.S. citizens to seek redress before the UN, but has not ratified the second, in part because of disagreements on the concept of economic rights. Which would you consider to be the rights that are clearly economic, those that are clearly not, and those that fall somewhere in between? Are these difficult to differentiate?

4. Even though these listed rights may seem extensive, some groups would ask for more; for example, Amnesty International would like to have added the right to refuse to kill. What other rights could you argue should be considered?

5. Although numbers vary widely, the number of native speakers of Mandarin Chinese is typically estimated as between two and three times that of English, with Spanish and English vying for second place among native speakers. English is estimated to be the language known by the largest number of speakers, including second-language speakers; however, the declaration has been translated into more than three hundred languages, largely to address the importance of having such information available in individuals' native languages. What are some challenges of translating information that is designed to prescribe equivalent behaviors around the globe?

The Freedom to Take Risks
PHILIP K. HOWARD

This article is excerpted from a chapter in the book Life without Lawyers, *written by, of all people, a lawyer. Philip K. Howard has been a longtime advocate of law reform, and he argues that "aspects of modern law undermine our freedoms." In Howard's view, too much dependence on law can abrogate personal freedoms and personal responsibilities. In quoting philosophers, politicians, safety experts, and others, Howard suggests to his readers that self-reliance can be difficult in an era of laws that can, in some cases, inhibit rather than promote the choices we make in daily life. In this reading, Howard chooses examples that support his claim that we need legal "green lights" as well as "red lights" in order to encourage risk. In what ways can risk be positive both locally and globally? As Howard makes his claims, consider what causes other than laws might be responsible for reduced risk-taking behaviors and whether this reduction is necessarily negative.*

---------------------- ◆ ----------------------

The houses on Wildemere Avenue in Milford, Connecticut, sit under the shade of towering hickory and oak trees. It's the kind of old-fashioned neighborhood where both young families and retired couples live next to one another, like a scene from a Norman Rockwell painting. You can practically see the young boy pulling his red wagon down the street.

Milford is the last place you would expect to see pushing the boundaries of social policy defining unacceptable risks of life. Since the 1960s, as we've seen, few areas of daily life have been immune from legal scrutiny. Food, drink, play, social relations of almost every sort, you name it. But the town fathers of Milford introduced a new area of legal scrutiny—nature itself.

In 2005, Una Glennon, a grandmother who lives on Wildemere Avenue, put in a pool for the enjoyment of her fourteen grandchildren. The hickory trees spread their branches all around her house. That was the problem. One of her grandchildren is allergic to nuts and can't play in the pool with the other children when the nuts are falling. Mrs. Glennon sent a letter to the mayor demanding the removal of three large hickory trees on the street near her house. What's a mayor to do? Allergy to nuts is indeed a serious risk to those who have it, and requires that parents or caretakers of children always carry a shot of epinephrine to counteract the reaction when there is unintended exposure. On the other hand, the neighbors on Wildemere Avenue weren't happy at the prospect of leaving a gap in the middle of the block, three stumps instead of a canopy of shade.

Where do you draw the line? Public choices are not usually matters of right and wrong. They require balance and trade-offs of one sort or another—here balancing the extra effort to safeguard the child, on the one hand, against the majesty of trees rising over sixty feet above Wildemere Avenue. Deciding between competing interests is one of the main jobs of government. But how does an official decide? The philosopher John Rawls famously suggested that social choices should be made behind a "veil of ignorance," where the decider here would imagine that he could end up in the position of either a tree lover or someone with a nut allergy.

The logical implications here would probably be enough to convince me. Cutting down trees to accommodate people with allergies could be ominous news for trees that reproduce themselves with nuts—walnut, chestnut, pine, pecan, and hazelnut as well as hickory trees. About one out of 200 Americans is allergic to tree nuts. Making all their neighborhoods safe from nuts could spawn a new logging industry. And what do we do about all the other serious allergies—say, bee stings, shellfish, and pollen? Do we start a national drive to obliterate bees? Doctors say that there is no safe zone for people with severe allergies; children with an allergy have to learn to be always on their guard. Balancing the risks of allergies against nature's realities should lead us down a path toward personal caution, not obliteration of nature.

Balancing these interests is not what happened in Milford, however. In the letter to the mayor, Mrs. Glennon enclosed a letter from a doctor suggesting the possibility of dire consequences to the child. Risk to the child, no matter how remote, was enough to make the mayor capitulate. The town ordered the trees chopped down. According to the mayor, he had no choice. "It really came down to taking a risk," he said, "that the child may be sick or even die."

Risk has become a hot button in public and private decisions. Press the risk button, and discussion pretty much ends. If there's a risk, better not do it. Part of the problem, as we've seen, is fear of lawsuits. The accusation "You took a risk" is reason enough to get sued. But there's something deeper that's infected our cultural psyche. There's a compulsion to move heaven and earth to eliminate a risk even if in the clear light of day, everyone agrees that the effect is a grotesque misallocation of resources. There was a panic to require flame-resistant pajamas for children in the early 1970s—at a cost seven times greater than the cost of smoke alarms that would save the same number of lives. Then it turned out that the flame retardant was carcinogenic, and it had to be banned. Certain pesticides that result in dramatically greater safety and increased crop productivity have been banned because of minuscule cancer risks. . . .

Risk, by definition, is a question of trade-offs and odds—accepting one set of risks in order to accomplish something (or in order not to incur worse risks). Build a heavy car for maximum safety and it may be less affordable, as well as burn more fuel. A key role of public leadership is to sort through these risks and put resources and legal protections where they are most effective. These are the choices we refer to as public policy. . . .

Risk, unfortunately, is inherent in all life choices. Every choice involves a risk. Every movement involves a risk. Doing nothing involves risk. Crossing the street, exercising, taking a job, getting married, all involve risks. Risk is just the flip side of opportunity—do away with risk, and we lose all chance for accomplishment. Safety itself, as I discuss shortly, is impossible without risk. The question with each choice is to weigh the risks and benefits, not reflexively to avoid risk. Using the logic of Milford, we might as well enact a legal ban on nut trees. Certainly this logic was not lost on the residents of Milford. The town hall received forty calls from residents asking whether they should chop down their hickory trees. . . .

THE NEED TO PROMOTE RISK

The surge in childhood obesity was the topic for a panel of health care leaders convened by Health and Human Services Secretary Tommy Thompson. The trend, they agreed, is unsettling—the rate of obesity in children has tripled in two decades. One in three is overweight, and one in six is obese. The harm to these individuals is inevitable. More than 70 percent will be overweight as adults, and most of these will suffer chronic illness as a result, including heart problems and type 2 diabetes. The harm to society is also frightening: The cost of obesity today is more than $100 billion—almost enough to provide health insurance to all Americans who don't have it, or to give each teacher in America a $30,000 raise. This self-inflicted cost will only rise as obese children become obese adults.

But what do we do about it? Lecturing kids about their diet is unlikely to be effective. More responsible marketing, such as selling juice instead of soda in school vending machines, is certainly useful, but only at the margin. Banning all the things that contribute to the trend would lead to a pretty bare landscape—candy, fast food, soft drinks, bread, video games, television, the Internet. . . . But most of us grew up with candy, soda, and fast food and didn't have this problem. The difference is how children spend their days. Obesity is mainly a cultural problem. Kids no longer find it fun or feel peer pressure to lead active lives.

Reversing this trend, the experts on the panel agreed, required reinstilling a culture of physical fitness. Almost fifty years ago JFK's President's Council on Youth Fitness, with the same goal, recommended installing monkey bars and other athletic equipment in playgrounds across the country. But they've all been ripped out. Why? Someone might fall and hurt himself.

Playgrounds are so boring, according to some experts, that no child over the age of four wants to go to them. Jungle gyms, merry-go-rounds, high slides, large swings, climbing ropes, even seesaws are, as they say, history. Recess in school is also not what it used to be. About 40 percent of elementary schools have eliminated or sharply curtailed recess. Dodgeball is gone. Tag has been banned in many schools.

Playgrounds are only the tip of the sedentary lifestyle. Children don't wander around the neighborhood anymore; one study found that the range of exploration from home by nine-year-olds is about 10 percent what it was in 1970. Only 15 percent of children walk or bike to school, compared to half in 1970. Kids have been taught that outside means danger—from cars, from adults, from the uncertainty of the real world; almost two-thirds of children think unknown adults pose a danger to them. The hovering parent wants control—unstructured play is too risky. "Countless communities have virtually outlawed unstructured outdoor nature play," Richard Louv observes in *Last Child in the Woods*. So what are children doing instead of wandering around, pushing their friends on swings or making mischief? Eight- to ten-year-olds spend an average of six hours per day in front of a television or computer screen. These trends, more than any others, account for the surge in obesity.

Safety is the reason for many of these changes in children's play opportunities. Ever since Ralph Nader exposed GM for making an unsafe car in the 1960s, safety has been a primary goal of public policy, right up there with individual rights. SAFETY might as well be a billboard that looms over almost any activity. AVOID RISK is its twin. Nothing in schools or camps or home activities occurs without people first looking up at those billboards and asking themselves whether, well, something might go wrong. Amen, you might say, especially with children, our most precious assets. This cult of safety, drawing out parents' worst fears, [now] envelops children in America. Better not let the dear darling out alone. Who knows what might happen out on the street?

It's hard to be against safety. Regulators should certainly try to keep us safe from hidden defects. We can hardly protect ourselves against lead paint on toys and other invisible flaws of mass-market products. But the Consumer Product Safety Commission (CPSC) and other safety groups go a lot farther than hidden defects. They want to protect against any activities that involve risks. The CPSC has standards that recommend removal of "tripping hazards, like . . . tree stumps and rocks." Many other organizations, public and private, also loudly champion the cause of ever-greater safety. The National Program for Playground Safety, at the University of Northern Iowa, advises that "Children should always be supervised when playing in the outdoor environment." Professor Neil Williams, at Eastern Connecticut State College, has created a Physical Education Hall of Shame, whose inductees include dodgeball, kickball, red rover, and tag.

Focusing on safety, it's hard to know where to stop. The drive toward eliminating risk grows ever more powerful, pushed by true believers and by people terrified by legal liability. Each new risk avoided ratchets up the stakes for the next one. Broward County has put up warnings on playgrounds admonishing children not to use equipment "unless designed for your age group." That's about as effective, I suspect, as warning fish that the lure is "harmful if swallowed." But we can't help ourselves. We've become safety addicts.

Something is wrong here. The headlong drive for safety has resulted in a generation of obese children who bear not only the risk, but the near certainty, of terrible health problems.

Safety, as it turns out, is only half an idea. The right question is what we're giving up to achieve safety. A playground may be designed to be accident-free, but be so boring that children don't use it. Conversely, a playground may serve its purpose perfectly, but there will be a certainty that every once in a while, a child will be hurt. Safety and risk always involve trade-offs—of resources, of efficiency, and, especially in the case of children, of learning to manage risk.

Taking risks, it also turns out, is essential to a healthy childhood. Risk in daily activities—running around in a playground, confronting classmates at recess, climbing trees, or exploring the nearby creek—is different from hidden product flaws. Learning to deal with these challenges is part of what children need—not only physically but socially and intellectually. "The view that children must somehow be sheltered from all risks of injury is a common misperception," says Professor Joe Frost, who ran the Play and Playgrounds Research Project at the University of Texas. "In the real world, life is filled with risks—financial, physical, emotional, social—and reasonable risks are essential to a child's healthy development.". . .

Socialization skills are learned not under adult supervision but by coping with other children. "The way young people learn to interact with peers is by interacting with their peers, and the only place this is allowed to happen in schools is at recess," observes psychology professor Anthony Pellegrini. "They don't learn social skills being taught lessons in class." "Life is not always fair," notes

Professor Tom Reed, an expert in early childhood education. "Things like this are learned on the playground." Dr. Stuart Brown, who led the commission trying to understand why Charles Whitman murdered fourteen people at the University of Texas in 1966, found that "his lifelong lack of play was a key factor in his homicidal actions." This was also true with other mass murderers. Dr. Brown went on to found the National Institute for Play, dedicated to understanding the cognitive and cultural benefits of play.

Being on your own is a critical component of play because, among other benefits, it makes you responsible for yourself. Responsibility, like risk, is intrinsically interesting. Instead we have trained children to believe that being on your own presents an ever-present danger of abuse by adults who are strangers. Milk cartons display photographs of abducted children, as if there's a scourge of kidnappers up from Mexico City or Manila intent on nabbing children in Akron and Atlanta. In fact, the chances of abduction by a stranger are about as small as getting hit by a meteorite, and dramatically smaller than having an accident when riding in a car with your parents. Contrary to popular wisdom, the National Crime Prevention Council advises that "If children need help—whether they're lost, being threatened by a bully, or being followed by a stranger—the safest thing for them to do in many cases is ask a stranger for help."

Perhaps the most surprising, and important, benefit of children's risk is this: Children's brains do not fully develop without the excitement and challenge of risk. A report from the American Academy of Pediatrics found that unsupervised play allows children to create and explore worlds of their own creation, helps them develop new competencies, teaches them to work in groups and to negotiate and resolve conflicts, and, perhaps most significant, is important for developing their cognitive capacity: Play "develop[s] their imagination, dexterity, and physical, cognitive, and emotional strength." Research at Baylor College of Medicine found that "children who don't play much or are rarely touched develop brains 20 percent to 30 percent smaller than normal for their age." Professor Joe Frost concludes: "Early experiences determine which neurons are to be used and which are to die, and consequently, whether the child will be brilliant or dull, confident or fearful, articulate or tongue-tied. . . . Brain development is truly a 'use it or lose it' process."

All these activities—merry-go-rounds, tag, climbing trees, wandering around on their own—involve risk. That's what's appealing. That's how kids stay healthy. That's what fires their neurons, leading to better brain development. That's how kids learn to smell danger, and to deal with difficult people. That's how kids learn confidence.

The error of the safety police was to move from protecting against hidden hazards to meddling in life activities where the risks are apparent. The most sacred of [CPSC's] sacred cows is that playgrounds should be covered with soft material, preferably rubber matting, to cushion the falls of the dear ones. "Asphalt and concrete are unacceptable. They do not have any shock absorbing properties. Similarly, grass and turf should not be used." It seems sensible that soft surfaces are best for toddlers who can't be expected to understand risk, and for equipment on which we expect children to be hanging upside down, like jungle gyms. But for almost everything else, the hard ground is just part of the risk calculus that kids, consciously or unconsciously, will factor into their play. I actually learned, all by myself, without any regulator's help, that concrete has no "shock absorbing properties."

I'm bracing myself for the return blast: More than 200,000 injuries per year on slides, swings, and climbing equipment! Not only that—there are fourteen deaths per year on playgrounds. I can practically hear the accusation now—that I'm in favor of kidocide, and that a generation of brain-damaged and lame children would be limping around America were it not for the vigilance of the safety police.

Yes, there are many accidents involving children on playgrounds. Whether the number is reasonable involves evaluating not only the positive benefits of risk, but also the universe of other life risks. It turns out that there are almost five times as many children's accidents in the home—over 200,000 on stairs alone, another 200,000 falling out of beds, 113,000 crashing off chairs, and almost 20,000 from falling television sets. What are the policy implications? Carrying the logic of safety to these home risks, we could mandate rubber floors, safety rails on beds, air bags on televisions, and, almost certainly, a ban on running at home.

What's going on in the child safety movement is not prudence, but something more akin to paranoia. Instead of safety, we are creating the conditions of danger: children who are not physically fit, have arrested social development, and don't have the sense or satisfaction of taking care of themselves. In the name of safety we're creating, in the words of Hara Marano, editor at large of *Psychology Today*, "a nation of wimps."

REBUILDING BOUNDARIES OF REASONABLE RISK

. . . . There's never been a time like this in American history. Society has lost its sense of balance on ordinary life choices. Many people no longer have a clear sense of what we should allow our children to do. Once fear sets in, and common sense capsizes, nothing short of leadership can make it upright again. Here are two changes I think are required.

1. *Law must reclaim its authority to draw enforceable boundaries of reasonable risk.* Prevailing judicial orthodoxy today allows anyone to sue for almost anything—allowing any injured person, in effect, to set unilaterally the agenda on risk for the rest of society. Just allowing the claim to go to the jury sets social policy. . . . Judges, legislatures, and regulators must take back the responsibility of drawing these boundaries.
2. *Create "Risk Commissions" to offer guidance on where to draw the lines.* Legislatures should set up nonpartisan risk commissions to offer guidance to courts and regulators for activities that have been most affected by legal fear, including for children's play and for physical contact with children. These risk commissions should be independent of existing safety agencies, which are dug in too deep to see the trade-offs. Standard-setting bodies are common in industry—for example, for industrial tools—and in professions such as medicine. The standards set by these bodies enjoy broad support and are considered authoritative by courts. If legislatures don't establish these independent risk commissions, then private groups should seize the authority by building broad-based coalitions that assert standards. Common Good, working with health care and child development organizations, has begun the process of creating a playbook of guidelines for healthy play.

In 2005, U.K. Prime Minister Tony Blair gave a speech on risk in which he observed that "something is seriously awry when teachers feel unable to take children on school trips, for fear of being sued" and that "public bodies . . . act in highly risk-averse and peculiar ways." Blair called for laws to "clarify the existing common law on negligence" and for issuance of "simple guidelines" on reasonable risks. He concluded with these thoughts:

> Government cannot eliminate all risk. A risk-averse scientific community is no scientific community at all. A risk-averse business culture is no business culture at all. A risk-averse public sector will stifle creativity and deny to many the opportunities to be creative. . . . We cannot respond to every accident by trying to guarantee ever more tiny margins of safety. We cannot eliminate risk. We have to live with it, manage it. Sometimes we have to accept: no-one is to blame.

In countries across the globe, children run and play all by themselves. In India unstructured play is considered an essential tool of child development. Germany has adventure playgrounds that are stocked with scrap lumber, nails, and hammers, so children can come and build things, and then tear them down and build something else. These are the children against whom our children will be competing. Are we really protecting our children, or are we putting them at risk of failure because they lack tools of self-reliance?

"The age cries out for all the freedoms," historian Jacques Barzun observed, "Yet it turns its back upon risk, the companion to free will." Accomplishment at all levels, as well as personal growth, requires looking at the challenges of life realistically, not succumbing to the cheap rhetoric of a safety utopia. People will disagree on where the lines will be drawn. Certainly the safety zealots will defend decades of a bubble wrap approach to child rearing. But that difference in view only underscores the need to reestablish sensible boundaries. More than at any time in recent memory, America needs legal red lights and green lights. Our freedom depends on it.

From Howard, Philip K. "The Freedom to Take Risks." Life without Lawyers: Liberating Americans from Too Much Law. *New York: Norton, 2009. 34–48. Copyright 2009 by Philip K. Howard. Used by permission of W. W. Norton & Company, Inc.*

Questions to Consider

1. Howard opens his chapter with Una Glennon's letter. In asking where we draw the line, Howard references John Rawls's idea of a "'veil of ignorance.'" Considering this stance, what argument would you make to resolve Ms. Glennon's problem if you were an environmentalist, the parent of a child with nut allergies, a neighbor, or a government official?

2. In discussing why children are not as active as they used to be, Howard claims that "safety is the reason for many of these changes in children's play opportunities." Has Howard sufficiently supported his generalization? What else might account for these changes? What other generalizations does he employ, and which might be useful to verify? Explain.

3. In the examples provided in this reading, Howard moves from Glennon's letter at one extreme to "adventure playgrounds" in Germany, where children can build with hammers and nails. In determining "enforceable boundaries of reasonable risk," as Howard suggests, would reasonable risk look like either of these two examples or like something else?

4. A number of terms are left undefined in Howard's text, such as *freedom, risk, safety,* and *sensible boundaries.* What definitions would work within the argument Howard has developed? Which would not?

5. Howard claims that "there's never been a time like this in American history." What do you think he means by this, and in what ways would you agree or disagree with this assessment?

A Platform for Love and Generosity: Law and Justice
THE EDITORS OF *TIKKUN* Magazine

On Tikkun *Magazine's masthead, "tikkun" is noted as meaning "to heal, repair, and transform the world." As part of its vision statement, the editors note that "worldwide economic and political problems are not solely external in nature, but reflect also distortions in how we experience each other and ourselves." To this end, the editors see changing our vision of ourselves and the world as an integral part of this transformative process, which includes economic, political, and legal changes. In this 2004 essay, the editors describe our legal culture as influencing a "fear of others" that they argue is ultimately destructive. As you read this essay, consider how workable the editors' suggestions would be. What would the world's legal systems look like if these suggestions were to be implemented?*

———————— ✦ ————————

We seek a fundamentally new direction in the way our society shapes its legal assumptions and a transformation in the practice of law. We are both proud of the accomplishments of the American system of justice and concerned to rectify its misuse in some areas (e.g., the torture and humiliation that takes place in some of our prisons—not only in Iraq but also in the United States—and the administration of law through police forces and courts that retain de facto racist and classist elements). We believe that, in its fundamental orientation to the world, our legal system reflects a worldview and helps create a reality that undermines rather than builds the possibility of genuine community and human connection. The changes that are needed go far beyond those sought by civil liberties groups—though we support their efforts to achieve greater fairness, to overturn repressive elements of the Patriot Act, and to overcome the use of the legal system as an instrument of repression (as, for example, under the current misuse of law by Attorney General Ashcroft and his Justice Department).

   When the Founding Fathers wrote the American Constitution and laid the groundwork for the development of our legal system, their main intent was to affirm the dignity of the individual against all forms of group coercion. As a result, they created a legal system that was focused almost entirely on protecting individual rights: to free speech, to the free exercise of religion, to assemble peacefully and seek redress of grievances, to have one's home protected from unreasonable searches and seizures, to be presumed innocent until proven guilty, to confront one's accusers if charged with a crime, and so forth.

This concern with individual rights extended also to the so-called private realm of the economy. Our Constitution protects the right to make contracts, the right to use one's property in any manner that one wishes so long as that use does not unreasonably interfere with the rights of others; the right to be justly compensated if the community determines it must take the individual's land for an important public purpose; and our law has come also to protect the right of people to freely associate through incorporation to pursue freely chosen private ends. The conception of justice that has largely shaped the development of American law since these beginnings has held that these various freedoms must be extended equally to all. This linkage of the idea of equality with equal liberty to compete in the marketplace has shaped the development of "equal protection" to include African-Americans, women, and others who in some way have suffered from prejudice that has restricted their "equality of opportunity." The current controversy surrounding the issue of gay marriage is essentially about liberty and equality defined in this way: in seeking the right to marry, gays and lesbians are asserting that they should have the same individual rights and freedoms that are granted to others.

While we recognize and support the liberal achievements of American law and support the world's continuing efforts to secure the blessings of liberty for all of humanity, we nevertheless insist that our law's emphasis on the individual has also proved to be destructive. In defining liberty and equality in terms that emphasize the pursuit of individual self-interest in a competitive marketplace, and in linking the meaning of liberty and equality with the individual's need to be protected against others, the legal system has legitimized Fear of the Other as preeminent over Love of the Other, and has minimized and even suppressed the longing of each of us to live in a loving and caring community founded upon social connection and cooperation.

We therefore say that what is needed today is an approach to law and justice that seeks to reconnect the Self with the Other and to link the pursuit of justice with healing the distortions in human interaction that have led us to equate individual rights with the pursuit of self-interest at the expense of others and the natural environment. We need to develop an approach to law that is guided by Martin Luther King Jr.'s definition of justice as "[l]ove correcting that which revolts against love"—a definition that begins with our connectedness to each other as social beings and points toward the creation of legal processes that increase empathy, mutual understanding, and compassion, rather than vindicating an adversarial conception of rights. Such an approach should conceive of the legal arena as the central public space where conflicts are healed through reconciliation, and where all of us can witness individuals overcoming their selfishness and their fear of the Other by seeing the Other as equally deserving of love and concern.

There are many examples of how this new "post-liberal" conception of law and justice is emerging within our society. The greatest single example is South Africa's Truth and Reconciliation Commission, in which the black majority of South Africa avoided much of the bloodshed that history would have taught us to expect following the dismantling of the brutal legacy of apartheid, by granting amnesty to those responsible for more [than] 22,000 acts of violence. In return they received public acknowledgment by the perpetrators of the wrongs they had committed under apartheid. The fastest growing legal movement in the United States is the Restorative Justice movement—an approach to crime and social injustice that emphasizes healing conflict through direct encounters between perpetrators and victims. Perpetrators must hear directly the suffering caused by their own actions and they are encouraged to accept responsibility, to apologize, to atone for their actions, and to seek forgiveness from those whom they have harmed. New developments in the related areas of Transformative and Understanding-Based Mediation are moving beyond the self-interest-based settlement-mediation model toward seeing conflicts as opportunities for people to grow through the achievement of empathy and understanding for others. The Collaborative Law movement is bringing together large groups of lawyers in Boston, Seattle, New York, and other major American cities who are rejecting adversarial litigation of conflicts in favor of legal resolutions that legitimize mutual respect, sensitivity, and cooperation.

We believe federal, state, and local governments must do all they can to give public legitimacy to these new movements that are linking law to the creation of community. We call for a modification of evidentiary rules regarding relevance away from the narrow empiricism of the current "fact-finding" process and toward the telling of meaningful stories or narratives that place disputes into their social and personal context, thereby revealing more of the full human meaning of each party's actions. The American Bar Association should modify its existing ethical rules governing the legal profession so that, in addition to having an acknowledged duty to the client and the court, a lawyer must also assume an ethical responsibility for the welfare of the broader community. In order to better accomplish this objective, the principle of a lawyer's "duty of zealous representation" should be reoriented so that it no longer is limited to advancing the individual self-interests of clients, but also includes an ethical obligation to work toward promoting substantive social justice, harmony, and the flourishing of the well-being of the community.

The American legal system should adopt and recognize as a new principle of tort law a duty to care for others in distress. This duty would be broader than the historical duty to rescue, but would be limited by a reasonableness condition subject to common law interpretation. The purpose of this duty would be to create a new ethos of responsibility for those who are in personal and economic crisis—the homeless, the infirm, the elderly, and family members.

"Law and Justice" in "A Platform for Love and Generosity." Editorial. Tikkun 19 August 2004. Online at www.tikkun.org/article/php?story= LawandJustice. Copyright 2004. Reprinted by permission of Tikkun: A Bimonthly Interfaith Critique of Politics, Culture, & Society.

Questions to Consider

1. The editors call their ideas "a fundamentally new direction" in the legal system. How would you describe these changes, and where and how could you see them implemented?

2. The dignity of the individual is seen as the basis for much of the founding documents and the developments in law in the United States. What mindset do the *Tikkun* editors claim this emphasis in law has led to, and why do they see this as problematic? With what examples would you argue in support of and against this claim?

3. After providing examples of how more community-oriented views have been used in South Africa and the United States, the editors call for avoiding what they describe as narrow fact-finding in favor of "meaningful stories or narratives." How is this approach evident in the examples provided? How could you see this emphasis working in traditional legal cases?

4. The editors argue that instead of lawyers zealously representing their clients, the lawyers should consider social justice. What problems might arise if each lawyer gets to decide what a socially just outcome would be in each case?

5. Consider what practices on your campus or in your locality are designed to avoid conflict and seek conciliation rather than emphasizing someone's winning a case or an argument. What are the advantages and limitations of such an attempt for consensus?

Making Connections

1. Make a list of the various roles you play—including student, brother, daughter, volunteer, employee, citizen of a city/state/nation, and so forth—and then note what rules govern these roles. What would you want to change, and why?

2. The "Fear of the Other" noted by the editors of *Tikkun Magazine* sounds somewhat like Philip Howard's argument about our worries about risks. In what ways are these writers arguing against similar problems? In what ways do their solutions differ?

3. If, as researcher Lera Boroditsky claims in her essay in Chapter 1, our language changes our perspectives of the world, how might our different languages continue to be an impediment to creating universal empathy or achieving universal rights? Are some core values more easily universalized than others?

4. Some texts represented here point out how countries are different from each other, such as the article on failing nations. Others, like the Universal Declaration of Human Rights, represent the similarity—or potential similarity—among nations. In what ways does it help to look at both kinds of comparisons in developing strategies to improve all nations?

5. Given the readings in this and the other chapters, how would you tally lists of both the useful and the problematic aspects of the law? Which would win out?

6. Each of the texts in this chapter suggests that certain attitudes can be particularly destructive to peace and order. What would you say these attitudes are, and how do we begin to change such attitudes, values, and worldviews?

7. Some of the readings represent single authors, and others a collaborative approach. Try writing a series of rules or regulations that you think should govern a situation you and your classmates consider problematic in your community. After you all come up with your separate lists, work together to compromise on a master list that is acceptable to everyone and is seen as being reasonable and potentially effective. How difficult is it to collaborate?

8. Some of the websites noted in this chapter allow you to compare the status of nations. Choose one country, perhaps one where your family originated. How is it different from the country in which you currently reside? What accounts for those differences? What would you say to a resident of that country to explain the importance of what you have in common?

9. In what ways does a global perspective of laws contribute to a more informed reflection on local rules and laws? What are the benefits of universal laws compared to local laws and vice versa?

10. How do laws in other countries differ from those in the United States on hotly debated topics such as gun control, separation of church and state, and gay marriage? Keeping in mind that some of these issues might arguably be covered by articles in the Declaration of Human Rights, could you write a specific and binding law on any of these topics that would be universal? Why or why not?

Endnote

These readings can provide a starting place for further inquiry about the law. Learning more about the authors, the cases they discuss, the concepts they reference, and the history behind the situations to which they refer will be useful in more fully understanding each of these texts. The law, for better or worse, is not something that can be easily boiled down to a few definitions or examples.

An entertaining way to learn more about the law—and to critique its representation—is what many of us have already discovered: television shows and movies. What do lawyers think of these? It's a mixed response, but many lawyers have favorites, even among characterizations considered less than realistic. The lawyers of the American Bar Association (ABA) have taken time away from their cases to compile lists of "The 25 Greatest Legal TV Shows" and "The 25 Greatest Legal Movies," which can be found respectively at the following sites:

www.abajournal.com/magazine/article/the_25_greatest_legal_tv_shows/
www.abajournal.com/magazine/article/the_25_greatest_legal_movies/.

Frank Beaver, a professor emeritus in screen studies at the University of Michigan, noted some of these films in a 2008 issue of *Michigan Today* Magazine along with two very early examples, one being an 1899 eleven-reel film covering *The Dreyfus Affair* by French director Georges Melies. Another, one of my favorites, is Carl Dreyer's *The Passion of Joan of Arc*. Though made as a silent film in 1928, it speaks volumes about the rigors of trial by inquisition.

In addition to its information on the entertaining aspects of the law, the website of the ABA, which describes its organization as "Defending Liberty, Pursuing Justice," offers a great deal of information on the law and a wealth of public resources at: www.americanbar.org/aba.html.